AF505640

What Can I Do Now?

Law

Books in the
What Can I Do Now? Series

Animal Careers
Animation
Art
Business and Finance
Computers
Education
Engineering, Second Edition
Environment, Second Edition
Fashion
Film
Health Care
Journalism, Second Edition
Law
Music
Nursing, Second Edition
Radio and Television, Second Edition
Safety and Security, Second Edition
Science
Sports, Second Edition
Travel and Tourism, Second Edition

What Can I Do Now?

Law

Ferguson Publishing
An imprint of Infobase Publishing

What Can I Do Now? Law

Copyright © 2010 by Infobase Publishing

All rights reserved. No part of this book may be reproduced or utilized in any form
or by any means, electronic or mechanical, including photocopying, recording, or
by any information storage or retrieval systems, without permission in writing from
the publisher. For information contact

Ferguson
An imprint of Infobase Publishing
132 West 31st Street
New York NY 10001

Library of Congress Cataloging-in-Publication Data

What can I do now? Law.
     p. cm. — (What can I do now? series)
  Includes bibliographical references and index.
  ISBN-13: 978-0-8160-8074-8 (hardcover : alk. paper)
  ISBN-10: 0-8160-8074-7 (hardcover : alk. paper) 1. Law—Vocational guidance—
United States—Juvenile literature. [1. Vocational guidance.] I. Title: Law.
  KF297.W48 2010
  340.023′73—dc22
                              2009038371

Ferguson books are available at special discounts when purchased in bulk quantities
for businesses, associations, institutions, or sales promotions. Please call our Special
Sales Department in New York at (212) 967-8800 or (800) 322-8755.

You can find Ferguson on the World Wide Web at http://www.fergpubco.com

Text design by Kerry Casey
Composition by Mary Susan Ryan-Flynn
Cover printed by Sheridan Books, Ann Arbor, Mich.
Book printed and bound by Sheridan Books, Ann Arbor, Mich.
Date printed: March 2010
Printed in the United States of America

10 9 8 7 6 5 4 3 2 1

This book is printed on acid-free paper.

Contents

Introduction

There are many people just like you who want to get involved with the law, whether in a courtroom, law office, or other setting. You may see a legal career in your future and wonder how you can get started right away, while still in high school. There are countless areas of the legal field in which you can work—areas that you can match to your skills and talents. All you need to begin is a general interest in the field. Although you will need a law degree before you can work as a lawyer, there are other options in the field that require less education. These include the careers of court reporter, paralegal, and legal secretary—all of which you can land by completing some postsecondary training.

There is absolutely no reason to wait until you graduate from high school to "get serious" about a career. That doesn't mean you have to make a firm, undying commitment right now. Gasp! Indeed, one of the biggest fears most people face at some point (sometimes more than once) is choosing the right career. Frankly, many people don't "choose" at all. They take a job because they need one, and all of a sudden 10 years have gone by and they wonder why they're stuck doing something they hate. Don't be one of those people! You have the opportunity right now—while you're still in high

school and still relatively unencumbered with major adult responsibilities—to explore, to experience, to try out a work path. Or several paths if you're one of those overachieving types. Wouldn't you really rather find out sooner than later that you're not cut out to be a lawyer after all, that you'd actually prefer to be a paralegal or a legal nurse consultant? Or even a court reporter?

There are many ways to explore the field of law. What we've tried to do in this book is give you an idea of some of your options. Section 1, What Do I Need to Know about the Legal Field?, will give you an overview of the field—a little history, where it's at today, and promises of the future; as well as a breakdown of its structure—how it's organized—and a glimpse of some of its many career options.

The Careers section includes 10 chapters, each describing in detail a specific legal career: court reporter, elder law attorney, intellectual property lawyer, judge, lawyer (which covers many specialties), legal nurse consultant, legal secretary, paralegal, prosecutor, and public defender. These chapters rely heavily on first-hand accounts from real people on the job. They'll tell you what skills you need, what personal qualities you must have, and what the ups and downs of the jobs are. You'll also find out about educational requirements—including specific high school and college classes—advancement possibilities, related jobs, salary ranges, and the employment outlook.

In keeping with the secondary theme of this book (the primary theme, for those of you who still don't get it, is "You can do something now"), Section 3, Do It Yourself, urges you to explore the law on your own and, if necessary, take charge and start your own programs and activities where none exist—school, community, or the nation. Why not?

The real meat of the book is in Section 4, What Can I Do Right Now? This is where you get busy and *do something*. The chapter "Get Involved" will clue you in on the obvious volunteer and intern positions, the not-so-obvious summer camps and summer college study, and other opportunities.

"Read a Book" is an annotated bibliography of books (some new, some old) and periodicals. If you're even remotely considering a career in law, reading a few books and checking out a few magazines is the easiest thing you can do. Don't stop with our list. Ask your librarian to direct you to more materials. Keep reading!

While we think the best way to explore the legal field is to jump right in and start doing it, there are plenty of other ways to get into the legal mind-set. "Surf the Web" offers you a short annotated list of Web sites where you can explore everything from job listings (start getting an idea of what employers are looking for now), to educational and certification requirements, to legal issues, to on-the-job accounts from those who work as pat-

ent lawyers, court reporters, and a variety of other professions.

"Ask for Money" is a sampling of law-related scholarships. You need to be familiar with these because you're going to need money for school. You have to actively pursue scholarships; no one is going to come up to you one day and present you with a check because you're such a wonderful student. Applying for scholarships is work. It takes effort. And it must be done right and often as much as a year in advance of when you need the money.

"Look to the Pros" is the final chapter. It lists professional and advocacy organizations you can turn to for more information about accredited schools, educational requirements, legal issues, career descriptions, salary information, job listings, scholarships, and more. Once you become a college student in a legal field, you'll be able to join many of these. Time after time, professionals say that membership and active participation in a professional organization is one of the best ways to network (make valuable contacts) and gain recognition in your field.

High school can be a lot of fun. There are dances and football games; maybe you're in band or play a sport. Great! Maybe you hate school and are just biding your time until you graduate. That's too bad. Whoever you are, take a minute and try to imagine your life five years from now. Ten years from now. Where will you be? What will you be doing? Whether you realize it or not, how you choose to spend your time now—studying, playing, watching TV, working at a fast food restaurant, hanging out, whatever—will have an impact on your future. Take a look at how you're spending your time now and ask yourself, "Where is this getting me?" If you can't come up with an answer, it's probably "nowhere." The choice is yours. No one is going to take you by the hand and lead you in the "right" direction. It's up to you. It's your life. You can do something about it right now!

SECTION 1

What Do I Need to Know About the Legal Field?

What do you think of when you hear the word *law*? Two well-dressed attorneys matching wits in front of a rapt jury in a packed courtroom? The traffic law you broke when you were caught driving 50 miles-per-hour in a school zone? A judge banging her gavel during a raucous trial? A celebrity lawyer explaining his or her client's latest bad behavior before a collection of TV cameras? The reality of legal work today is actually much more diverse and complex than these examples suggest. Millions of people work in the legal field in literally thousands of different ways. Some work in courtrooms, others in law offices or the halls of Congress. You probably already know about the work of lawyers and judges, but did you know that paralegals and legal secretaries are needed to help lawyers conduct research and handle office tasks? Court reporters are needed to record courtroom testimony and any other events that occur during a trial? Legal educators are needed to teach students about the law? Legal nurse consultants are needed to provide medical expertise to lawyers in medical malpractice cases? Legal writers are needed to convey legal information to lawyers and the general public? This list of law professions may surprise you, and we haven't even mentioned the dozens of specialties for lawyers—from entertainment and environmental lawyers, to defense and prosecuting attorneys, to intellectual property and real estate lawyers. In short, a wealth of diverse legal careers is available to people with any educational background, skill set, or interest.

GENERAL INFORMATION

Our legal system includes statutes (laws) enacted by legislatures (Congress) and decisions handed down by the courts (judicial system). The law provides us with guidelines and rules to live by in our personal, social, and business activities. When someone doesn't follow the laws or a law is unclear, our legal system includes ways to settle disputes and resolve conflicts. The law in the United States is based on democratic principles, and its goal is to protect individual rights and ensure a just and free society.

Throughout history, societies have established systems of law to govern people. One of the earliest known codes of law is the Code of Hammurabi developed circa 1800 B.C. by the Babylonians. Roughly 400 years later, Moses was given and then introduced the Ten Commandments, which have become the foundation of Judeo-Christian ethics and the basis of our current legal system.

The ancient Greeks and Romans set up the first schools of law for young boys to learn the many skills involved in pleading a case. To be an eloquent speaker was a great advantage. The Greeks focused their training on thinking logically, another important part of debating and proving matters of the law.

In the late 1700s and early 1800s the French emperor Napoleon organized and refined European law into what became known as the Napoleonic Code. The Napoleonic Code of law is based more on common sense than on specific legal theories.

In America's early days, settlers lived under the English Common law that they

Lingo to Learn

acquit If the court (either judge or jury) decides that the defendant is not guilty, the individual is acquitted and set free.

affidavit A written statement detailing facts that are needed as evidence or supporting material in a court case. The statement is made under oath.

arraignment The hearing set aside for the court to officially charge a suspect and hear the suspect's plea of guilt or innocence.

bar examination To become licensed to practice law, it is necessary to pass the bar examination. Bar exams usually last more than one day and test the taker's knowledge of many different legal topics.

bench The actual seat that the judge sits on, but more often used to refer to the person of the judge or the judge's authority.

bench trial A trial decided by a judge instead of a jury.

damages Money paid to the person who wins a lawsuit against another person. The money is awarded to pay for the injury or loss caused by the losing party of the lawsuit.

hung jury At the end of a court trial, the jury is expected to review the evidence and give the court a final decision. If the jury cannot make that final decision, it is called a hung jury.

indictment The grand jury returns this statement of charges if it believes a suspect is guilty.

jurisprudence The study of law.

moot court A mock court conducted with hypothetical cases to train law students.

plea bargain When the defendant in a criminal case pleads guilty to a lesser charge in exchange for a shorter sentence. The result is that the defendant is guaranteed punishment, although perhaps not as severe as it could have been without the plea bargain. The prosecution gets the assurance of a conviction and the defendant avoids the risk of a more severe penalty.

retainer An advance fee paid to a lawyer to ensure that the lawyer will represent the client and that the lawyer will get paid.

testimony A declaration made under oath by a witness in response to questions from attorneys.

torts Wrongs against individuals.

brought with them to the New World. This common law began under Henry II in England and established standard punishments for certain crimes. This common law was later modified by the Articles of Confederation and then the Constitution.

In areas of the United States that were originally controlled by the Spanish, such as California and Texas, traces of Spanish law still exist. Similarly, because Louisiana was controlled by the French, it still uses a more French than English legal system. But in all cases, the laws of other countries and other times were adapted by legislatures to fit the changing needs and customs of American society. Our legal system today is called statutory because lawmakers enact statutes to govern us.

Several fields of law have been practiced in the past and continue to be practiced today. The two most well-known fields are *criminal law* and *civil law*. Criminal law focuses on crime; that is, acts committed in violation of a law. This field of law is concerned with an individual's relation to society; in fact, criminal acts are considered offenses against all members of a society, even if the acts were committed against only one person. Anyone who breaks criminal laws may be punished with prison time or fines. Civil law focuses on relationships between individuals. Most civil law addresses written contracts, wrongs against individuals (or torts), and property issues. Breakers of civil law cannot be imprisoned or fined, but they may have to pay money as a result of the decision of the court. Other fields of law include administrative law, constitutional law, tax law, maritime law, and labor law.

STRUCTURE OF THE INDUSTRY

In addition to the U.S. judicial system (which will be covered later in this section) and traditional law firms, the legal industry includes opportunities in many other fields, such as library science, publishing, education, entertainment, and politics. Other than judges, the main players in the legal profession are lawyers. Supporting these main players are paralegals, legal secretaries, court reporters, bail bondsmen, process servers, and other specialists that each play an important role in the legal system. (See the Careers section later in this article for descriptions of job duties for these and other legal professionals.)

Because of the many different types of laws and the various situations and people they are applied to, lawyers have opportunities to practice law in a variety of areas. Most lawyers base this choice on what subject they are interested in, the people they want to work with, and where they want to live while working. The possibilities include working for a private company, a government agency, a corporate law firm, or a public interest law firm. In addition, lawyers may serve as judges or become instructors and professors in colleges or universities.

Over the years, most lawyers have chosen to go into private practice; that is, devoting full time to providing legal services for private clients. These are the lawyers most average people contact when they need legal advice or services. The majority of private-practice lawyers work by themselves, without the immediate assistance of any partners (although they may have salaried associates). Others work with colleagues in law firms that range in size from two attorneys to as many as several hundred. Typically, law firms are composed of partners, who own the practice and share expenses and earnings on an agreed basis, and associates, who are salaried lawyers working for the firm and usually expect to become partners themselves someday.

Probably the most essential segments of the legal system, however, are the courts. After all, without courts and judges to preside over them, there would be no use for lawyers and support professionals. On the federal level, the judicial system is made up of a series of courts. The Supreme Court is the highest court of the land and rules on issues related to the U.S. Constitution. The Supreme Court is made up of nine justices, appointed by the president with consent of the Senate, who review selected decisions made at the state level.

The Circuit Court of Appeals deals with appeals of decisions made by the district courts and reviews judgments of lower courts.

The Best Law Schools, 2009

Each year *U.S. News & World Report* ranks law schools in the United States. To create the rankings, the magazine's editors ask law school deans, program directors, and senior faculty to rate the quality of other law programs. They also survey hiring managers regarding the quality of their new hires and analyze statistical data such as the average time it takes law graduates to get jobs and their state bar exam passage rates. This data reflects, to some extent, the quality of the law schools they attended. The following law schools were ranked as the best in 2009. *U.S. News & World Report* encourages aspiring law students to use this information to supplement, not replace, their own research and deliberations about what is the best school (and fit) for them.

1. Yale Law School (New Haven, Conn., http://www.law.yale.edu)
2. Harvard Law School (Cambridge, Mass., http://www.law.harvard.edu)
3. Stanford Law School (Stanford, Calif., http://www.law.stanford.edu)
4. Columbia Law School (New York, N.Y., http://www.law.columbia.edu)
5. New York University School of Law (New York, N.Y., http://www.law.nyu.edu)
6. University of California—Berkeley School of Law (Berkeley, Calif., http://www.law.berkeley.edu)
6. University of Chicago Law School (Chicago, Ill., http://www.law.uchicago.edu)
8. University of Pennsylvania Law School (Philadelphia, Pa., http://www.law.upenn.edu)
9. University of Michigan Law School (Ann Arbor, Mich., http://www.law.umich.edu)
10. Duke University (Durham, N.C., http://www.law.duke.edu)
10. Northwestern University School of Law (Chicago, Ill., http://www.law.northwestern.edu)
10. University of Virginia School of Law (Charlottesville, Va., http://www.law.virginia.edu)

The district courts are the third level of the federal court system, servicing approximately 100 zones, or districts, across the country.

Each state also has its own judicial system, which is separate from the federal system. Most civil and criminal cases are tried in state courts. These cases can move on to a federal court if they are related to an issue concerning the U.S. Constitution. Most cities also have municipal courts to handle minor cases.

CAREERS

There are many career options in law, from becoming a judge to working as a support staff member in a law firm. A short sampling of the many career opportunities in law follows in the paragraphs below.

Court (Pre-Trial and Trial) and Law Office Support Professionals

Bail bondsmen pay the bail to allow someone who has been arrested and is awaiting trial to go free for the time being. In exchange, the person who was arrested agrees to pay the bondsman a certain percentage of the bond assigned by the court.

Process servers are licensed by the courts to serve legal papers to the people or corporations that are involved in legal disputes.

Bailiffs are court officers that keep the peace of the court, make sure witnesses are ushered in and out of the courtroom, hand evidence directly to the witnesses, and maintain order.

Court clerks perform administrative and clerical duties at courthouses.

Court administrators manage all non-judicial administrative activities in a courtroom.

Court or *judiciary interpreters* work in courtrooms and at attorney-client meetings, depositions, and witness preparation sessions. They translate spoken passages of a foreign language into another specified language.

Court reporters document the events in court for the official record by transcribing or otherwise recording the words and actions of the judge, attorneys, and witnesses.

Paralegals, also called *legal assistants,* are a lawyer's assistant. Paralegals do things that lawyers would do themselves if they didn't have the help of an assistant. Whether it be interviewing witnesses, examining documents, drafting agreements, or conducting research, the paralegal's work saves a lawyer's time and energy, and makes the paralegal indispensable to the task of getting the job done.

Legal secretaries help lawyers by performing administrative and clerical duties in a law office. They are sometimes called *litigation secretaries* or *trial secretaries.*

Legal receptionists receive visitors at law offices. They also answer telephones, take and distribute messages for lawyers and other employees at law firms, and make sure no one enters the office unescorted or unauthorized.

Legal administrators, also known as *law office managers,* oversee daily operations in a legal department or law office.

Demonstrative evidence specialists create exhibits—such as graphs, illustrations, photographs, charts, and computer-generated graphics—for presentation during court trials.

Legal videographers record statements of witnesses in criminal or civil cases.

Trial consultants help lawyers develop trial strategies that will help them win cases.

Judges and Lawyers

Judges can be elected or appointed to their positions. They preside over every type of case that appears in court. Even though many have to run for election, judges are supposed to be nonpartisan and are not associated with a particular political party.

Bankruptcy lawyers help individuals and corporations obtain legal protection from creditors under existing bankruptcy laws and with debt repayment and financial reorganization.

Corporation lawyers, also known as *corporate lawyers*, advise corporations concerning their legal rights, obligations, or privileges.

Criminal attorneys deal with offenses against society such as murder, rape, arson, and theft. They defend the accused suspects.

District attorneys, also called *prosecuting attorneys*, are elected officials, representing the people of a city, county, state, or federal government. They gather evidence that may incriminate the accused and try to convince a judge to grant an indictment.

Elder law attorneys specialize in providing legal services for the elderly and, in some cases, the disabled.

Intellectual property lawyers focus on helping their clients with patents, trademarks, and copyright protection. *Patent lawyers* specialize in patent law. They secure patents for inventors from the U.S. Patent Office and prosecute or defend cases of patent infringement.

International lawyers specialize in the body of rules that are observed by nations in their relations with one another.

Probate lawyers specialize in planning and settling estates. They draw up wills, deeds of trust, and similar documents for clients.

Public interest lawyers provide a wide range of services to those who otherwise could not afford legal representation. *Public defenders* are specialized public interest lawyers who have been chosen by the court to represent those unable to afford private counsel.

Real estate lawyers draw up legal documents and act as agents in various real estate transactions, such as when people buy or sell their homes.

Tax attorneys handle cases stemming from problems such as income tax and estate tax issues.

Title attorneys deal with titles, leases, contracts, and other legal documents pertaining to the ownership of land and gas, oil, and mineral rights.

Other law specialties include maritime, insurance, employment, entertainment industry, and personal injury law.

Additional Opportunities

Researchers, writers, editors, and *proofreaders* are responsible for preparing the thousands upon thousands of legal publications that are produced every year.

Legal reporters gather and analyze information about law-related topics and write stories for publication or for broadcasting.

Legal Profession Still Lacking Diversity

Although the percentage of minorities in the legal profession has increased in recent years, they are still underrepresented in terms of total percentage of the U.S. population, according to a survey of firms by the National Association for Law Placement. In fact, only 5.92 percent of partners at law firms in 2008 were minorities. Only 19.08 percent of associates at law firms in 2008 were minorities. Asian/Pacific Islanders made up 9.05 percent of associates; African Americans, 4.75 percent; and Hispanic Americans, 3.86 percent.

The American Bar Association offers information on programs to advance diversity in the legal profession at its Web site (http://www.abanet.org/lawyer.html).

Law librarians organize and administer the numerous libraries of law books throughout the country. Many large law firms have their own libraries staffed with law librarians.

Legal nurse consultants are nurses who have a comprehensive understanding of medical issues and trends. They are members of a litigation team that deals with medical malpractice, personal injury, and product liability lawsuits as well as other medically related legal cases.

Forensic accountants and auditors use accounting principles and theories to support or oppose claims being made in litigation.

College law professors instruct students in legal procedures, terminology, and techniques. They lecture classes, lead small seminar groups, and create and grade examinations.

Patent agents assist clients by obtaining patents for new inventions such as electronics, medications, or machinery. They must be registered by the U.S. Patent & Trademark Office to prosecute patent applications.

Legislators are elected to represent the districts and regions of cities and counties within their state. The primary function of all legislators, on both the state and national levels, is to make laws. With a staff of aides, senators and representatives attempt to learn as much as they can about the bills being considered. They research legislation, prepare reports, meet with constituents and interest groups, speak to the press, and discuss and debate legislation on the floor of the House or Senate.

Lobbyists work to influence legislation on the federal, state, or local level on behalf of clients. Nonprofit organizations, labor unions, trade associations, corporations, and other groups and individuals use lobbyists to voice concerns and opinions to government representatives. Some lobbyists have law degrees; others have degrees in public policy, government, or other fields.

EMPLOYMENT OPPORTUNITIES

Law professionals are employed in government in almost all types of law and by a variety of government agencies, including the Internal Revenue Service, Department of Commerce, Department of Justice, Department of Homeland Security, Department of the Interior, Environmental Protection Agency, and the Federal Drug Administration. A vast number of law professionals work in the local, state, and federal court systems as well. Many legal professionals today find work in the private sector for large and small firms and corporations. Others work in private practice.

Legal professionals are employed in a variety of other industries, including health care, education, the environment, entertainment, and publishing.

INDUSTRY OUTLOOK

As laws become more complicated and lawsuits more prevalent, legal services will continue to expand. According to the U.S. Department of Labor, employment of lawyers is expected to grow about as fast as the average for all careers through 2016. As the population grows and the economy expands, many more lawyers and other legal personnel will be needed to focus on such areas as elder, health care, antitrust, environmental, international, and intellectual-property law.

Lawyers who want to become judges will face stiff competition, since employment of judges is expected to grow more slowly than the average through 2016 due to budgetary restrictions at all levels of government. Continuing public concerns about crime, safety, and efficient administration of justice should spur demand, but job growth will be limited by public budgetary pressures.

Employment for paralegals and legal assistants is expected to grow much faster than the average for all occupations through 2016. They will continue to find excellent employment opportunities with private law firms, and there will be increasing opportunities with corporate legal departments, insurance companies, real estate and title insurance firms, and banks. Paralegals who graduate from well-respected paralegal training programs and/or those with previous experience (in other words, a quality apprenticeship or internship) will find the best jobs.

Employment for court reporters is expected to grow much faster than the average through 2016 due to an increasing number of criminal court cases and civil lawsuits at both the state and federal levels.

SECTION 2

Careers

Court Reporters

SUMMARY

Definition
Court reporters record every word at hearings, trials, depositions, and other legal proceedings by using a stenographic machine or other technology.

Alternative Job Titles
CART providers
Digital reporters
Digital transcribers
Electronic reporters
Electronic transcribers

Stenographic court reporters
Voice writers

Salary Range
$25,360 to $49,710 to $83,500+

Educational Requirements
Some postsecondary training

Certification or Licensing
Recommended (certification)
Required by certain states (licensing)

Employment Outlook
Much faster than the average

High School Subjects
English (writing/literature)
Foreign language
Government
Law

Personal Interests
Computers
Current events
Law

A client contacted Janet Harris, a court reporter and owner of Harris Reporting Company, to record five days of video depositions in Ireland. "The plaintiff came to his brother's wedding in the U.S. and was involved in a car accident that prevented him from returning to his job as an anti-terrorist officer in Ireland," she recalls. "The only way for him to recover damages was to sue in the United States, but he could not afford to bring all his treating doctors and all his Irish family members who witnessed the car accident to the United States."

Janet's client wanted her to videotape their testimony and play it back in front of a jury at her local courthouse. "Video testimony from outside the United States had never happened before in our local circuit court," she says, "and I had never traveled outside the U.S. before, so I said I would do it. I learned about different voltage power in Ireland, that I would need a power adapter to use my equipment and all my supplies for NTSC video (the format for video in the United States). I felt completely prepared. Two days before I was scheduled to leave, I had a dream that my camera didn't work when I arrived in Ireland. So I purchased batteries for my tape deck and five camera batteries and charged them to have one full day of battery power."

When she arrived in Ireland, Janet tested the equipment in her hotel room and disaster struck: The power adapter started smoking. "I knew I would have one day of power," she says, "but now my adapter was shot so I couldn't recharge any of the batteries." In the end, she found a Sony dealer in town that was willing to loan her an adapter that she could use for charging the batteries. "The video depositions went smoothly. I played back all the videos before a jury on a large screen with a projector, and was even able to use my sound system to accommodate two live witnesses who were testifying by phone from outside the country. The plaintiff won his case.

"There have been many times since then that I have been asked if I could make a record in an unusual setting, and I enjoy the challenge of finding a way to accomplish it using technology."

WHAT DOES A COURT REPORTER DO?

When people think of the career of *court reporter,* they most often think of professionals sitting in the courtroom silently reporting what is said by the judge, defendant, lawyers, expert witnesses, and anyone else involved in the case. While that is true, it is only part of the court reporter's job. Much more work is done after the court reporter leaves the trial or hearing. Moreover, there are several methods of court reporting (such as real-time, electronic, and voice-writing) in addition to stenography. (These will be discussed later in this section.)

To Be a Successful Court Reporter (All Specialties), You Should...

- work well under pressure
- be able to meet deadlines
- be accurate and attentive to detail
- be able to use technology effectively to do your job
- have patience
- be familiar with a wide range of medical and legal terminology
- be ethical
- have excellent communication skills
- be a team player
- be willing to continue to learn throughout your career

In the courtroom, court reporters capture and preserve testimony and legal arguments and produce a verbatim, certified transcript. Many court reporters use combinations of letters or shorthand forms of complete words to record what is said as quickly as it is spoken on a stenographic machine (which looks like a miniature typewriter). The stenographic machine has 24 keys on its keyboard. Each key represents a single letter. Unlike a typewriter, however, the court reporter using a stenographic machine can press more than one key at a time to represent different combinations of symbols. Each letter or combination of letters represents a different sound, word, or phrase. As testimony is given, the reporter strikes one or more keys to create a phonetic representation of the testimony on a strip of paper, as well as on a computer hard drive inside the stenograph machine. The court reporter later uses a computer to translate and transcribe the testimony into legible, full-page documents or stores them for future reference. People in court may speak at a rate of between 250 and 300 words per minute, and court reporters must record this testimony word for word, and quickly.

Accurate recording of a trial is vital because the court reporter's record becomes the official transcript for the entire proceeding. In the U.S. legal system, court transcripts can be used before and after the trial for many important purposes. All proceedings that occur before a trial takes place are usually transcribed by the reporter and used for impeachment purposes during the trial. If a case is appealed, for example, the court reporter's transcript becomes the foundation for any further legal action. The appellate judge refers to the court reporter's transcript to see what happened in the trial and how the evidence was presented.

Because of the importance of accuracy, a court reporter who misses a word or phrase must interrupt the proceedings to have the words repeated. The court reporter may be asked by the judge to read aloud a portion of recorded testimony during the trial to refresh everyone's memory. Court reporters must pay close attention to all the proceedings and

be able to hear and understand everything. Sometimes it may be difficult to understand a particular witness or attorney due to poor diction, a strong accent, or a soft speaking voice. Nevertheless, the court reporter cannot be shy about stopping the trial and asking for clarification.

Court reporters must be adept at recording testimony on a wide range of legal issues, from medical malpractice to income tax evasion. In many cases, court reporters report the entire trial—including voir dire (the process in which prospective jurors and expert witnesses are questioned to determine if they can be fair during a trial), opening and closing statements, testimony, and legal arguments—for all types of cases, including murder trials, probate hearings, and domestic cases (such as child custody hearings or even parental termination cases). Witnessing tense situations and following complicated arguments are unavoidable parts of the job. The court reporter must be able to remain detached from the drama that unfolds in court while faithfully recording all that is said.

After the trial or hearing, the court reporter has more work to do. Using a CAT (computer-aided transcription) program, the stenograph notes are translated to English. The majority of these translated notes are accurate. This rough translation is then edited either by the court reporter or by a *scopist*—an assistant to the court reporter who edits and cleans up the notes. If a stenograph stroke does not match a word in the court reporter's CAT dictionary during translation, it will show up still in stenograph note form. The court reporter must manually change these entries into words and update the dictionary used in translating. If there are any meanings of words or spellings of names that are unfamiliar to the court reporter, research must be done to verify that the correct term or spelling is used. The court reporter then proofreads the transcript to check for any errors in meaning, such as the word *here* instead of the word *hear*. If necessary or requested by the lawyer or judge, special indexes and concordances are compiled using computer programs. The last step the court reporter must take is printing and binding the transcript to make it an organized and usable document for the lawyers and judge.

In some states, the court reporter is responsible for swearing in the witnesses and documenting items of evidence.

In addition to stenographic court reporting, several other court-reporting techniques have emerged in recent years. (Although there is some debate in the court reporting community regarding the definition of a court reporter, we have included the following court reporting specialties because the U.S. Department of Labor classifies them as court reporters.) In real-time court reporting, the court reporter types the court proceedings on a stenograph machine, which is connected to a computer. The letters/strokes that the court reporter types on the stenograph machine are converted to English that can be read in real-time by those involved in the case. This process is known as Communications Access Real-Time Translation (CART). In addition to its use in court (providing a real-time screen for deaf and hard-of-hearing individuals), CART is used in meet-ings, seminars, and educational settings. Broadcast captioners use the same real-time technology and caption live television broadcasts.

In electronic reporting (also known as e-reporting), the *electronic reporter* uses audio equipment to record court proceedings. The court reporter oversees the recording process, takes notes to identify speakers and clarify other issues, and ensures that the recording is of good quality. This process speeds the proceedings along because the court reporter rarely, if ever, has to ask speakers to repeat their testimony because they are speaking too quickly, have an accent, or are using complex terminology. Testimony can also be played back by judges, counsel, and members of the jury (in special circumstances) upon request. E-reporters known as *electronic transcribers* create a written transcript of the recorded proceeding. They are responsible for document formatting, identifying speakers, and ensuring that spelling in the document is correct. Sometimes reporting and transcribing are done by the same individual. Contact the American Association of Electronic Reporters and Transcribers for more information on this court-reporting specialty.

In voice writing, a court reporter wears a hand-held mask (known as a voice silencer or stenomask) that is equipped with a microphone, and repeats the testimony of all parties involved in the trial. They identify each speaker and describe pertinent activities that are taking place in the courtroom. Some *voice writers* translate the voice recording in real-time using computer speech recognition technology.

To Be a Successful Voice Writer, You Should...

- be able to listen and speak at the same time
- be able to speak very quickly
- have a large vocabulary
- be able to use technology effectively to do your job

Others wait until after the proceedings to create the translation using voice recognition technology or by doing the translation manually. Voice writers must be able to listen and speak at the same time, be able to speak very quickly, and have a large vocabulary. Voice writers are employed in trials, depositions, public and administrative hearings, courts at all levels, grand jury proceedings, and U.S. Senate hearings. More than 25 states allow voice writers to practice in their judicial systems. Contact the National Verbatim Reporters Association for a complete list.

Courtrooms and offices are usually pleasant places to work. Under typical conditions, a court reporter can expect to work a standard 40 hours per week. During lengthy trials or other complicated proceedings, court reporters often work much longer hours. They must be present before and after the court is actually in session and must wait while a jury is deliberating. "The hours for a freelance court reporter vary weekly," says Janet Harris. "Once a reporter is on the job, you are required to stay until the testimony concludes. This is not always predictable." A court reporter often must be willing to work irregular hours, including some evenings. "An official court reporter works in a courtroom setting usually during regular business hours," says Janet, "and is responsible for producing transcripts during non-business hours." Court reporters must be able to spend long hours transcribing testimony with complete accuracy. Some court reporters, especially those employed as freelance reporters and those who are working for a traveling circuit judge, will have to travel. Normally, a court reporter will experience some down time without any transcript orders and then be hit all at once with several. This uneven workflow can cause the court reporter to have odd hours at times.

Court reporters must also have a degree of financial and business acumen. They will need to maintain paperwork for record-keeping and tracking invoices, income, and expenses.

Long hours of sitting in the same position can be tiring and court reporters may be bothered by eye, neck, and back strain. Court reporters who use the stenographic court-reporting technique also risk repetitive motion injuries, including carpal tunnel syndrome. The constant pressure to keep up and remain accurate can be stressful as well.

WHAT IS IT LIKE TO BE A COURT REPORTER?

Janet Harris, an electronic reporter and transcriber, has been the owner of Harris

Reporting Company for 19 years. She has worked in the field since 1985. "The main duty of a court reporter is to create a verbatim record of a proceeding and ensure that the transcript is accurate," she says. "In the digital reporting profession, I am responsible for creating an accurate, high-quality, multi-channel recording, preserving the recording, and producing a verbatim transcript. As in any business, a freelance reporter needs to master business management skills, as well. The most satisfying accomplishment in my career has been being a part of creating the profession. I love to find ways to use technology in my job to be more efficient and produce work for clients regardless of where I am physically."

Janet works from her home or wherever she has Internet access. "Two main databases essentially run my online office," she explains. "One is for scheduling and maintaining billing and transcript records, and the other is for transferring audio/video to clients and transcribers. Every day I enter information into the database to schedule new jobs, assign work to transcribers, upload audio, scan notes or exhibits for transcribers, and print and bill completed transcripts so clients have access to their transcripts from any computer. As a sole proprietor, I manage all phone calls and maintain all business records and accounting. Some days I am out of the office on site recording depositions. Usually these take place in a lawyer's or doctor's office. But on occasion I have recorded at different locations—the office or home of a witness, inside a prison, or at the bedside of a witness unable to attend court."

To Be a Successful Electronic Reporter or Transcriber, You Should...

- be able to take notes quickly and accurately
- be able to use technology effectively to do your job
- be a good speller

DO I HAVE WHAT IT TAKES TO BE A COURT REPORTER?

Because part of a court reporter's work is done within the confines of a courtroom, being able to work under pressure is a must. Court reporters need to be able to meet deadlines with accuracy and attention to detail. As stated previously, a court reporter must be highly skilled at the stenograph machine and other technology used to record court proceedings. A minimum of 225 words per minute is required from a beginning stenographic court reporter.

Court reporters must be assertive enough to ask for clarification if a term or phrase goes by without the reporter understanding it. Court reporters must be as unbiased as possible and accurately record what is said, not what they believe to be true.

Court reporters should also be patient, seek to attain perfection in every aspect of their work, have the ability to work closely with judges and other court officials, and be familiar with a wide range of medical and legal terms.

"This career requires professionalism, respect for the law and its procedures, a detail-oriented nature, good organization skills, computer skills, and the ability to maintain confidentiality, meet deadlines, and work under pressure," says Janet Harris.

Gerie Bunch is an official court reporter in Quincy, California, and the chair of the California Court Reporters Association's Support Our Students Committee. She has worked in the field since 1985. Gerie says that the most important professional qualities for court reporters are "having good ethics, being accurate, being timely in preparation of transcripts and arriving to work, and treating everyone equally and respectfully."

Joyce Martin, president of the Colorado Court Reporters Association and a member of the Advisory Board of the Denver Academy of Court Reporting, believes that the most important personal and professional qualities for court reporters are "teamwork, promptness, perfectionism, professionalism, association membership, and a detail-oriented nature."

HOW DO I BECOME A COURT REPORTER?
Education
High School

To prepare for postsecondary study, you must first earn a high school diploma or its equivalent. Take as many advanced English classes as you can and strive to become a master at grammar and spelling. Typing classes and computer classes will provide you with a foundation in using computers and a head start in keyboarding skills. Classes in government and business will be helpful as well. Training in Latin can also be a great benefit because it will help you understand the many medical and legal terms that are used during court proceedings. Knowledge of foreign languages can also be helpful because as a court reporter, you will often transcribe the testimony of non-English speakers with the aid of court-appointed translators.

"I have participated in many career days at our local college and high school," says Gerie Bunch. "I let the students know that they need to be good spellers, have a broad vocabulary, need to know sentence structure and grammar, and have some education in anatomy and math; so basically, all those things that are taught in high school would go into being a successful reporter."

Postsecondary Training

Stenographic court reporters are required to complete a specialized training program in shorthand reporting. These programs usually last between two and four years and include instruction on how to enter at least 225 words a minute on a stenograph machine. Other topics include computer operations, transcription methods, English grammar, and the principles of law. For court cases involving medical issues, students must also take courses on human anatomy and physiology. Basic medical and legal terms are also taught.

Voice-writing training can typically be completed in nine months to a year, while e-reporting skills can be learned in three to six months. Both voice writers and e-reporters also learn how to use their respective technologies via in-house training while on the job.

About 130 postsecondary schools and colleges have two- and four-year programs in court reporting; approximately 70 of these programs are approved by the National Court Reporters Association (NCRA). Many business colleges offer these programs. As a court-reporting student in these programs, you must master machine shorthand and real-time reporting. The NCRA states that to graduate from one of these programs, you must be able to type at least 225 words per minute and pass tests that gauge your written knowledge and speed. "Students need to be dedicated and committed to practicing in order to attain the speed necessary to graduate," says Joyce Martin. "Just like a musician or athlete, it takes a lot of daily practice and commitment."

Certification or Licensing

The NCRA offers several levels of certification for its members. To receive the registered professional reporter certification, you must pass tests that are administered twice a year at more than 100 sites in the United States and overseas. The registered merit reporter certification means you have passed an exam with speeds up to 260 words per minute. The registered diplomate reporter certification is obtained by passing a written knowledge exam. This certification shows that the court reporter has gained valuable professional knowledge and experience through years of reporting. The certified real-time reporter certification is given to reporters who have obtained the specialized skill of converting the spoken word into written word at 96 percent accuracy. Several other specialized certifications also are available for court reporters.

The American Association of Electronic Reporters and Transcribers offers the following voluntary certifications: certified electronic court reporter, certified electronic court transcriber, and certified electronic court reporter and transcriber. The National Verbatim Reporters Association offers the following voluntary certifications: certified verbatim reporter, certificate of merit, and real-time verbatim reporter. Contact these organizations for information on requirements for each certification.

Some states require reporters to be notary publics or to be licensed through a state certification exam. Currently, more than 40 states grant licenses in either shorthand reporting or court reporting, although not all of these states require a license to work as a court reporter. Licenses are granted after the court reporter passes state examinations and fulfills any prerequisites (usually an approved shorthand reporting program).

Internships and Volunteerships

An internship during college is the best way to get your foot in the door and gain on-the-job experience. Your college career services office or court reporting program director can direct you to internship opportunities. Additionally, you should contact local court systems to ask if internships are available.

Another way to learn more about opportunities in the field is to contact a local court reporter to see if he or she can suggest any volunteer opportunities. You might be able to do basic office work (answering phones, filing, etc.) for a court reporter with a large practice. If you can't find an opportunity with a court reporter, try to find a volunteer position with a law firm or at your local courthouse to gain a general introduction to the legal field.

WHO WILL HIRE ME?

Many of the 19,000 court reporters employed in the United States work for city, county, state, or federal courts. Others work for themselves as freelancers or as employees of freelance reporting agencies. These freelance reporters are hired by attorneys to record the pretrial statements, or depositions, of experts and other witnesses. When people want tran-scripts or recordings of other important discussions, freelance reporters may be called on to record what is said at business meetings, large conventions, or similar events.

Most court reporters work in middle- to large-sized cities, although they are needed anywhere a court of law is in session. In smaller cities, a court reporter may only work part time.

A relatively new application of court-reporting skills and technology is in the field of television broadcast captioning. Using specialized computer-aided transcription systems (real-time), reporters can produce captions for live television events, including sporting events and national and local news, for the benefit of the deaf and hard-of-hearing community.

After completing the required training, court reporters usually work for a free-lance reporting company that provides court reporters for business meetings and deposition settings on a temporary basis. Qualified reporters can also contact these freelance reporting companies on their own. Joyce Martin entered the career of court reporting by substituting in courts throughout Colorado. "I then applied for and was hired by the city of Aurora," she recalls. "After getting married and having two daughters, I decided to stay home and teach at the local court reporting college part time. Fourteen years ago, I applied for and was offered an officialship position by a district court judge at the Arapahoe County District Court, one of the busiest counties in Colorado, where I continue to work. I also provide Communication Access Real-Time Translation to a hard-of-hearing judge in a domestic relations division. This allows him to read the spoken word—instantaneously enabling him to read the testimony of witnesses, the arguments made by the litigants, make proper rulings on objections, and issue his orders."

Occasionally a court reporter will be hired directly out of school as a courtroom official, but ordinarily only those with several years of experience are hired for full-time judiciary work. A would-be court reporter may start out working as a medical transcriptionist or other specific transcriptionist to get the necessary experience. Others might begin work as paralegals or legal secretaries in a law firm. Janet Harris was working as a legal secretary in a law firm when she received her first job offer. "The court reporting company we contracted services with hired me as the result of a casual discussion during a break in the proceeding," she says.

Career services counselors at your court reporting school can assist you in locating your first job. Also, try looking in the Yellow Pages for the names of potential employers. The Internet is also a rich source of information on career leads. The American Association of Electronic Reporters and Transcribers, the National Court Reporters Association, the National Verbatim Reporters Association, and the United States Court Reporters Association offer job listings at their Web sites.

WHERE CAN I GO FROM HERE?

Court reporters with a large amount of experience and skill may be promoted to

a larger court system or to an otherwise more demanding position, with a corresponding increase in pay and prestige. Those employed by a freelance company may be hired permanently by a city, county, state, or federal court. Those with experience working in a government position may choose to become a freelance court reporter and thereby have greater job flexibility and perhaps increase their income. Those with the necessary training, experience, and business skills may decide to open their own freelance reporting company.

According to a study funded by the National Court Reporters Foundation, court reporters advance by assuming more responsibility and greater skill levels; that

---

The Benefits of Association Membership

Joyce Martin, president of the Colorado Court Reporters Association, details the importance of membership in professional associations:

Association membership is vitally important to the success of one's career. Associations are created to provide networking opportunities, to provide education for their members, and to advocate on behalf of the profession, when necessary. A great quote I like to use for association participation is from Theodore Roosevelt, who once said, "Every man owes a part of his time and money to the business or industry in which he is engaged. No man has a moral right to withhold his support from an organization that is striving to improve conditions within his sphere."

gives the court reporter credibility in the eyes of professionals in the legal system. Those advanced responsibilities include real-time reporting, coding and cross-referencing the official record, assisting others in finding specific information quickly, and helping the judge and legal counsel with procedural matters.

Court reporters can also follow alternative career paths as legal and medical transcriptionists, captioning experts, and cyber-conference moderators.

WHAT ARE THE SALARY RANGES?

Earnings for court reporters vary based on their skill, speed, and experience, as well as where they live. Those who are employed by large court systems generally earn more than court reporters in smaller communities. Court reporters earned a median annual income of $49,710 in 2008, according to the U.S. Department of Labor. The lowest-paid reporters earned less than $25,360 annually, while the highest-paid had annual earnings of more than $83,500. Official court reporters not only earn a salary, but also a per-page fee for transcripts. Freelance court reporters are paid by the job and also per page for transcripts.

Court reporters who work in small communities or as freelancers may not be able to work full time. Successful court reporters with jobs in business environments may earn more than those in courtroom settings, but such positions offer less job security.

Those working for the government or full time for private companies usually receive health insurance and other benefits, such as paid vacations and retirement pensions. Freelancers may or may not receive health insurance or other benefits, depending on the policies of their agencies.

WHAT IS THE JOB OUTLOOK?

Employment of court reporters should grow much faster than the average for all careers through 2016, according to the U.S. Department of Labor. Job opportunities should be greatest in and around large metropolitan areas, but qualified court reporters should be able to find work in most parts of the country. Court reporters who use their skills to produce captioning for live and taped television programs, which is a federal requirement for all television programming, and those who create real-time translations for the deaf and hard-of-hearing in legal and academic settings, will be in high demand.

Job prospects will be strongest for court reporters with experience and advanced training. Because of the reliance on computers and other technology in many aspects of this job, computer training and proficiency are important. Court reporters who are certified—especially with the highest level of certification—will have the most opportunities to choose from.

As court reporters continue to use cutting-edge technology, such as real-time technology, to make court proceedings clearer and more accurate, the field itself should continue to grow. "Digital court reporting is a new industry and employment opportunities are on the rise," says Janet Harris. "Courts, administrative agencies, municipalities, corporate boardrooms, and private reporting agencies are the most common users of digital reporting technology. Due to the industry's relatively new start, employment in this field can only grow."

"Because of the implementation of real-time reporting, which provides the courts and attorneys with an immediate view of the testimony, we have a very good future," predicts Gerie Bunch. "There is not a type of software available that can do what court reporters do with real-time. Though there are often threatened cutbacks and layoffs, judges and attorneys realize the value of what we provide and often insist on using court reporters. Additionally, the California Court Reporters Association has a very powerful lobbying force, which has protected reporter jobs for more than 100 years."

Elder Law Attorneys

SUMMARY

Definition
Elder law attorneys provide legal services for the elderly and, in some cases, the disabled.

Alternative Job Titles
Elder lawyers

Salary Range
$54,460 to $110,590 to $1,000,000+

Educational Requirements
Law degree

Certification or Licensing
Voluntary (certification)
Required by all states (licensing)

Employment Outlook
About as fast as the average

High School Subjects
English (writing/ literature)
Government
Law
Speech

Personal Interests
Law
Writing

"People I meet who are not clients often tell me about their challenges with their own families," says Daphne Moritz, an elder law attorney. "Part of that is its own reward. People know what I do and they tell me their stories. They do not always become new clients, but sometimes they do. Mostly, I know that people can turn to me when they need the services that I provide, which can really help them in their lives."

WHAT DOES AN ELDER LAW ATTORNEY DO?

Elder law attorneys focus on the needs of their elderly clients, using a variety of legal tools and techniques to meet their goals in an efficient, fiscally responsible, and legally sound manner. Elder law attorneys deal with all of the legal needs of their clients. Because of this, they have many responsibilities. They may help one client with estate planning; they may counsel another client about planning for mental incapacity and compose an alternative decision-making document that will allow another family member, for example, to make decisions about that client's health care; and they may assist yet another client in planning for possible long-term care needs, including nursing home care. Locating the appropriate type of care, coordinating private and public resources to finance the cost of care, and working to ensure the client's right to quality care are all part of the elder law practice.

Elder law attorneys must know the law's position on a variety of issues, including health and long-term care planning, surrogate decision-making (that is, when the client has appointed someone, most likely a relative, to make financial or other decisions when the client is unable to), obtaining public benefits (including Medicaid, Medicare, and Social Security), managing diminished capacity (such as when the client can no longer think clearly), and the conservation and administration of the older person's estate (including wills, trusts, and probate). In advising about these matters, elder law attorneys must know about the tax consequences for clients when they decide on a certain action (such as putting money in a trust); attorneys must also recognize when they need to seek out more sophisticated tax information from an expert and do so for the best interests of their clients. In addition, elder law attorneys must be able to recognize cases of abuse, neglect, and exploitation of an older client. An elder law attorney must also be familiar with professional and nonlegal resources and services that are publicly and privately available to meet the needs of the older person. Elder law attorneys can then refer clients to these resources, which may include adult day care centers, community transportation, and food services. Elder law encompasses more than just legal planning; it deals with a larger realm of life planning.

In many cases, a crisis is what brings a new client to an elder law attorney. Common situations include middle-income families concerned about paying for a parent's long-term care and nursing home care; families with an older member whose ability to think clearly and live independently is diminishing; older people wanting to ensure that their wishes are respected when their health deteriorates; families struggling with retirement and/or assisted-living decisions, contracts, and expenses; and families or seniors faced with issues of age discrimination, exploitation, or abuse.

Elder law attorneys must conduct their practices ethically. They must understand their clients, know which confidences can be shared with which family members, and know when and how to seek the advice of other professionals, whether about medical, financial, insurance, or tax issues, to best meet the needs of their clients. The attorney must also recognize situations where a client's wishes clash with those of the family and then determine the best way of handling the issues to most effectively serve the client.

Lawyers typically enjoy a pleasant, although busy, work environment. Law offices are usually designed to impress clients and can be quite comfortable. Lawyers may also spend significant time in law libraries or record rooms or in the homes and offices of clients. Courtrooms are usually orderly and efficient workplaces. However, many elder law attorneys never work in a courtroom, and, unless directly involved in litigation, they may never work at a trial.

Working hours for most lawyers are usually regular business hours. Many lawyers,

To Be a Successful Elder Law Attorney, You Should...

- be highly knowledgeable about elder law

- care deeply about the welfare of your clients

- enjoy meeting new people

- be able to find creative solutions to difficult situations

- be a good listener

- be diplomatic

- always present a professional image

- be willing to continue to learn throughout your career

however, have to work long hours when a client's case demands it, spending evenings and weekends preparing cases and materials and working with clients. Besides the time spent working directly on a client's needs, elder law attorneys must also stay current with the latest developments in the field. They do this by attending seminars and reading industry publications, such as *Eye On Elder Issues,* an e-newsletter published by The National Academy of Elder Law Attorneys.

Elder law attorneys, more than other types of lawyers, can expect to put in more hours visiting their clients in their homes or care facilities, since traveling to the attorney's office may be challenging for some clients. Attorneys who special-

ize in elder law should be prepared for the realities of life for the elderly, as they are likely to be exposed to various types and stages of illness or infirmity and environments that can be disturbing to some.

WHAT IS IT LIKE TO BE AN ELDER LAW ATTORNEY?

Daphne Moritz is an elder law attorney in Woodstock, Vermont. She works at the Law Offices of Mark E. Melendy, P.L.L.C., a firm that provides legal services primarily in the areas of estate planning, trusts, estate administration, nonprofit law, business succession planning, corporate law, tax, real estate, and land use. Her work day begins at about 8:30 A.M. "Once I am at the office I check in with staff and attorneys, turn on my computer, read the mail and begin planning my responses, check voice mail and make return calls as needed, read e-mail and respond as necessary, check my 'to-do' list, my 'tickler' to see what needs immediate attention, and work through my daily action plan.

"During the day I draft documents for clients, including wills, trusts, advance directives, powers of attorney, guardianship directives, etc. I also work on probate administration documents. I often speak with nursing home personnel, senior centers, assisted living facilities, state agencies, financial advisers, accountants, the Internal Revenue Service, and professionals whose work interfaces with mine. I confer with other attorneys in my office on various concepts and directions and challenges, and I research as needed."

On certain days, Daphne meets with clients. "These meetings," she explains, "may be initial consultations in which we go over the client's personal and financial information and begin strategizing their goals and objectives. Other times our meetings are informational and advisory. Still other times I have signing meetings during which time we go through the formalities of completing the client's documents."

Daphne says that her type of work only occasionally requires her to go to court to represent clients. These court appearances generally relate to guardianship matters. She may also visit a client where he or she lives, particularly if the client resides in a nursing home or assisted living facility. "I have assisted clients with their moves and managing their finances to ensure they can continue living in comfort and dignity as they age," she says.

Because she has a small firm and is an entrepreneur, Daphne also devotes a portion of each week to marketing. "I take referral sources to lunch, develop speaking engagements and make presentations, write articles, and work on our Web site and newsletter," she says. "I am preparing to launch a blog on legacy advising. I scour the *Wall Street Journal*, *New York Times*, and local papers and the Internet and listen to public radio for topics of interest and to stay informed about the financial markets, the general economy, and trends. I am very interested in using social media and utilizing the Internet as a new legal practice frontier.

"Toward the end of the day I make sure I organize myself for the following day. I work from my home office one day per week. Some evenings I attend events geared toward estate planners."

Daphne says that there are many pros to working as an elder law attorney. "You get to help people, meet new people, develop lasting relationships with clients and their families, and you act as adviser, teacher, and guide. This is the best type of law to practice if you are a compassionate, patient, and loving person who is most interested in helping individuals and families solve their problems."

When asked to cite negative aspects of a career in elder law, Daphne says that she hasn't seen a downside yet. "However," she says, "there is a very technical aspect of this work and so there are times when clients have a hard time grasping this information no matter how well you try to convey it. Also, the rules and regulations change frequently and, although lawyers keep in step, it again is difficult to convey a complex regulatory change to a client. You must be very patient with clients and their families. Often resolutions take time. Finally, sometimes it is difficult to help people in crisis. When people are very ill it is generally very difficult for the family and the individual emotionally, and it certainly is difficult for them to understand the technical aspects of estate planning or state benefit programs. As their attorney, you have to be there for them in whatever capacity you can. I do not view this as a con, only as a challenge."

DO I HAVE WHAT IT TAKES TO BE AN ELDER LAW ATTORNEY?

All lawyers have to be strong communicators, have good interpersonal skills, and be able to find creative solutions to problems. Elder lawyers, however, need to have some special skills and personality characteristics. They should care deeply about the welfare of their clients. "I have the personality more of a social worker than a traditional lawyer," says Charlie Robinson, an elder law attorney since 1985. "And the opportunity to help families in distress from chronic illness and disability fits me." Daphne Moritz agrees. "The type of law that I practice has a very human quality to it," she says. "Compassion is a very good quality in this practice area. You do not have to be naturally extroverted, but it helps if you enjoy meeting new people." Elder law attorneys also need to understand how the aging process may affect a client's mind and body, how conflicts can arise among family members regarding the best interests of an elderly member, and how the family's wishes sometimes are in conflict with those of the older person. "You have to be willing to work with families who do not always agree about the best course of action—help them work through conflict to reach an end that works," says Daphne.

This work also requires perceptiveness, ethics, and diplomacy. Daphne believes that listening to and truly understanding a client is one of the most important skills for an elder law attorney. "You have to be a very active listener and hone those specific skills," she says. "It isn't just listening, it is about making sure you 'get' what your clients are after, that they know you get it, and that you are able to give them counseling they seek to ensure that their needs are

> ## Advice for Students
>
> Daphne Moritz offers the following advice to students as they graduate and look for jobs in this field:
>
> - Always be curious about life and learning.
>
> - Be creative.
>
> - Love to learn.
>
> - Ask questions.
>
> - Build networks and connections using all means available—both in person and via technology.
>
> - Strive to be great at what you do and be valuable in your chosen field.

met. You always have to be professional in your mannerisms, your dress, and the way in which you convey information. You have to be empathetic and address clients in a way that you would want others to address you. Never speak disparagingly about colleagues or clients, and maintain client confidentiality."

Daphne also believes that to be a successful elder law attorney, "you have to be willing to read a lot, be interested in much detail, and be skilled in analyzing complex information about property distribution, legislation, case law, the tax code, and other rules and regulations. You should have an entrepreneurial spirit, be nimble and flexible in your approach to a variety of people, and understand who you want your clients to be and learn to attract them to you. Above all, you have to have a passion for this work. Love it, live it."

HOW DO I BECOME AN ELDER LAW ATTORNEY?

Education

Daphne Moritz graduated from Vermont Law School with a juris doctor and a master's degree in environmental law. "In college and law school stay broad minded," she advises. "In college, take courses in many areas and become knowledgeable about human behavior. Try to get internships and summer jobs that will help you develop strong communication skills with a variety of people. Develop your writing skills. During your high school, college, and law school years do not devote all of your time to absorbing only the minute details of the law. Make sure that your human relationship skills are very strong. The best lawyers combine a deep knowledge of the law and proficiency in their practice areas with empathy for their client's situation."

High School

To become a lawyer you will need to earn a college degree and a law degree after you graduate from high school. To start preparing for this later education and career, take a college preparatory curriculum, including math, science, and even a foreign language, while in high school. Be sure to take courses in social studies, government, history, and economics to prepare for law studies. English courses are also important for building your writing, researching, and speaking skills. And because lawyers often use technology to research and interpret the law, take advantage of any computer-related classes or experience you can get. Even surfing the Internet can provide experience in doing online research.

Postsecondary Training

To enter a law school that has been approved by the American Bar Association, you must satisfactorily complete at least three, and usually four, years of college work. Most law schools do not specify any particular courses for prelaw education. The traditional majors for college students intending to pursue a postgraduate law degree are history, English, philosophy, political science, economics, and business. Other successful law students have focused their undergraduate studies in areas as diverse as art, music theory, computer science, engineering, nursing, and education. A college student planning to specialize in elder law might also take courses significantly related to that area, such as social sciences, psychology, economics, and health care.

To gain admission to law school, most programs require applicants to take the Law School Admission Test (LSAT). The LSAT tests students on analytical thinking, writing, and problem-solving skills. Most full-time law degree programs take three years to complete.

There are currently 200 law schools in the United States that have been approved by the American Bar Association. State authorities approve additional programs, many of them part-time or night school programs that can be completed in four years. You should contact law schools you are interested in to find out specific requirements for their programs. College guidance counselors and professors may also be valuable sources of information.

The first year of typical law school programs consists of required courses, such as legal writing and research, contracts, criminal law, constitutional law, torts, and property. First-year law students are required to read and study thousands of legal cases. The second and third years are usually focused on specialized courses of interest to the student. In the case of elder law, students might take course work in public policy, health law, medical ethics, and geriatrics.

Upon completing law school, students usually receive the juris doctorate (J.D.) degree or bachelor of laws (LL.B.) degree.

Certification or Licensing

To obtain a law license, lawyers (regardless of their specialization) must be admitted to the bar association of the state in which they will practice. Bar admission standards in most states require that students graduate from an approved law school and that they pass a bar examination in the state in which they intend to practice. These exams, usually lasting two days, have questions about various areas of the law, such as constitutional law and criminal law. The tests may also include an essay section and a professional responsibility section. It is important to note, however, that each state sets its own standards for taking the bar exam, and a few states allow exceptions to the educational requirements. For example, a small number of states allow a person who has spent several years reading law in a law office and has some law school experience to take the state bar exam. A few states allow people who have completed law study through correspondence programs to take the bar. In addition, some states require that newly graduated lawyers serve a period of clerkship in an established law firm before they are eligible to take the bar examination. Because of such variations, you will need to contact the bar examiners board of your state for specific information on its requirements.

Specialized voluntary certification is available for elder law attorneys. The National Elder Law Foundation (NELF) offers certification to attorneys who have been in practice for five years or longer, have spent at least 16 hours per week (over three years) practicing elder law, have handled at least 60 elder law matters, and have had at least 45 hours of continuing legal education in elder law. To obtain certification, applicants must also pass an examination. After five years, certified attorneys must be recertified to maintain their status.

Internships and Volunteerships

Try to land an internship or clerkship through your college's law program or your college's career services office. You can also try to get part-time or summer work in a lawyer's office. You may only answer phones, file office papers, or type letters, but this work will give you excellent exposure to the profession. The American Bar Association provides information on clerkships and internships (including those for law students who are interested in elder law) at its Web site, http://www.abanet.org.

It is also important for you to obtain experience working with the elderly, either on a paid or a volunteer basis. "Work or volunteer at a senior center or an assisted living facility," advises Daphne Moritz. "Make yourself available to seniors in your community. Peruse the AARP Web site and other sites devoted to helping seniors." By working with the elderly population, you will start to learn about their specific needs, concerns, and opinions.

"Find a law practice devoted to elder law and see if you can get a job shadowing, community-based, or service learning opportunity with that office," recommends Daphne. "Another place to develop knowledge is often with legal aid (senior law project, etc.). If you do land such a position, show your initiative. Additionally, make sure the attorney you work with gives you actual work to do—brings you to see clients where they are and to office meetings."

WHO WILL HIRE ME?

The National Academy of Elder Law Attorneys (NAELA) reports that its current membership is 4,400. In addition, there are thousands of attorneys who practice elder law as a part of a law practice that encompasses a range of other areas.

The majority of practicing elder law attorneys in the United States work in private practice, either in law firms or alone. While it may seem that the best employment possibilities might be found in large cities and metropolitan areas, there is also fierce competition in these places. Many attorneys practice elder law in addition to other areas of law. Additionally, clients often come to their regular attorneys for

elder issues that arise in their lives. Since elder law is so client-oriented, the logical approach is to practice where there is a large population of elderly people; therefore, smaller, more rural areas offer numerous opportunities. In addition, the cost of living is lower in these areas, and since the majority of people seeking elder law attorneys are not wealthy and cannot pay astronomical fees, the elder law attorney will find living on a typical income easier in these areas.

After graduation from law school, a lawyer's first task is to pass the state bar examination. A new lawyer will often find a job with a law firm, doing research for other lawyers until passing the bar examination and becoming licensed to practice law. Beginning lawyers usually do not go into solo practice right away. It is difficult to become established, and the experience of working beside established lawyers is helpful to the fledgling lawyer. Newly hired lawyers typically do research and routine work at first. Specialization usually occurs after a lawyer has some experience in general practice, although lawyers at smaller firms might find themselves guided to particular areas earlier. After a few years of successful experience, a lawyer may be ready to go out on his or her own.

Many new lawyers are recruited directly from law school by law firms or other employers. Schools sponsor job fairs in which recruiters meet with and possibly interview potential hires. Local and state bar associations can also provide job leads.

To start building a practice in elder law, take as many cases that fall into the realm of elder law as you can and become a member of the NAELA. When you have enough experience under your belt and meet the necessary qualifications, become certified as an elder law attorney with the NELF.

Charlie Robinson believes that it is very helpful for new lawyers to begin participating in local, state, and national bar activities in elder law. "You meet the best and brightest in the field," he explains, "and may very well find someone who will mentor a new elder law attorney past some of the pitfalls. There are also a number of treatises on the subject now. Also, there are elder law courses available at many law schools."

WHERE CAN I GO FROM HERE?

There are many opportunities for lawyers with exceptional ability. New lawyers generally start out doing routine research tasks, but as they prove themselves and develop their abilities, opportunities for

---

Did You Know?

According to the National Academy of Elder Law Attorneys, elder law attorneys are experts in the following areas:

- age discrimination
- disability planning
- elder abuse/neglect
- entitlement programs
- estate and gift tax planning
- estate planning and probate
- guardianship/conservatorship
- housing
- insurance
- long-term care financing
- Medicaid
- medical decision making
- Medicare
- retirement benefits

advancement will arise. They may be promoted to junior partner in a law firm or establish their own practice focused on elder law.

Advancement for elder law attorneys can involve working at a larger firm, opening one's own firm, or taking leadership positions in nonprofit organizations that serve to advance education and competence in the field. There are many opportunities to make a contribution to the elderly population by working to support or change the laws and policies that affect senior citizens. In this unique area of legal practice, the potential for reward, although usually not as financially large as other areas of the law, is great.

WHAT ARE THE SALARY RANGES?

Beginning lawyers earn a relatively modest salary, but the potential for higher earnings builds quickly with solid experience. The median salary for all lawyers was $110,590 in 2008, according to the U.S. Department of Labor, although some senior partners earned more than $1 million a year. Ten percent of lawyers earned less than $54,460.

According to the National Association for Law Placement, median salaries for new lawyers were $95,000 in 2006, with salaries ranging from $50,000 to $135,000 based on the size of the firm. Although salaries for private practice law are attractive, it is important to remember that lawyers just starting out may barely make ends meet for the first few years. Most law school graduates carry upward of $70,000 in student loans. Thus, although many

> ### Fact
> By 2020 the number of people in the United States who are over the age of 65 is expected to double, according to the Federal Interagency Forum on Aging-Related Statistics. This suggests that there will be strong opportunities for elder law attorneys.

graduates may want to work in public service and government law, many take jobs in private practice in order to gain a stronger financial foothold.

Incomes for elder law attorneys vary greatly but generally are less than those of their colleagues working with wealthy clients, such as corporate lawyers representing major companies.

Benefits and bonuses vary widely in this field. Many attorneys are sole practitioners and therefore don't receive company benefits such as paid vacation, health insurance, and retirement plans. Generally, lawyers who are partners in larger firms may enjoy more generous benefits packages and perks than those with a solo practice.

WHAT IS THE JOB OUTLOOK?

The demand for all lawyers is expected to grow as fast as the average for all careers through 2016, according to the U.S. Department of Labor, but those in the specialty of elder law will have the advantage of a rapidly growing elderly population, increasingly complex laws, and unprecedented health care issues. All of these factors combine to make for a substantial client base in need of elder law attorneys. It is estimated that 40 percent of people over 65 will require a nursing home or other long-term care at some point, but few of them have planned financially for that eventuality. People are living longer and encountering a variety of health care problems, many of them debilitating. The sheer numbers of elderly people alone point to a promising future in this career.

However, the outlook is also affected by governmental changes and public policy. Since a majority of elder law clients are seeking legal advice and assistance for Medicare/Medicaid issues, the outlook for the profession is significantly affected by changes in law. "We have significant challenges to our health care system in this country, particularly in how we care for the chronically ill and disabled," says Charlie Robinson. "There are going to be many fighting over resources barely sufficient for current numbers in the health care system. That suggests to me that there will be room for advocates to do well by doing good for awhile."

Many people do not seek out an elder law attorney in particular for issues such as long-range planning, asset protection, guardianship, and probate practices; rather, they are likely to bring these issues to their regular attorney. In other words, attorneys who may not specialize in elder law often handle a large number of cases involving elder law issues.

The large number of law school graduates each year has created strong competition for jobs, and new attorneys, even those with an eye toward elder law specialization, will initially encounter strong competition for jobs.

Intellectual Property Lawyers

SUMMARY

Definition
Intellectual property (IP) lawyers focus on the protection of creative thought. They may work with patents to protect their clients' inventions and discoveries; copyrights to protect works their clients have authored, such as music or computer programs; and trademarks to protect brand names and symbols associated with their clients' businesses. IP attorneys may also work with companies to protect their trade secrets.

Alternative Job Titles
Intellectual property attorneys
Patent lawyers

Salary Range
$77,000 to $119,000 to $200,000+

Educational Requirements
Bachelor's degree (any major is appropriate for general IP lawyers; patent attorneys need a degree in science, engineering, or physics)
Law degree

Certification or Licensing
Required

Employment Outlook
Faster than the average

High School Subjects
English (writing/literature)
Government
Law
Speech

Personal Interests
Current events
Law
Writing

"One of the most rewarding parts of my job happens every day, when clients call me and I am able to provide them with legal counseling and insight to help them run their advertising and marketing promotions," says Lisa Thomas, an advertising and privacy lawyer and partner at Winston & Strawn LLP, one of the 50 largest law firms in the world. "I'm thrilled that my clients count on me as a valuable resource, and am honored in the trust they place in me to help them bring their ideas to fruition. For example, I have clients that design and launch new interactive Web sites and mobile sites, and they call me to ask me what type of content should be placed on the site, how the site should function for legal compliance, and whether (and what kinds of) disclaimers need to be on the site. It's rewarding to have the chance to look at these programs before they launch, and I often get to see

> ## To Be a Successful Intellectual Property Lawyer, You Should...
>
> - be attentive to detail
> - have excellent communication skills
> - be organized
> - be willing to continue to learn throughout your career
> - have knowledge of one or more foreign languages

the latest and greatest technology six to 12 months before everyone else!"

WHAT DOES AN INTELLECTUAL PROPERTY LAWYER DO?

Intellectual property lawyers protect a client's creative interests, whether those interests are to patent a new product or to ensure that a copyright hasn't been infringed upon. IP lawyers may work in all areas of intellectual property law; however, many lawyers specialize in patent, trademark, copyright, or licensing law. Whichever area the IP attorney focuses on, some job duties are the same across the board. One of the IP lawyer's main tasks is to counsel clients. Usually this counseling concerns whether the intellectual property can be patented, trademarked, or copyrighted; the best method

of protection for the individual property; and whether the product or idea being discussed will infringe on someone else's patent, trademark, or copyright. Another major task for an IP lawyer is the drafting of legal documents, such as patent applications and licensing agreements.

The IP lawyer also serves clients by being their advocate before administrative bodies and courts. The IP lawyer's goal is to secure the rights of the client and then protect those rights if others violate them. Conversely, if the IP lawyer's client is accused of violating someone else's intellectual property rights, the IP lawyer defends the client.

IP lawyers may help their clients choose an Internet domain name or a trademark. They are often asked to review press releases, advertising copy, and other official documents to ensure that there are no intellectual property problems.

IP lawyers work with a wide range of clients, from an author or individual inventor to the highest manager of a large corporation. Those who are employed by corporations are usually in-house counsels concerned with decisions affecting the use of intellectual property within the company. IP lawyers working in academia assist scientists and researchers by identifying products and inventions that have potential in the marketplace.

The majority of IP lawyers focus on patent law. A patent lawyer works with an inventor from the early stages to decide if the invention has a chance of being granted a patent. If so, the attorney drafts and files a patent application with the United States Patent and Trademark

Office (USPTO). The lawyer then works with the patent examiner to try to get the patent approved. If a patent is issued, the lawyer has succeeded; if it is not, the attorney can appeal the decision to the Patent Office's board of appeals. If the lawyer and client are again denied a patent, they can appeal to the United States Court of Appeals for the Federal Circuit. Once a patent is approved, the patent lawyer may continue to be involved by investigating and developing licensing agreements.

If a client believes his or her rights to intellectual property have been infringed upon, the IP attorney must try to prove that someone else has taken or used the client's intellectual property without consent. On the other hand, if a client is accused of infringing on another's intellectual property rights, the lawyer must try to prove that the item in question didn't deserve a copyright, patent, or trademark in the first place or that the protection is invalid. Although lawsuits are commonplace today, most IP lawyers consider litigation the last step and try to settle differences outside the courtroom.

IP attorneys, like lawyers in other areas, have heavy workloads and work long hours. IP lawyers may spend hours studying documents with few breaks. Many law firms establish weekly goals for their lawyers that include the number of hours billed to the client. Some of these goals can be extremely demanding. Most of the lawyer's time is spent indoors meeting with clients, researching, or arguing in court. Depending on their position in the company or firm, IP lawyers may lead a team of lawyers or supervise a group of paralegals and associates.

WHAT IS IT LIKE TO BE AN INTELLECTUAL PROPERTY LAWYER?

Linda Norcross is an associate at Lewis & Roca LLP in Las Vegas, Nevada. "I have worked in the field for a little more than eight years," she says, "first as a paralegal, then law clerk, and finally as an attorney. There is never a dull moment, and no such thing as a typical day. My specialty (and passion) is trademark prosecution. I do everything involved in the life cycle of a trademark, from conducting searches to determine infringement risk and registrability of a proposed trademark, to filing federal and state trademark applications. Federal trademark prosecution requires several steps between filing and registration. I prepare arguments in response to office actions rendered by the USPTO, and am involved in opposition and cancellation proceedings before the Trademark Trial & Appeal Board, which is the administrative arm of the USPTO. The most fun part is being able to advise people about protecting their brand portfolios, which are a significant asset."

Celina Diaz is an intellectual property lawyer at Carstens & Cahoon, LLP in Dallas, Texas. "I have worked in the IP field for about 16 months now," she says, "having switched fields two years after law school. I am the type of person who enjoys multitasking and taking on new challenges. I wanted to become an intellectual property lawyer because I felt it would provide me with the opportunity to keep up with changes in science and technology, as well as the challenge of keeping up with the changing laws and rules of the patent world. There is always something new to learn in the IP world and always interesting people to meet and help with protecting their intellectual property."

Celina's workdays are typically filled with patent prosecution matters. "Despite how the phrase 'patent prosecution' sounds, this is nothing like the criminal prosecution you see on *Law and Order*," she explains. "Patent prosecution is basically the back and forth communication between a patent examiner and an inventor, or his/her agent or attorney. Before a patent application is issued a patent, a patent attorney will correspond with an examiner at the USPTO regarding the novelty and/or non-obviousness of an invention. I may spend the day writing a patent application, responding to an office action and/or reviewing prior art (such as other patents, applications, or any other materials) to figure out whether an application should be filed for a particular invention, given other inventions or ideas out there like it. I often get to taste new products and tinker with new gadgets before they hit the public, but I especially enjoy seeing the success of the products that I have helped protect and knowing that I have helped clients with an important aspect of their business."

Although she mainly works with patent prosecution, Celina spends some of her time on other matters, such as litigation or drafting assignment or license documents. "Patent litigation relates to the infringement of issued patents," she explains. "I like this balance because the litigation side teaches me what pitfalls to avoid when writing applications so as to help clients avoid similar problems in the future. Depending on where you work or who your client is, patent prosecution may be more predictable in terms of work hours, which allows for steady work days, better-planned vacations, and more family time when you need it. On the other hand, with litigation, you get the opportunity to enforce your clients' intellectual property rights, which can also be exciting."

Jennifer Rogers is a patent attorney at Shumaker & Sieffert, P.A., a small patent law firm in St. Paul, Minnesota. Her firm focuses on helping companies get their technology patented. Its recent clients have included Medtronic, Qualcomm, Juniper Networks, and 3M Company. "Among the things I like the most about my job," she says, "are the opportunity to constantly learn about new areas of technology, the opportunity to work as a professional, and the fact that patent law is less contentious and confrontational than other areas of law. Also, the schedule I keep as a patent prosecution attorney is fairly predictable. My firm does not handle any litigation, which can involve a much more unpredictable and time-consuming schedule. Among the things that I like least about my job are the fact that it can require long hours at times, and that it can be tough to block off time to take vacations.

"One of the most rewarding things that has happened to me while working in this field is having the opportunity to become involved in the leadership in my law firm and working on shaping policies for the firm. The firm I work for was founded in 2001, so it is a relatively new firm. It has grown quite a bit since its inception. I have been in charge of coordinating our recruiting efforts for the past few years. I have enjoyed working at a place that is small enough where I feel like I have a voice and can put forth suggestions that will make a difference in how things are done."

Donna Mason is an associate at Brundidge & Stanger, P.C. in Alexandria, Virginia. "I currently work in the field of intellectual property law, specifically in the field of patent prosecution," she says. "I have nearly 10 years of experience—including two-and-a-half years as a patent examiner at the USPTO, and the remainder of my experience has primarily been as a patent attorney in private practice."

Donna attended Vanderbilt University, where she completed a double major in electrical and biomedical engineering. After graduating from college, she worked as an electrical engineer in the field of nuclear electrical engineering at Virginia Power Company. "I became interested in patent law while working as an engineer," she says. "Although I enjoyed the technical aspects of my job, I wanted to channel my interest in technology in a different manner, but I did not know how to do so until I discovered the field of patent law. After working for

> ### Did You Know?
>
> According to the Franklin Pierce Law Center, the United States is the largest producer of intellectual property in the world.

three years as an engineer, I made the decision to attend law school. I obtained a J.D. degree from Vanderbilt University School of Law, and then a year later I obtained an LL.M. degree in patent and intellectual property law from The George Washington University Law School in Washington, D.C.

"As a registered patent attorney, I prepare and prosecute patent applications, which are directed to inventions in a wide range of technologies. I argue back and forth with patent examiners at the USPTO in an attempt to obtain patents for our clients. I have some experience in trademarks and copyrights, but my main focus is patent law."

Donna says that one of the most rewarding things about working in the field is the opportunity she has received to travel to Japan. "One of our clients is a Japanese company," she explains, "and members of our firm regularly travel to Japan to conduct meetings with our client. I have always associated Japan with innovation and advanced technologies. With my interest in technology, it has been a delight for me to visit a place that I consider to be at the forefront of technology."

DO I HAVE WHAT IT TAKES TO BE AN INTELLECTUAL PROPERTY LAWYER?

IP lawyers should have excellent written and oral communication skills. In fact, the American Bar Foundation says a recent survey shows that law firms are more interested in these skills than the overall legal knowledge of the interviewee. Also, having command of foreign languages is crucial because IP lawyers work with products and ideas in international markets. Intellectual property lawyers need

Advice for High School Students

The editors of *What Can I Do Now? Law* asked Celina Diaz and Donna Mason to provide advice to young people who are interested in pursuing careers in the field.

Celina Diaz, Carstens & Cahoon, LLP, Dallas, Texas:

Figure out what you enjoy doing, and life will be more enjoyable. If you like science or physics, don't be afraid to take as many science and math courses as you can. It will only make you more marketable as a patent attorney. Mock trials will also provide real hands-on experience and will give you a better idea of whether or not you prefer litigation over prosecution, or even whether you prefer to spend your days with a little bit of both. It is never too early to get involved in these activities. At best, it will give you a leg up on the competition; at worst, you make some good friends or connections that can help at some point down the road.

Donna Mason, Brundidge & Stanger, P.C., Alexandria, Virginia:

A career in intellectual property law is very rewarding, and it is filled with different specialties and types of practices. However, to obtain career satisfaction, you should determine what area of this field you are most interested in and in what type of environment you want to practice. For instance, whether you decide to practice patent law, trademark law, copyright law, or a combination of these three branches of intellectual property law, you must also decide whether you prefer litigation, patent prosecution (i.e., drafting and prosecuting patent applications), or licensing (i.e., drafting and negotiating intellectual property law-related contracts). You should also consider the advantages and disadvantages associated with practicing in a small, mid-sized, or large firm, a corporate office, and academia. The type of law you practice, combined with the environment in which you practice, are important factors in career satisfaction.

Throughout my career path as an engineer, a patent examiner, and a patent attorney, I have been either the only woman or one of few women working in my profession, within my immediate work group. Thus far, no negative experiences have generated from my being in the minority.

However, I would encourage women to seek out other women as mentors to help develop a network of contacts that can provide valuable resources when trying to meet one's professional goals. Talking to someone who has already done what you want to do is invaluable.

to be organized, attentive to detail, and willing to continue to learn throughout their careers.

HOW DO I BECOME AN INTELLECTUAL PROPERTY LAWYER?

Education

High School

Because intellectual property often deals with creations in the scientific, engineering, literary, and music worlds, a background in any of those areas will be helpful. If you are interested in combining a certain area with practicing law, you should focus on that area while in high school. Take as many science courses as possible in order to learn basic scientific principles that will help you as you draft patent applications. Take courses in business, accounting, computers, government, and English as well. "Excelling in English, especially writing, would be very helpful," advises Linda Norcross. "If your school district offers a magnet program or even elective classes specializing in law, definitely look into it."

"The most valuable lesson I learned in high school was to question the sources I read," says Lisa Thomas. "Never take anything at face value, something that is so easy to do today where the Internet gives us unprecedented access to written information. Look at who wrote the materials. Ask yourself if they have the background, education, and knowledge to be a trusted source. Whenever possible, go to the primary source. So, for example, instead of reading an article about a new law, read the new law. I never thought when in high school that I would become a lawyer, but in retrospect, I realize that the love of learning—and of asking questions—made this the perfect career for me."

Karin Kennedy, an intellectual property lawyer at Christopher & Weisberg, P.A. in Fort Lauderdale, Florida, advises high school students to work hard and study hard. "There is a lot of competition for seats at universities," she says. "In order to compete, you need to have great grades and test scores. Also be involved in school activities. Make the time to go to meetings and socials and participate, because it will not only help you professionally, but you will also make great friends for life."

Postsecondary Training

As in other areas of law, IP lawyers most often complete an undergraduate degree and then graduate from law school. For most types of intellectual property law, the undergraduate degree does not have to have a special focus. The exception to that is patent law. If you want to become a patent lawyer, you should major in science, engineering, or physics. Other technology-related majors will also be helpful. Some students pursue a double major in order to increase their skills and make themselves more attractive to employers. "While I was getting my electrical engineering degree, I discovered that physics was quite fascinating," recalls Karin. "So I decided to major in both fields. I had to work summers to make ends meet, and now I see that this was a blessing in disguise. I spent a summer at IBM, another at DaimlerChrysler, another at Tektronix, and that gave me the advantage of having industry experience, even though I was just a college student. When I graduated and started applying for jobs, that experience helped me tremendously."

To apply to almost any law school, you must first pass the Law School Admission Test (LSAT). The LSAT is an aptitude test used to predict how successful an individual will be in law school. Most law schools teach courses in intellectual property law, and some have IP sections and degrees, such as Columbia Law School, Franklin Pierce Law Center, and George Mason University School of Law.

Asked if she would do anything differently in law school, Celina Diaz says that she "probably would have taken the patent bar sooner; if not before law school, then just after my first year of law school. I believe this would have given me more exposure to the patent rules early on. In addition, once you pass the patent bar, you become a *patent agent,* able to prepare, file, and prosecute patent applications. This would allow you to start accumulating experience and expertise with patent prosecution. This would also give a better picture of whether this field is the right fit for you."

During law school, it is also a good idea to seek employment as a student associate at an intellectual property firm to gain experience in the field. Ceyda Azakli Maisami, a law student in Suffolk University Law School's evening division, is a student associate at Finnegan, Henderson, Farabow, Garrett & Dunner, LLP in Cambridge, Massachusetts. Ceyda offers the following thoughts on her experience at the firm: "Practicing law is a very fast-paced job, full of cases (projects) with hard deadlines, which requires time management, discipline, and commitment. It is definitely not a 9 A.M.-to-5 P.M. job. Even though law has rules and precedence, everything can be very gray. Most of the time, there is no one right answer, and a better structured and presented argument wins. I really enjoy strategy construction, persuasive writing, and oral arguments. Moreover, I enjoy being surrounded by very intelligent and hardworking people."

Certification or Licensing

After graduating from law school, you will be eligible to take the bar exam in any state. After passing the bar, you will be sworn in as an attorney and will then be eligible to practice law. Patent attorneys who practice patent law before the USPTO must go a step further and obtain additional certification. Would-be patent lawyers must pass the patent bar exam. According to the American Bar Association, you must hold a bachelor's degree in engineering, physics, or the natural sciences (such as chemistry and biochemistry), hold a bachelor's degree in another subject, or have passed the Engineer in Training test in order to be eligible to take the patent bar exam.

Internships and Volunteerships

IP law is a perfect career for someone who is interested in both science and technology and legal areas. Because of this duality, you can explore the career by focusing on the law side or on the science/technology side. To get experience on the law side, seek internships with law offices in your area. As in any area of law, internships and clerkships are usually the path to a quality job. For those interested in patent law specifically, applying for a clerkship in the United States Court of Appeals for the Federal Court in Washington, D.C., is a great way to gain experience. To apply for an unpaid, part-time internship during law school or soon after graduation, you should write directly to the court about six months in advance. To gain a full-time, paid clerkship position, law students should inquire sometime before the end of their second year. You can also apply for clerkships and internships with law firms. Another way to break into the IP law field is to get a job at the USPTO. Working directly with patents will put you in a better position for an IP job later in your career.

You may be able to get a part-time job as a legal assistant. Also check out your local business college for special prelaw programs that offer introductory law courses to the public. If you can't get any hands-on experience right away, ask your guidance counselor for help in setting up a tour of a local law office or arranging for an interview with a law professional. Any experience you can get writing technical or legal documents can also help, so don't rule out temporary jobs in any kind of business office.

If you have another interest that you hope to combine with law, try to get some hands-on experience in that area as well. If you are interested in science, for instance, join the science club at your school. Ask your science teacher about planning a field trip to anywhere you can learn about engineering. Take initiative and start an inventors club with your classmates to come up with new ideas and products.

Ceyda earned a B.S. degree in electrical engineering and a B.A. in economics from Bucknell University. "While studying at Bucknell, I worked at the Small Business Development Center on campus as an engineering consultant. My responsibilities included interacting with inventors to understand their ideas (utility and design), and performing market and patent searches to see if the ideas were novel. If we believed the idea could succeed in the marketplace, we would build their prototypes and test for feasibility. This was a great way to learn more about patent law and client interaction. Moreover, I volunteered at Lewisburg Prison Project as an intern. My role was to work with staff attorneys and respond to client questions and requests. In this position, I learned more about the administrative side of the legal practice, and also rules of civil procedure applicable to pretrial."

WHO WILL HIRE ME?

Intellectual property lawyers are employed by major corporations, law firms, universities, and government agencies. Some may also own their own business. The main employer of IP attorneys, however, is the USPTO, which is part of the Department of Commerce. The USPTO employs lawyers as trademark examiners, patent examiners, and more. Other departments in the government that employ IP lawyers include the Departments of Defense, Interior, Justice, and Energy. IP lawyers can also find employment in the United States Copyright Office.

Although IP attorneys are in steady demand throughout the United States, most work in large cities where major corporations are headquartered. Other strong employment centers for IP lawyers include Washington, D.C., because of the government agencies located there, and Silicon Valley, California, because of its concentration of computer-related industries.

Celina Diaz advises law students and new graduates to be visible in the field. "Get your name out there by writing articles on IP topics and meeting as many people in the field as you can," she says. "Not only will fellow IP attorneys know where the next job is, but they can also provide great advice on everything from firm reputations to the best networking groups for you. Also, look into conferences in cities or geographical areas you are interested in living so you can start making some connections there and begin learning more about how the courts there weigh in on different issues. IP conferences can cost an attorney at least $600 to get up-to-date advice on prosecution and/or litigation matters. However, in many cases, law students can attend for just $50."

WHERE CAN I GO FROM HERE?

At law firms, IP lawyers start out as entry-level associates and then advance as their experience and job performance allows. Associates who build a strong track record and who have many years of experience can become partners in a law firm. IP lawyers who work for universities may advance from assisting scientific and engineering groups to becoming professors of IP law or program heads. Whether in corporations, government agencies, or law firms, most IP lawyers, like other types of lawyers, are given more high profile cases and more important clients as they become more experienced.

The Benefits of Association Membership

The editors of *What Can I Do Now? Law* asked Jennifer Rogers, a patent attorney at Shumaker & Sieffert, P.A. for her thoughts on the value of membership in professional associations.

I am a member of two professional law associations: the Minnesota Intellectual Property Law Association and the American Intellectual Property Law Association. I think that association membership is relatively important to career development, and to some extent to career success, although I'm sure you could have a successful career without being a member of these associations. It is just so important to get out and meet people and make connections. You never know where the connections will lead in the future, but professional associations provide good opportunities for networking and relationship building. I have found it helpful to become involved in the associations' committees, which is where a lot of the opportunities are for meeting people and building relationships as you work together to put together programming or other projects.

"In five or 10 years," says Jennifer Rogers, "I see myself either becoming a partner in my law firm, or working as a patent attorney somewhere outside of a law firm, such as intellectual property counsel at a company. I am still at the early part of my legal career right now, so it is a little hard for me to visualize where I will be in 10 years. Nonetheless, I enjoy the field I am in and I can see myself continuing at the firm I'm with right now. The people I work with are pleasant and have in common a desire to produce a high-quality work product and a dedication to client satisfaction."

WHAT ARE THE SALARY RANGES?

The average salary for an IP attorney in corporate offices and patent firms is $119,000 per year, according to the American Intellectual Property Law Association. IP lawyers fresh out of law school can expect to earn between $80,000 and $85,000, and those with the most experience and success can earn more than $180,000 per year. The median income for partners in private law firms is $200,000 or more per year, while associates' salary is about $77,000. IP lawyers who own their own practices usually earn $100,000 per year while salaries for those who work in law firms and corporations averaged slightly higher.

Almost all corporations, firms, and government agencies provide medical insurance, vacation, sick days, and holidays. Partners in large firms can expect other perks as well, including company cars, spending allowances, bonuses, and more, depending on the firm.

WHAT IS THE JOB OUTLOOK?

Employment for intellectual property lawyers is expected to remain good through the next decade. The worldwide growth of the computer industry, the electronics industry, and the Internet have provided a great amount of work for IP lawyers. As new computer software and online media enters the market, IP lawyers will be needed to protect it. According to the American Bar Association, even if other markets that use the services of lawyers are softened by recession, the demand for IP lawyers will remain high. Because there will always be a need to protect the creative resources of the people, there will also be a need for IP lawyers. "I think the employment outlook is very positive," says Linda Norcross. "Technology is constantly changing and the law needs to keep up with the changes. There will always be a new spin on existing technology, and good lawyers will be needed to protect the people who invent the technology and the brands created to promote it."

Judges

SUMMARY

Definition
Judges are appointed or elected officials who preside over municipal, state, county, and federal courts. They apply the law to citizens and businesses and oversee court proceedings according to the established law. Judges also give new rulings on issues not previously decided.

Alternative Job Titles
Justices
Magistrates

Salary Range
$32,290 to $110,220 to $200,000+

Educational Requirements
Bachelor's degree
Law degree (federal and state judges)

Certification or Licensing
Required

Employment Outlook
More slowly than the average

High School Subjects
English (writing/literature)
Government
History
Law

Personal Interests
Current events
Law
Reading/books

"I'll never forget the time I gave a speech to a group of high school students and met a young woman, a Vietnamese refugee, who was about to graduate," recalls Tam Nomoto Schumann, a judge in the Superior Court of Orange County, California. "She remarked how she felt inspired after seeing me, an Asian woman, in a position of authority. Her unforgettable words were 'America is truly a great country because someone like me could be a judge.'"

WHAT DOES A JUDGE DO?

Judges are most often lawyers who have either been elected or appointed, and preside over federal, state, county, or municipal courts. Federal and state judges are usually required to have a law degree; approximately 40 states allow those with a bachelor's degree and work experience to hold limited-jurisdiction judgeships.

Judges administer court procedures during trials and hearings and establish new rules on questions where standard procedures have not previously been set. They read or listen to claims made by parties involved in civil suits and make decisions based on facts, applicable statutes, and prior court decisions. They examine evidence in criminal cases to see if it supports the charges. Judges listen to the pre-

Another Judicial Career Opportunity: Judicial Referee

Katherine J. Garza is a referee in the Juvenile Division of the Lake Superior Court in Crown Point, Indiana. She has worked in the field since January 2007. She discussed her career with the editors of *What Can I Do Now? Law*.

Q. What is a referee?

A. A referee is a judicial officer who presides over pending cases and makes decisions regarding those cases. All orders issued by a referee require the countersignature of a judge.

Q. What made you want to enter the field?

A. Prior to working in the juvenile system I practiced civil litigation, mainly representing defendants in commercial lawsuits. Although I liked the work very much, I did not have a chance to interact with many individual clients or see the personal impact of my work because most of my clients were corporations. I decided to work in the juvenile system so that I could have more interaction with individuals, in particular children. Every day I interact with children and their families and assist these families in solving any problems they are encountering. Although all of the parties are not always happy with my decisions, I strive to do what is best for the child in every case. I find my work in the juvenile system to be very professionally rewarding.

Q. What are your typical daily job responsibilities?

A. I, along with the judge and five magistrates, hear a range of cases, including: paternity, delinquency, children in need of services, guardianships, adoptions, termination of parental rights, and protection orders. We hear the cases on a daily basis and make determinations of the cases and draft corresponding orders. Outside of the courtroom we also perform a variety of other functions throughout the year. This includes sitting on community boards, consulting with the local bar association concerning best legal practices, applying for grant money to improve court services and systems, attending and presenting at various speaking engagements, and interacting with state agencies.

Q. What is your work environment like?

A. I work in the Juvenile Justice Complex, which includes eight courtrooms, a juvenile detention center, juvenile prosecutor's office, juvenile probation office, and Court Appointed Special Advocate office. The Juvenile Justice Complex is a very pleasant place to work, as everyone is here to assist children and their families. I am fortunate to work for a very talented and caring judge, Mary Beth Bonaventura. She has dedicated her career to doing what is best for children, and I believe her philosophy trickles down to everyone else at the Juvenile Justice Complex.

Q. What advice would you give to high school students who are interested in a legal career?

A. Any high school student interested in a legal career should take government

(continues)

sentation of cases, rule on the admission of evidence and testimony, and settle disputes between attorneys. They instruct juries on their duties and advise them of laws that apply to the case. They sentence defendants found guilty of criminal charges and decide who is responsible in nonjury civil cases. Besides their work in the courtroom, judges also research legal matters, study prior rulings, write opinions, and keep abreast of legislation that may affect their rulings. They must also manage staff.

Some judges have other titles such as *magistrate* or *justice,* and preside over a limited jurisdiction. Magistrates hear civil cases in which damages do not exceed a prescribed maximum, as well as minor misdemeanor cases that do not involve penitentiary sentences or fines that exceed a certain specified amount.

Some courts, such as small claims, family, or surrogate, may have evening hours to provide flexibility to the community. Criminal arraignments may be held at any time of the day or night. Court hours for most judges are usually regular business hours, with a one-hour lunch break.

WHAT IS IT LIKE TO BE A JUDGE?

Tam Nomoto Schumann has been a judge for 30 years. "In fact, I was the youngest judge ever appointed in the state of California—at the age of 28," she says. "I was actually appointed to the position by the governor of California. He sought more diversity on the bench and really wanted all nationalities to be represented. As a qualified Asian-American woman, I fit the bill." In addition to serving in the Superior Court of Orange County, Judge Schumann is also the president of the American Judges Association. Before becoming a judge, she served as a deputy in the Orange County Counsel's Office and was in private practice.

Judge Schumann believes that there are many pros to working in the field. "As a judge," she says, "you are viewed as a role model and have a moral integrity to uphold. I also love having the opportunity to interact with others, helping people in need, and the sense of contributing to society."

Being a judge can be very stressful at times. "The job comes with a huge amount of stress—especially cases that deal with family law," says Judge Schumann. "In such cases, I am always aware that the outcome of the trial may change peoples' lives."

DO I HAVE WHAT IT TAKES TO BE A JUDGE?

"You need to be a good listener, attentive to detail, and compassionate above all," says Judge Schumann. "It's also important to leave your 'bad days' at home. Many of our decisions hold great impact to others—you have to stay focused and make

The Supreme Court: Facts and Traditions

- The Supreme Court was created by the Judiciary Act of September 24, 1789. It is the highest court of the land and rules on issues related to the U.S. Constitution.

- The Supreme Court is made up of nine justices, appointed by the president with consent of the Senate, who review selected decisions made at the state level.

- Justices are appointed for life.

- Every justice has been a lawyer, but there is no constitutional requirement that this is required.

- The justices have worn black robes in court since at least 1800.

- At the beginning of each session and private conference, all nine judges shake hands. This symbolic action, called the "conference handshake," is done as a reminder that while they may disagree regarding a case, they should embrace a "harmony of purpose."

- The youngest justice ever appointed to the court was Joseph Story, age 32. Horace Lurton, age 65, was the oldest justice ever appointed.

- Justice William O. Douglas had the longest tenure serving on the court—36 years and six months.

- Thurgood Marshall was the first African-American justice. He was appointed in 1967.

- Sandra Day O'Connor was the first female justice. She was appointed in 1981.

- The Supreme Court receives approximately 7,000 petitions annually. Only 80 or so are taken for oral argument.

Source: U.S. Supreme Court, Supreme Court Historical Society

studied, impartial judgments. This is so important. For many people, coming to trial and standing before a judge is a first-time event. I have to always keep in mind that my decision may make a grave impact on their lives. They deserve my full undivided attention."

Judges must also be effective communicators, work well with others, be decisive and diligent, and have strong organization skills.

HOW DO I BECOME A JUDGE?

Education

High School

Most judges first practice as lawyers before being elected or appointed to the bench. You will need to earn a high school diploma and a college degree, as well as complete three years of law school, to become a lawyer. A high school diploma is a first step on the ladder of education that a lawyer must climb. "Students should take high school classes such as English, history, or any courses that will help develop strong writing and speaking skills," says Judge Schumann. "Also, any classes with a civic background are recommended. This is a highly competitive field and gaining admission into law school is quite hard. I would recommend that students find ways not only to stand out scholastically, but also to stand apart from other applicants extracurricularly. Seek out leadership opportunities by joining clubs and associations."

Speech courses are also helpful to build strong communication skills necessary for the profession. Also take computer-related courses because lawyers and judges often use technology to research and interpret the law.

Postsecondary Training

To enter any law school approved by the American Bar Association, you must satisfactorily complete at least three, and usually four, years of college work. Most law schools do not specify any particular courses for prelaw education. Usually a liberal arts track is most advisable, with courses in English, history, economics, social sciences, logic, and public speaking. A college student planning on specialization in a particular area of law, however, might also take courses significantly related to that area, such as economics, agriculture, or political science. Those interested should contact several law schools to learn more about any requirements and to see if they will accept credits from the college the student is planning to attend.

The American Bar Association has approved 200 law schools in the United States. Other law schools, many of them night schools, are approved by state authorities only. Most ABA-approved law schools, however, do offer night sessions to accommodate part-time students. Part-time courses of study usually take four years.

In law school, you will take required courses such as legal writing and research, contracts, criminal law, constitutional law, torts, and property. During your second and third years, you may focus on areas that you are particularly interested in, such as evidence, business transactions and corporations, or admiralty. The study of cases and decisions is of basic importance to the law student, who will be required to read and study thousands of these cases. A degree of juris doctor (J.D.) or bachelor of laws (LL.B.) is usually granted upon graduation. Some law students considering specialization, research, or teaching may go on for advanced study.

Most law schools require that applicants take the Law School Admission Test, where prospective law students are tested on their critical thinking, writing, and reasoning abilities.

Judge Schumann received both a bachelor of arts in history and a juris doctor degree from the University of California—Berkeley.

Federal courts and agencies have their own rules regulating admission to practice. Other requirements vary among states. For example, Vermont, New York, Washington, Virginia, California, Maine, and Wyoming allow a person who has spent several years reading law in a law office but has no college training, or who has a combination of reading and law school experience, to take the state bar examination. Few people now enter law practice in this manner.

A few states accept the study of law by correspondence. Some states require that newly graduated lawyers serve a period of clerkship in an established law firm before they are eligible to take the bar examination.

Almost all judges appointed or elected to any court (except those holding limited-jurisdiction judgeships) must be lawyers and members of the bar, usually with many years of experience.

Judges are often required to take continuing education courses throughout their careers. Many also read industry publications, such as *Criminal Justice*, *The Federal Lawyer*, and *The National Law Journal*, in order to stay up-to-date regarding developments in the field. See Section 4, What Can I Do Right Now?, for information on these and other legal publications.

Certification or Licensing

In order to practice as a lawyer, you will need to apply for admittance into the bar of your state. This involves graduating from an approved law school and passing a written examination. In a few states, graduates of law schools within the state are excused from these written examinations.

After lawyers have been admitted to the bar in one state, they can practice in another state without taking a written examination if the states have reciprocity agreements; however, they will be required to meet certain state standards of good character and legal experience and pay any applicable fees. There is no specific certification or licensing available for judges.

Internships and Volunteerships

Landing an internship at the undergraduate level or in law school is an excellent way to learn more about the field and make valuable contacts in the legal industry. One example of an internship program is the ABA's Judicial Intern Opportunity Program, a "full-time, six-week minimum summer program open

> ## Quote
>
> "I consider trial by jury as the only anchor ever yet imagined by man, by which a government can be held to the principles of its constitution."
>
> —Thomas Jefferson, 3rd president of the United States

to all first- or second-year minority and/or financially disadvantaged law students who want to do legal research and writing for state or federal judges." Visit http://www.abanet.org/litigation/jiop for more information.

If you are unable to land an internship, try volunteering with a legal organization in your community. "Community work or volunteerism will not only help others, but also creates a unique background for law school applicants," says Judge Schumann.

WHO WILL HIRE ME?

There are approximately 51,000 judges employed in the United States. Judges and magistrates work for federal, state, and local levels of government. About 53 percent of all judges work for state and local government.

The career of judge is not an entry-level position. Judges typically start out as lawyers and only after years of experience and careful study of the law are appointed or elected to the bench.

The first steps in entering the law profession are graduation from an approved law school and passing a state bar examination. Beginning lawyers usually work as assistants to experienced lawyers. At first they do mainly research and routine work. After a few years of successful experience, they may be ready to go out on their own. Other choices open to the beginning lawyer include joining an established law firm or entering into partnership with another lawyer.

WHERE CAN I GO FROM HERE?

Judges usually advance from lower courts to higher courts either in terms of the matters that are decided or in terms of the level—local, state, or federal. Some judges leave the profession and become college professors, legal commentators or writers, or run for political office, among other career paths.

WHAT ARE THE SALARY RANGES?

Judges earned median annual salaries of $110,220 in 2008, according to the U.S. Department of Labor. Salaries ranged from less than $32,290 to more than $162,140. According to the Administrative Office of the U.S. Courts, federal district court judges earned an average of $169,300 in 2008. The chief justice of the U.S. Supreme Court earned $217,400, while associate justices of the Supreme Court earned $208,100, in 2008. A survey conducted by the National Center for State Courts reports that the 2008 average salaries for associate judges in the states' highest courts ranged from \$106,185 to \$218,237. At the state level, judges serving in intermediate appellate courts earned salaries that ranged from \$105,050 to \$204,599, and in general jurisdiction trial courts, salaries ranged from \$99,234 to \$178,789.

Judges usually receive paid vacations and holidays, sick leave, hospitalization and insurance benefits, and pension programs.

WHAT IS THE JOB OUTLOOK?

Employment of judges is expected to grow more slowly than the average for all occupations through 2016, according to the U.S. Department of Labor. Budgetary cuts may limit the hiring of new judges at all levels, but especially at the federal level. Despite this prediction, demand for judges should grow as the public focuses more on crime, as well as seeks to litigate disputes that were previously handled out of court.

Employment will also grow as a result of demographic shifts in the U.S. population; more judges will be needed to handle immigration- and elder law-related issues. The number of people immigrating and seeking to immigrate to the United States has increased in recent years. By 2020, the number of people in the United States who are over the age of 65 is expected to double, according to the Federal Interagency Forum on Aging-Related Statistics. Both of these trends will fuel employment growth for judges in these specialties. Medical science, electronic commerce, and information technology are other areas in which judges will be needed. Most positions will open as judges retire or leave the field to go into the private sector (which is more lucrative). There may be an increase in judges in cities with large population growth, but competition will be high for any openings.

Lawyers

SUMMARY

Definition
Lawyers serve in two capacities in our legal system: as advocates and as advisers. As advocates, they represent the rights of their clients in trials and depositions or in front of administrative and government bodies. As advisers, attorneys counsel clients on how the law affects business or personal decisions, such as the purchase of property or the creation of a will. Lawyers represent individuals, businesses, and corporations.

Alternative Job Titles
Attorneys

Salary Range
$54,460 to $110,590 to $1,000,000+

Educational Requirements
Law degree

Certification or Licensing
Required

Employment Outlook
About as fast as the average

High School Subjects
English (writing/ literature)
Government
Law
Speech

Personal Interests
Current events
Law
Writing

One of Mary Rose Silva's most rewarding experiences as a lawyer came when she worked as an environmental attorney for the Illinois Attorney General's Office. "I came to work there just out of law school," she recalls, "and the first day on the job I was given 13 cases to handle on my own. It was scary to be thrown into litigation so quickly, but I truly enjoyed the experience, and it made me a better lawyer."

WHAT DOES A LAWYER DO?

No matter what their specialty, a lawyer's job is to help clients know their rights under the law and then help them achieve these rights before a judge, jury, government agency, or other legal forum, such as an arbitration panel. Lawyers may represent individuals or businesses. For individuals they may be trustees, guardians, or executors; they may draw up wills or contracts or advise on income taxes or on the purchase or sale of a home. For businesses, they manage tax matters, arrange for stock to be issued, handle claims cases, represent the firm in real estate dealings, and advise on all legal matters. Some lawyers work solely in the courts; others carry on most of their business outside of court, doing such tasks as drawing up mortgages, deeds, contracts, and other legal documents or by handling the background work necessary for court cases, which might include researching cases in a law library or interviewing witnesses. A number of lawyers work to establish and enforce laws for the federal and state governments by drafting legislation, representing the government in court, or serving as judges.

Lawyers can also take positions as *professors* in law schools. Administrators, research workers, and writers are also important to the profession. Administrative positions in business or government may be of a nonlegal nature, but the qualities, background, and experience of a lawyer are often helpful in such positions.

Other individuals with legal training may choose not to practice but instead opt for careers in which their background and knowledge of law are important. These careers include tax collectors, credit investigators, FBI agents, insurance adjusters, process servers, and probation officers.

Some of the specialized fields for lawyers include the following:

Civil lawyers work in a field also known as private law. They focus on damage suits and breach-of-contract suits; prepare and draw up deeds, leases, wills, mortgages, and contracts; and act as trustees, guardians, or executors of an estate when necessary.

Criminal lawyers, also known as *defense lawyers,* specialize in cases dealing with offenses committed against society or the state, such as theft, murder, or arson. They interview clients and witnesses to ascertain facts in a case, correlate their findings with known cases, and prepare a case to defend a client against the charges made. They conduct a defense at the trial, examine witnesses, and summarize the case with a closing argument to a jury.

Prosecutors, also known as *prosecuting attorneys* or *district attorneys*, represent cities, counties, states, or the federal government in court proceedings. They gather and analyze evidence and review legal material relevant to a lawsuit. Then they present their case to a grand jury, which decides whether the evidence is sufficient for an indictment. If it is not, the suit is dismissed and there is no trial. If the grand jury decides to indict the accused, however, the case goes to court, where the district attorney appears before the judge and jury to present evidence against the defendant.

Probate lawyers specialize in planning and settling estates. They draw up wills, deeds of trust, and similar documents for clients who want to plan for giving their belongings to their heirs when they die. Upon a client's death, probate lawyers vouch for the validity of the will and represent the executors and administrators of the estate.

Bankruptcy attorneys assist their clients, both individuals and corporations, in obtaining protection from creditors under existing bankruptcy laws and with financial reorganization and debt repayment.

Corporation lawyers, sometimes known as *corporate lawyers*, advise corporations concerning their legal rights, obligations, or privileges. They study constitutions, statutes, previous decisions, ordinances, and decisions of quasi-judicial bodies that are applicable to corporations. They advise corporations on the pros and cons of prosecuting or defending a lawsuit. They act as agent of the corporation in various transactions and seek to keep clients from expensive litigation.

Maritime lawyers, sometimes referred to as *admiralty lawyers*, specialize in laws regulating commerce and navigation on the high seas and any navigable waters, including inland lakes and rivers. Although there is a general maritime law, it operates in each country according to that country's courts, laws, and customs. Maritime law covers contracts, insurance, property damage, and personal injuries.

Intellectual property lawyers focus on helping their clients with patents, trademarks, and copyright protection. (See the article, Intellectual Property Lawyers, for more information on this career.) *Patent lawyers* are intellectual property lawyers who specialize in securing patents for inventors from the United States Patent and Trademark Office and prosecuting or defending suits of patent infringements. They prepare detailed specifications for the patent, and may organize a corporation or advise an existing corporation to commercialize on a patent. Biotechnology patent law is a further specialization of patent law. *Biotechnology patent lawyers* specialize in helping biotechnology researchers, scientists, and research corporations with all legal aspects of their biotechnology patents.

Elder law attorneys are lawyers who specialize in providing legal services for the elderly and, in some cases, the disabled. (See the article Elder Law Attorneys.)

Tax attorneys handle cases resulting from problems with inheritance, income tax, estate tax, franchises, and real estate tax, among other things.

Insurance attorneys advise insurance companies about legal matters pertaining to insurance transactions. They approve the wording of insurance policies, review the legality of claims against the company, and draw up legal documents.

An *international lawyer* specializes in the body of rules that are observed by nations in their relations with one another. Some of these laws have been agreed to in treaties, and some have evolved from long-standing customs and traditions.

Securities and exchange lawyers monitor individuals and corporations involved in trading and oversee their activities to make sure they comply with applicable laws. When corporations undergo takeovers and mergers, securities and exchange lawyers are there to represent the corporations' interests and fulfill all legal obligations involved in the transaction.

Real estate lawyers handle the transfer of property and perform such duties as searching public records and deeds to establish titles of property, holding funds for investment in escrow accounts, and acting as trustees of property. They draw up legal documents and act as agents in various real estate transactions.

Title attorneys deal with titles, leases, contracts, and other legal documents pertaining to the ownership of land and gas, oil, and mineral rights. They prepare documents to cover the purchase or sale of such property and rights, examine documents to determine ownership, advise organizations about legal requirements concerning titles, and participate in trials or lawsuits in connection with titles.

Other lawyers may specialize in environmental, employee benefits, entertainment, or health law.

It is important to note that once you are licensed to practice law, you are legally qualified to practice any one or more of these and many other specialties. Some general practitioners handle both criminal and civil matters of all sorts. To become licensed, you must be admitted to the bar of that state. Bar examiners test the qualifications of applicants. They prepare and administer written exams covering legal subjects, examine candidates orally, and recommend admission of those who meet the prescribed standards.

Offices and courtrooms are usually pleasant, although busy, places to work. Lawyers also spend significant amounts of time in law libraries or record rooms, in the homes and offices of clients, and sometimes in the jail cells of clients or prospective witnesses. Many lawyers never work in a courtroom. Unless they are directly involved in litigation, they may never participate in a trial.

Some courts, such as small claims, family, or surrogate, may have evening hours to provide flexibility to the community. Criminal arraignments may be held at any time of the day or night. Court hours for most lawyers are usually regular business hours, with a one-hour lunch break. Often lawyers have to work long hours, spending evenings and weekends preparing cases and materials and working with clients. In addition to the work, lawyers must always

To Be a Successful Lawyer, You Should...

- have strong communication skills, both written and oral
- be able to think on your feet
- be a creative problem solver
- have strong ethics
- be organized
- be confident in your skills and abilities
- have a thick skin because the practice of law can sometimes be an adversarial process
- be willing to continue to learn throughout your career

keep up with the latest developments in the profession. Also, it takes a long time to become a qualified lawyer, and it may be difficult to earn an adequate living until a lawyer gets enough experience to develop an established private practice.

Lawyers who are employed at law firms must often work grueling hours to advance in the firm. Aspiring lawyers should expect to spend long weekend hours doing research and interviewing people, when necessary.

WHAT IS IT LIKE TO BE A LAWYER?

Patrick McKenna is an assistant chief counsel with the U.S. Department of

Homeland Security, Immigration and Customs Enforcement (ICE). He has been a lawyer for approximately eight years. In addition to working for ICE, Patrick has also worked as a state criminal prosecutor. "I became a lawyer for numerous different reasons," he explains. "First, I have always been fascinated with the constitution and the rule of law in the United States. It seemed logical to choose a field where I could explore my interests further. Second, I had two uncles who were attorneys (both of whom worked in the criminal litigation field) who seemed happy and very excited about their careers. Their enthusiasm for the profession drew me to law as well.

"Primarily, I represent the United States in the administrative removal of criminal aliens. Meaning, I litigate on behalf of the United States in removal proceedings before an immigration judge. These proceedings are completely separate from criminal proceedings, where guilt and punishment are determined. In immigration court, the judge determines if an alien is allowed to remain in the United States or if he or she must be removed."

Patrick's secondary duties include providing training and advice to ICE special agents about a variety of criminal law matters and initiating civil denaturalization proceedings against individuals who obtained their U.S. citizenship illegally or improperly.

"I am very lucky in that I really enjoy my job," says Patrick. "Daily, I deal with both criminal and immigration law; these are the two areas of law that I find the most fascinating. I litigate, meaning that I am in court arguing my positions, which I find

Advice for Aspiring Lawyers

Mary Rose Silva, a lawyer for nearly 16 years, offers the following advice to young people who are interested in pursuing a career in law:

Go into law if being a lawyer is truly what you want to be. People go into law for various reasons. Some people go into it for the money; others go into it as a "Plan B" for their career choice. But in reality, I see too many attorneys who are unhappy with their jobs because they went into law for other reasons than truly wanting to practice law. If you're going to be happy with what you do, do what makes you happy. Another piece of advice is to visit the county courts and see what lawyers do. Watching the court process is fun, interesting, and enlightening.

very rewarding. The work is fast paced, and I like thinking on my feet. Working for the federal government also has definite advantages. Though I do not receive the same salary as some of my classmates at large law firms, I am compensated fairly, work reasonable hours, and receive great benefits. The only con I have experienced is dealing with the negative stereotype some members of the public have about ICE and the federal immigration system."

Mary Rose Silva is a staff attorney at McDermott Will & Emery in Chicago. She has worked as lawyer for almost 16 years, and has practiced in several areas of law, including environmental, insurance defense, ethics, and litigation. "As a staff attorney," she explains, "my main responsibility is to assist the trial attorneys at the firm during 'discovery' (the stage in litigation where plaintiffs and defendants are supposed to produce to each other documents and facts relevant to the case). Given the technology we have now, most of the documents that the attorneys get are in electronic format (i.e., scanned documents or emails). The number of documents may range from a few thousand to hundreds of thousands, depending on the complexity of the case. A typical day generally involves meeting with the trial attorneys to determine what sort of documents have been provided by the client; analyzing what documents may be relevant to the case; establishing a protocol in reviewing the potentially relevant documents; setting up a database where the documents are contained; and reviewing the documents in accordance to the protocol that has been set up. Review of the documents can take months. Since my job is working in litigation and with a trial team, the kinds of cases I get vary depending what case is going to trial. So one project could involve environmental pollution, the next one could involve medical malpractice. The variety keeps things interesting."

DO I HAVE WHAT IT TAKES TO BE A LAWYER?

Lawyers have to be effective communicators, work well with people, and be able to find creative solutions to problems, such as complex cases. They should also have strong ethics. "Though it is a cliché, an attorney must be ethical," says Pat-

rick McKenna. "It is a stressful field, and there is sometimes pressure to cut corners. You will see attorneys do the wrong thing because it is easy or because it will benefit them monetarily. A good attorney is one who does the right thing, even when it is not in his or her best interest, because it is the right thing."

Patrick says that another trait that comes in handy for lawyers is a thick skin. "The court process is an adversarial process pitting attorneys against each other. The process, at times, can get heated, but you cannot take it personally or it can affect your life outside work."

HOW DO I BECOME A LAWYER?
Education
High School

A high school diploma, a college degree, and three years of law school are minimum

---

Did You Know?

Abraham Lincoln, the 16th president of the United States, was also a lawyer. During his 25-year law career, he was involved in approximately 5,000 cases. In fact, Lincoln was one of the most successful lawyers in Illinois during his time. Visit http://showcase.netins.net/web/creative/lincoln.html to learn more about this fascinating man and read some advice he gave on being a lawyer.

requirements for a law degree. A high school diploma is a first step on the ladder of education that a lawyer must climb. If you are considering a career in law, courses such as government, history, social studies, and economics provide a solid background for entering college-level courses. "Generally, students who want to go to law school shouldn't worry too much about what classes they take in high school," advises Patrick McKenna. "Instead, they should take (and excel in) the classes they find interesting."

Speech courses are also helpful to build the strong communication skills necessary for the profession. "Classes or extracurricular activities that involve public speaking will benefit anyone who wants to be an attorney," says Patrick. "Being able to speak in front of a crowd is a skill that for most individuals only develops with practice. I was a shy person in high school and avoided public speaking at all costs. This avoidance lasted through college. By the time I was in law school, my skills as an orator were far below that of my classmates who had participated in activities such as debate and drama. It took years to become comfortable speaking in public. I believe that if I would have started practicing public speaking in high school, the transition would have been much smoother."

Also take advantage of any computer-related classes or experience you can get, because lawyers often use technology to research and interpret the law, from surfing the Internet to searching legal databases.

Postsecondary Training

To enter any law school approved by the American Bar Association, you must sat-isfactorily complete at least three, and usually four, years of college work. Most law schools do not specify any particular courses for prelaw education. Usually a liberal arts track is most advisable, with courses in English, history, economics, social sciences, logic, and public speaking. A college student planning on specialization in a particular area of law, however, might also take courses significantly related to that area, such as economics, agriculture, or political science. Those interested should contact several law schools to learn more about any requirements and to see if they will accept credits from the college the student is planning to attend.

Currently, 200 law schools in the United States are approved by the American Bar Association; others, many of them night schools, are approved by state authorities only. Most of the approved law schools, however, do have night sessions to accommodate part-time students. Part-time courses of study usually take four years.

Law school training consists of required courses such as legal writing and research, contracts, criminal law, constitutional law, torts, and property. The second and third years may be devoted to specialized courses of interest to the student, such as evidence, business transactions and corporations, or admiralty. The study of cases and decisions is of basic importance to the law student, who will be required to read and study thousands of these cases. A degree of juris doctor (J.D.) or bachelor of laws (LL.B.) is usually granted upon graduation. Some law students considering specialization, research, or teaching may go on for advanced study.

Most law schools require that applicants take the Law School Admission Test (LSAT), where prospective law students are tested on their critical thinking, writing, and reasoning abilities.

Federal courts and agencies have their own rules regulating admission to practice. Other requirements vary among the states. For example, Vermont, New York, Washington, Virginia, California, Maine, and Wyoming allow a person who has spent several years reading law in a law office but has no college training, or who has a combination of reading and law school experience, to take the state bar examination. Few people today enter law practice in this manner.

A few states accept the study of law by correspondence. Some states require that newly graduated lawyers serve a period of clerkship in an established law firm before they are eligible to take the bar examination.

Certification or Licensing

Every state requires that lawyers be admitted to the bar of that state before they can practice. They require that applicants graduate from an approved law school and that they pass a written examination in the state in which they intend to practice. In a few states, graduates of law schools within the state are excused from these written examinations. After lawyers have been admitted to the bar in one state, they can practice in another state without taking a written examination if the states have reciprocity agreements; however, they will be required to meet certain state standards of good character and legal experience and pay any applicable fees.

Internships and Volunteerships

Donna Mason, a patent attorney at Brundidge & Stanger, P.C. in Alexandria, Virginia, participated in internships as an undergraduate and while in law school. "As an undergraduate student," she says, "I participated in internships in the field of electrical engineering. One summer, I worked at Alabama Power Company, and the next summer I worked at Southern Natural Gas Company. These internships provided me with a great opportunity to get a real-world view of what it was really like to work as an engineer, particularly in a corporate environment. As a law student, I participated in a number of internships in the legal field. I clerked for a judge, and I performed legal research and writing assignments for an entertainment law attorney, a state employee association, the city of Nashville, and a general practice firm. At the general practice firm, I gained my first experience in patent law. It was that experience in patent law that solidified my decision to practice in the field of intellectual property law."

During law school, Patrick volunteered at a law clinic helping to explain the immigration process to individuals. "Volunteering is the best way for students to gain experience," he says, "and experience is always the key to landing a job. This will show future employers that you have long been interested in that area of law and were passionate enough about the subject matter to work without compensation."

WHO WILL HIRE ME?

Approximately 761,000 lawyers are employed in the United States. About 75 percent of them work in private practice, either in law firms or alone. The others are employed in government, often at the local level. Lawyers working for the federal government hold positions in the Departments of Justice, Treasury, Homeland Security, and Defense, as well as in other agencies such as the Environmental Protection Agency. Lawyers also hold positions as house counsel for public utilities, transportation companies, banks, insurance companies, real estate agencies, manufacturing firms, welfare and religious organizations, and other businesses and nonprofit organizations.

The first steps in entering the law profession are graduation from an approved law school and passing a state bar examination. Beginning lawyers usually do not go into solo practice right away. It is often

Law School Survey of Student Engagement

Nearly 67 percent of first-year law students say that they have to work harder than they expected to meet faculty expectations, according to the latest *Law School Survey of Student Engagement* (LSSSE). This percentage decreases to 52 and 47 percent, respectively, for second- and third-year law school students. The annual survey, which is administered by the Center for Postsecondary Research at Indiana University at Bloomington, aims to "provide data to law schools to improve legal education, enhance student success, inform accreditation efforts, and facilitate benchmarking efforts." Some promising findings from the survey include:

- More than 90 percent of students in their first year of law school regularly come to class prepared.

- More than 90 percent of students feel that their law school provides them with a "broad legal education."

- Three-quarters of students report that their law school education has helped them to become clearer and more effective writers.

- Approximately 50 percent of third-year law students "participate in a clinical or pro bono project as part of a course or for academic credit."

- Seventy-six percent of full-time students believe that their school "substantially emphasizes encouraging the ethical practice of law."

There were also a few disappointing findings detailed in the survey, including:

- Twenty-five percent of third-year law students come to class unprepared.

- Sixty-percent of law students at all levels report that their institution "places a substantial emphasis on memorizing facts, ideas, or methods to repeat them in pretty much the same form."

- Twenty-four percent of respondents report that their law school has not provided them with the necessary counseling to help them afford a legal education.

In 2008 more than 29,000 law students participated in the survey, which has been conducted since 2003. Visit http://lssse.iub.edu for the latest survey.

difficult to become established, and additional experience is always helpful to the blossoming lawyer. Also, most lawyers do not specialize in a particular branch of law without first gaining experience. Beginning lawyers usually work as assistants to experienced lawyers. At first they do mainly research and routine work. After a few years of successful experience, they may be ready to go out on their own. Other choices open to beginning lawyers include joining an established law firm or entering into partnership with another lawyer. Positions are also available with banks, business corporations, insurance companies, private utilities, and with a number of government agencies at different levels.

Many new lawyers are recruited by law firms or other employers directly from law school. Recruiters come to the school and interview possible hires. Other new graduates can get job leads from local and state bar associations.

WHERE CAN I GO FROM HERE?

Lawyers with outstanding ability can expect to go a long way in their profession. Novice lawyers generally start as law clerks, but as they prove themselves and develop their abilities, many opportunities for advancement will arise. They may be promoted to junior partner in a law firm or establish their own practice. Lawyers may enter politics and become judges, mayors, congressmen, or other government leaders. Experienced lawyers can also find top positions in business.

Lawyers working for the federal government advance according to the civil service system.

WHAT ARE THE SALARY RANGES?

Incomes generally increase as the lawyer gains experience and becomes better known in the field. The beginning lawyer in solo practice may barely make ends meet for the first few years. According to the National Association for Law Placement, the median salary for new lawyers was $95,000 in 2006, with salaries ranging from $50,000 to $135,000 based on the size of the firm.

Experienced lawyers earn salaries that vary depending on the type, size, and location of their employers. According to the U.S. Department of Labor, the 2008 median salary for lawyers was $110,590, although some senior partners earned more than $1 million per year. The lowest-paid lawyers earned less than $54,460. General attorneys working in the federal government received $123,660 in 2008. State and local government attorneys generally made less, earning $80,890 and $89,320, respectively, in 2008.

Benefits for lawyers include paid vacation, retirement or pension plans, and health, disability, and life insurance.

WHAT IS THE JOB OUTLOOK?

Employment for lawyers is expected to grow about as fast as the average for all careers through 2016, according to the

Occupational Outlook Handbook, but large numbers of law school graduates have created strong competition for jobs. Continued population growth, typical business activities, and increased numbers of legal cases involving health care, antitrust violations, the environment, intellectual property, international law, venture capital, energy, elder law, and sexual harassment, among other issues, will create a steady demand for lawyers. Law services will be more accessible to the middle-income public because of the popularity of prepaid legal services and clinics. However, stiff competition has and will continue to urge some lawyers to look outside the legal profession for employment. Administrative and managerial positions in real-estate companies, banks, insurance firms, and government agencies are typical areas where legal training is useful.

The top 10 percent of the graduating seniors of the country's best law schools will have more opportunities with well-known law firms and jobs on legal staffs of corporations, in government agencies, and in law schools in the next few decades. Lawyers in solo practice will find it hard to earn a living until their practice is fully established. The best opportunities exist in small towns or suburbs of large cities, where there is less competition and new lawyers can meet potential clients more easily.

Graduates with lower class rankings and from lesser-known schools may have difficulty in obtaining the most desirable positions.

Legal Nurse Consultants

SUMMARY

Definition
Legal nurse consultants are experienced nurses who assist litigation teams with cases.

Alternative Job Titles
None

Salary Range
$30,000 to $50,000 to $100,000+

Educational Requirements
Postsecondary nursing training; clinical nursing experience plus some training in legal issues or legal nurse consulting

Certification or Licensing
Voluntary (certification)
Required (licensing as a nurse)

Employment Outlook
Faster than the average

High School Subjects
Anatomy and Physiology
Biology
Chemistry
English (writing/literature)
Health
Law
Mathematics

Personal Interests
Current events
Helping people: physical health/medicine
Law

If you love nursing, research, and have a bit of detective in you, you might be interested in a career as a legal nurse consultant.

Barbara Levin, a legal nurse consultant since 1988, used all of her talents on a case that involved the review of medical records regarding a 31-year-old woman who was in a motor vehicle accident. The woman had sustained numerous orthopedic injuries, including a right femur fracture, left tibia/fibula fracture, left humerus fracture, right radial fracture, and a pelvic fracture. She underwent several surgeries to repair her fractures and

was sent home from the hospital. Seven days later, she died of massive blood clots, which broke off from her leg and lodged in her lung.

"I was hired by the plaintiff attorney and was asked to comment about the nursing care delivered to this woman in the hospital," Barbara recalls. "While reviewing the woman's medical records, I found a 'needle in the haystack.' She was at high risk for developing deep vein thrombosis and had initially been placed on a blood thinner medication for only three days instead of her entire hospitalization and recuperation. In addition, she

To Be a Successful Legal Nurse Consultant, You Should...

- have strong organizational skills
- be able to explain medical issues and procedures to people with nonmedical backgrounds
- have good critical-thinking skills
- be reliable
- be attentive to detail
- have excellent communication skills
- be able to handle deadline pressure
- be able to work well with many types of people

never worked with physical therapy and was sent home via an ambulance to stay in a hospital bed. Both parents needed to care for her and there were no home services arranged to assist the family with the care." The prolonged immobility, lack of physical therapy, and other factors placed this woman at high risk for developing blood clots. "This woman was not a candidate to be discharged home," Barbara says. "Instead, she should have been transferred to a rehabilitation facility and continued on the blood thinner medication. This would have helped protect her against the development of blood clots."

Barbara testified on many aspects of this case regarding standards of nursing practice. "As a result of my testimony," Barbara says, "the case settled during mediation for an undisclosed amount of money."

WHAT DOES A LEGAL NURSE CONSULTANT DO?

Legal nurse consultants are members of a litigation team that deals with medical malpractice, personal injury, and product liability lawsuits as well as other medically related legal cases. They may be employed independently on a contract or retainer basis; or they may be employed by law firms, insurance companies, corporations, government agencies, or as part of a risk management department in a hospital. Legal nurse consultants are trained nurses who have a thorough understanding of medical issues and trends. They utilize their clinical experiences, knowledge of health care standards, and medical resources to assist litigation teams and to act as liaisons between the legal and health care communities. Their primary roles are to evaluate, analyze, and render informed opinions regarding health care. They practice in both plaintiff and defense capacities in collaboration with attorneys and others involved in legal processes.

Legal nurse consultants' job responsibilities vary depending on the case and its medical implications. When working on cases, they may conduct client interviews, which involve talking to people who feel they have legal claims against medical facilities, physicians, or nurses. They may research past medical cases and treatments. They often advise attorneys regarding medical facts, treatments, and other medical issues that are relevant to the cases. Legal nurse consultants obtain and organize medical records and locate and procure evidence. They may identify, interview, and retain expert witnesses. Assisting with depositions and trials, as well as developing and preparing exhibits for jury or judge trials, are also aspects of this role.

As part of legal teams, legal nurse consultants are often required to do considerable research and paperwork. They must gather information and write reports.

Independent legal nurse consultants must also be responsible for getting their work done within strict deadlines. They often work under a contract and must produce the records, information, and reports within a specified time frame. In addition, they must generate their own clients if they have an independent practice. This requires an entrepreneurial spirit combined with a business mindset, so independent legal nurse consultants need to learn and practice business skills, such as marketing, sales, and record keeping.

WHAT IS IT LIKE TO BE A LEGAL NURSE CONSULTANT?

Mindy Cohen is the president of the American Association of Legal Nurse Consultants (AALNC) and the founder and president of Mindy Cohen & Associates, a legal nurse consulting firm in Villanova, Pennsylvania. "I was always interested in law school, but did not want to be a lawyer," she recalls. "I loved being a nurse, not only the patient care aspects but the knowledge and critical thinking involved in nursing as well. I saw legal nurse consulting as a way of combining my interest in law and passion for nursing."

When asked what she likes most about the field, Mindy cites its diversity, challenging nature, and the opportunities it provides for flexibility and independence. "Legal nursing is a field of diverse opportunities," she says. "You can run your own business, work for a law firm or insurance company, specialize in risk management or corporate compliance in a health care facility, or work in technology in the courtroom related to medical cases, just to name a few options. The field is also very challenging. Every case is different and presents unique issues. The process can vary somewhat between cases, but you are never bored or feel like you are doing the same thing day in and day out. The field also allows you both flexibility and independence—particularly when in an independent practice, when you can set your own hours and schedule, which allows you to fit other activities into your day. A strong work ethic is required to ensure you do get the work done in a timely manner. For some, this element could be considered a con."

Mindy says that some of her most rewarding moments as a legal nurse consultant are when she finds something in medical records that the attorney was not aware of. "I can explain it effectively so that the attorney can make an informed decision on how to proceed with a case," she explains. "For instance, my most memorable case was working on the defense side of a personal injury motor vehicle case, where I was involved in numerous aspects—identifying and working with multiple medical experts, preparing timelines and medical summaries, bringing in a life care planner, and analyzing pain and suffering issues. The demand was in the mid-eight figures, and the settlement was in the mid-seven figures. I loved being involved in multiple facets of the case, the challenge and complexity of the issues, and my firm's contributions were significant in bringing the settlement in at a fair amount. It is very rewarding to know your work makes a difference."

Mindy says that there are some drawbacks to work as a legal nurse consultant. "For those in private practice," she says, "there are the challenges of building a business and the lack of a dependable steady income (at least initially). With consulting work, you cannot always control when the work comes in, and it is likely at times that you may experience periods of feast or famine. Additionally, since legal nursing is relatively new, there are many attorneys in parts of the U.S. that are not aware of the value that nurses bring to medically related cases. However, this is rapidly changing. Finally, there are instances where work needs to be done in a very short window of time. This can be stressful and is unavoidable. Due to the nature of legal work, certain deadlines cannot be missed or the entire case will be jeopardized."

Barbara Levin is a past president of the American Association of Legal Nurse Consultants and is currently the clinical

Related Jobs

- advanced practice nurses
- clinical nurse specialists
- criminal investigators
- critical care nurses
- detectives
- emergency nurses
- geriatric nurses
- home health care and hospice nurses
- lawyers
- legal secretaries
- licensed practical nurses
- neonatal nurses
- nurse anesthetists
- nurse assistants
- nurse managers
- nurse-midwives
- nurse practitioners
- occupational health nurses
- oncological nurses
- paralegals
- psychiatric nurses
- registered nurses

scholar of the Orthopaedic Trauma Unit at Massachusetts General Hospital in Boston, Massachusetts. "I started in the field," she explains, "when an attorney contacted me to review medical records regarding a pedestrian who was struck by a motor vehicle and sustained numerous orthopedic injuries. My role was to explain the injuries and long term/short term goals for the person's future health."

Barbara works on a variety of cases with clients across the United States. "Every day brings new beginnings," she says. "Some days I review medical records exclusively, while other days I participate in conference calls with attorneys, and at times their clients, to educate them on the variety of issues. Much of my time is spent researching various data for cases including research studies. I also serve as an expert witness by testifying on standards of care issues." Barbara also attends independent medical examinations (IMEs) and writes detailed reports. Her business focuses on a variety of practice areas, including personal injury, medical malpractice, mediation/arbitration, IMEs, and limited criminal-related work. "Several years ago I expanded my practice to include participation at court mediations," she says. "This is a wonderful opportunity to serve as the educator on the various health issues to both parties, as well as the mediator or judge."

DO I HAVE WHAT IT TAKES TO BE A LEGAL NURSE CONSULTANT?

To be a successful legal nurse consultant, you should enjoy organizing information, writing reports, explaining medical issues and procedures to people with nonmedical backgrounds, and be able to handle multiple tasks under deadline pressure. You should also have strong reasoning skills, self motivation, and the ability to work well with many types of people.

If you currently practice as a nurse, you should enjoy working with people and be able to give directions as well as follow instructions and work as part of a health care team. "Anyone interested in becoming a legal nurse consultant should have a fascination and a strong desire to continue learning because new tests, procedures, and technologies are

The History of Legal Nurse Consulting

Nurses have served as expert witnesses in nursing malpractice cases for many years. But it was not until the early 1970s, according to the American Association of Legal Nurse Consultants (AALNC), that nurses began to receive compensation for providing this much-needed expertise to the legal community. As nursing and medical malpractice litigation increased in the 1980s, more nurses were needed to serve as expert witnesses in legal proceedings. During this time, according to the AALNC, nurses also began assisting lawyers with understanding medical records and literature, hospital policies and procedures, and medical testimony. Law firms quickly realized that legal nurse consultants were a knowledgeable, cost-effective alternative to physician consultants and began to hire these professionals to assist them with not only nursing and medical malpractice issues, but also personal injury and criminal cases.

The American Association of Legal Nurse Consultants was founded in 1989 to serve the professional needs of legal nurse consultants.

continually being developed," says Barbara Levin.

Mindy Cohen believes that the most important personal and professional skills for legal nurse consultants are accountability, a commitment to excellence, the ability to think critically, attentiveness to detail, excellent writing and communication skills, and an ability to meet short deadlines.

HOW DO I BECOME A LEGAL NURSE CONSULTANT?
Education

High School

While in high school, take mathematics and science courses, including biology, chemistry, and physics. Health courses will also be helpful. English and speech courses should not be neglected because you must be able to communicate well with attorneys and other legal professionals. Business and accounting classes can provide you with the basic tools necessary to run a business.

Postsecondary Training

Legal nurse consultants must first become registered nurses. There are three ways to become a registered nurse—a two-year associate's degree program at a junior or community college, a two- or three-year diploma program at a hospital, or a bachelor's degree program at a college or university. All the programs include supervised, hands-on training in a hospital setting.

All legal nurse consultants must have clinical nursing experience. They draw on this work experience to present cases and testify. It is imperative that they have up-to-date medical knowledge that they can utilize. Legal nurse consultants should have work experience in critical care areas such as hospital emergency rooms, intensive care units, and obstetrics, since these are the areas that are most likely to be involved in litigation.

There are a variety of ways to obtain the education to become a legal nurse consultant. Legal education is not a prerequisite, although many legal nurse consultants acquire knowledge of the legal system by consulting with attorneys, taking classes, and attending seminars. You must evaluate your preferred method of learning—do you prefer a classroom setting, online courses, or textbooks? Barbara recommends that you first join the AALNC and then join your local chapter. This association helps support all levels of legal nurses, ranging from the beginner to the most advanced. The AALNC is the professional organization recognized by the American Nurses Association and offers an online course for new and seasoned legal nurses.

A few colleges (such as Bergen Community College, Kent State University, and Madonna University) offer associate's degrees and advanced certificates in legal nurse consulting.

While some independent legal nurse consultants maintain their clinical practices, others may depart from this arena and work exclusively as legal nurse consultants. It is important for legal nurse consultants to maintain up-to-date knowledge of the current practices in health care. "Remaining abreast of the current health care literature is really integral to the success of my business," Barbara Levin says. "Much time is devoted to reading clinical nursing journals, legal nursing journals, medical journals, and books. In addition, I attend a variety of conferences yearly and participate on many committees." Many legal nurse consultants read the *Journal of Legal Nurse Consulting*, which is published by the AALNC, to stay up to date regarding developments in the field.

Certification or Licensing

You must pass a licensing exam to become a nurse. Licensing is required in all 50 states, and license renewal or continuing education credits are also required periodically. In some cases, licensing in one state will automatically grant licensing in reciprocal states. For further information, contact your state's nursing board. (See the National Council of State Boards of Nursing's Web site at http://www.ncsbn.org for contact information.)

The legal nurse consultant certified (LNCC) program is the only certification in legal nurse consulting recognized by the American Association of Legal Nurse Consultants. Administered by the American Legal Nurse Consultant Certification Board, it is the only legal nurse consulting certification approved by the American Board of Nursing Specialties because it meets their stringent criteria. The LNCC program promotes the recognition of experience and knowledge of the legal nurse consulting specialty practice of nursing. The certification is renewed every five years through continuing education or reexamination and continued practice in the specialty.

Internships and Volunteerships

As part of your basic nursing program, you will be required to complete several nursing internships, or clinical rotations.

The Benefits of Association Membership

The editors of *What Can I Do Now? Law* asked Mindy Cohen, president of the American Association of Legal Nurse Consultants, to detail the benefits of association membership for people in the field:

As a member of the American Association of Legal Nurse Consultants, you can increase your legal, nursing, and medical knowledge, expand your network of contacts (approximately 3,600 members and 45 chapters around the country), and stay up to date on the cutting edge topics affecting legal nurse consultants. We offer seminars/conferences, a variety of publications, discounts on products and services of use to legal nurse consultants, access to other members for networking and resources, and access to your information is available to potential clients.

Membership in the AALNC is very important to career success. Professional development opportunities (products, conferences, etc.) enable you to develop your skills and expertise to excel at what you do. Networking opportunities have allowed me to grow my business through obtaining referrals from other legal nurses and hiring colleagues for needs in my business that are beyond my expertise. The association has also provided opportunities to serve the profession as a volunteer, educator, and author—all of which have enriched my professional development and enhanced my professional reputation for excellence.

Usually these clinicals are set up through the college or university to be completed at a hospital or other health care facility.

You might also want to pursue an internship or a volunteer opportunity with a law firm that specializes in medical malpractice or related issues.

WHO WILL HIRE ME?

The only way to become a registered nurse is through completion of one of the three kinds of educational programs plus passing the licensing examination. Registered nurses may apply for employment directly to hospitals, nursing homes, and companies and government agencies that hire nurses. Jobs can also be obtained through school career services offices, by signing up with employment agencies specializing in placement of nursing personnel, or through each state's employment office. Other sources of jobs include nurses' associations, professional journals, and newspaper want ads.

Mindy Cohen landed her first job by making numerous calls to attorneys, friends, and acquaintances to investigate the idea of legal nursing. "One of the attorneys I spoke with happened to have a case involving a child," she recalls, "and my specialty in nursing was pediatrics. I reviewed the medical records and wrote a report about what happened to the child, explaining why the care given to the child was below the acceptable standard of nursing care. I was so excited, yet nervous, too, because I had not done this before. It was prior to any training I received and I was eight-and-a-half months pregnant,

so I had other things on my mind. Since I was within my clinical expertise, I was confident in my opinions. The attorney could not believe this was my first case. I was so proud. The case settled quickly for more than half-a-million dollars. The attorney was thrilled, and I was hooked on legal nurse consulting."

Barbara Levin landed her first job as a legal nurse consultant through networking. "Since then," she says, "I have taken many opportunities to network with my colleagues, nursing staff, and attorneys, and this is how I receive my work. In addition, I have had opposing counsel as well as judges contact me to later work on their cases."

Nurses who are interested in becoming legal nurse consultants should plan their transition into the field carefully. "You really need to have a firm nursing foundation of about five years with a clinical nursing position before venturing into legal nursing," advises Barbara. "Joining the American Association of Legal Nurse Consultants will assist you in many ways, including education, networking, and business development. When you decide to enter this field, do not quit your regular job until you have enough work to sustain you."

Barbara says that there are numerous legal practice specialties within legal nursing. "To quote from the Scope and Standards of Legal Nurse Consulting, 'the legal nurse consultant practices in a variety of settings including law firms, government offices, insurance companies, hospital risk-management departments, forensic environments, and as self-employed practitioners. They serve as a liaison between the legal and health care communities and between the consumer and health care or legal communities. Legal nurse consultants provide consultation and education to legal, health care professionals and others in litigation related to illness or injury including areas such as personal injury, product liability, medical malpractice, workers' compensation, toxic torts, risk management, medical professional licensure investigation, and criminal law.'" Other responsibilities include legal writing, medical record analysis, literature research, report preparation, and locating and working with expert witnesses.

WHERE CAN I GO FROM HERE?

Administrative and supervisory positions in the nursing field go to nurses who have earned at least a bachelor of science in nursing (BSN). Nurses with many years of experience who are graduates of a diploma program may achieve supervisory positions, but requirements for such

Nurse Legal Consulting Education

Only a few colleges offer associate's degrees and advanced certificates in legal nurse consulting, including:

Bergen Community College
400 Paramus Road
Paramus, NJ 07652-1508
201-447-7100
http://www.bergen.edu
Degree available: Associate's

Johnson County Community College
12345 College Boulevard
Overland Park, KS 66210-1299
913-469-8500
http://www.jccc.net/home/depts/1245
Degree available: Advanced certificates (legal nurse consultant, legal nurse consultant entrepreneurship)

Kent State University
Kent, OH 44242-0001
330-672-3000
http://www.kent.edu
Degree available: Advanced certificate

Madonna University
36600 Schoolcraft Road
Livonia, MI 48150-1176
800-852-4951
http://www.madonna.edu/pages/
npcertificate.cfm
Degree available: Advanced certificate

Roger Williams University
One Old Ferry Road
Bristol, RI 02809-2923
800-458-7144
http://www.rwu.edu/academics/
departments
Degree available: Advanced certificate

University of Toledo
2801 West Bancroft
Toledo, OH 43606-3390
800-586-5336
http://www.utoledo.edu/hshs/
paralegal
Degree available: Advanced certificate

promotions have become more difficult in recent years and in many cases require at least the BSN.

Legal nurse consultants with considerable experience may advance to supervisory positions or move on to open their own consulting companies.

WHAT ARE THE SALARY RANGES?

According to several sources, independent legal nurse consultants may be paid on an hourly basis that can range from $60 to $250 per hour. The fee depends on the type of services they are performing, such as testifying, reviewing records, or doing medical research, and also reflects their experience and reputation. In addition, fees vary in different parts of the country. Some legal nurse consultants may work on a retainer basis with one or more clients.

Many legal nurse consultants who work for law firms and other businesses and institutions may be employed full time or part time. Their salaries vary by experience, geographic location, and areas of expertise. The full-time salary range, according to various sources, is from under $50,000 to a small percentage making more than $100,000. Some litigation situations may require that consultants work overtime.

General employment benefits such as health and life insurance, vacation time, and sick leave may be offered to full-time legal nurse consultants.

WHAT IS THE JOB OUTLOOK?

Nursing specialties will be in great demand in the future. The U.S. Department of Labor reports that employment of registered nurses will grow much faster than the average for all occupations through 2016. As long as there is litigation involving medical issues, one can expect this specialty nursing field to continue to grow.

Legal Secretaries

SUMMARY

Definition
Legal secretaries assist lawyers by performing the administrative and clerical duties in a law office or firm.

Alternative Job Titles
Litigation secretaries
Trial secretaries

Salary Range
$29,670 to $50,250 to $95,990

Educational Requirements
Some postsecondary training

Certification or Licensing
Recommended

Employment Outlook
About as fast as the average

High School Subjects
Computer science
English (writing/literature)
Government
Law

Personal Interests
Law
Writing

Patricia Infanti works at Ballard Spahr Andrews & Ingersoll, LLP, a large law firm with 12 offices across the country. She has been a legal secretary since 1977. "Working for a large firm is a wonderful opportunity because large firms offer so many benefits and services that a small law firm simply cannot afford," she says. "I work with two well-known real estate attorneys, one of whom I've been with for more than 13 years, and one associate. The atmosphere of my department is pleasant and all of us consider ourselves professionals and work well with each other. I feel confident in saying that I will probably stay with this firm until I retire. I truly love my profession and wish that more competent young people would see it as I do and choose being a legal secretary as a viable, worthwhile profession."

WHAT DOES A LEGAL SECRETARY DO?

Legal secretaries are responsible for not only handling the duties of a general secretary, but also all the specific responsibilities that come with working for a lawyer. Although every law office or firm may vary in the exact duties required for the position, in general, most legal secretaries spend their time managing information that comes in and goes out of the law office. Legal secretaries may type letters and legal documents, such as subpoenas, appeals, and motions; handle incoming

To Be a Successful Legal Secretary, You Should…

- be knowledgeable regarding legal terminology and court structures and practices
- be able to prioritize and balance different tasks under deadline pressure
- be detailed oriented
- be able to follow directions, but also work on your own, when necessary
- have strong communication skills
- have the ability to get along with many types of people
- be willing to learn throughout your career

and outgoing mail; maintain a detailed filing system; and deliver legal documents to the court. Besides these duties, legal secretaries spend much of their time making appointments with clients and dealing with client questions. The legal secretary is a sort of personal assistant to one or more lawyers as well, and must maintain the calendars and schedules for the office. It is important to know where your attorney can be found or whether another attorney can assist the client.

Legal secretaries may also be asked to conduct research for the cases that are current within the office. They may research and write legal briefs on a topic or case that is relevant to the lawyer's current cases. Legal secretaries spend many hours researching cases in law libraries, public libraries, and on the Internet. Part of this research includes scouring legal journals and magazines looking for relevant laws and courtroom decisions that may affect the clientele.

Legal secretaries also must keep and manage detailed files and records. They help lawyers locate information such as employment, medical, and criminal records. They also keep records from all previous clients and court cases for future use. Legal secretaries must also track and use various forms, such as trial request, client application, and accident report forms.

Legal secretaries spend much of their workday using a computer. They spend lengthy periods of time typing or writing, which may cause hand and wrist strain. Long hours staring at a computer monitor may also cause eyestrain. Legal secretaries work with lawyers, other legal secretaries, clients, court personnel, library personnel, and other support workers. Senior legal secretaries supervise some legal secretaries; others are left largely unsupervised. Most legal secretaries are full-time employees who work a 40-hour week. Some are part-time workers who move into full-time status as they gain more experience. Because the legal secretary's work revolves around the lawyer, many secretaries work long hours of overtime.

Legal secretaries may work at small, single attorney firms, mid-sized firms, or large law firms with offices throughout the United States.

WHAT IS IT LIKE TO BE A LEGAL SECRETARY?

Julie Abernathy has been a legal secretary since 1974. "I currently work for a large firm based out of Dallas, Texas—Haynes and Boone, LLP—but am working in their Austin office," she says. "I have worked for Haynes and Boone for approximately eight years. I am currently employed in the Business Litigation Section of my firm. Prior to my employment at Haynes and Boone, I worked for Jackson Walker, LLP. The majority of my legal experience has been in small firms consisting of one to five attorneys. For 16.5 years I worked for a firm that specialized in administrative law. After that exciting legal experience, I chose to work for an attorney who went out on her own and devoted her practice primarily to estate planning and probate. I found that specialty very rewarding and fulfilling. However, my true love is litigation."

Julie, who is also the president of the National Association of Legal Secretaries (NALS), says that there is no typical day on the job. "That in itself is what I love most about my career," she says. "Each case is different from the next, and each client is unique in their/its own way. I typically interact with the clients, prepare correspondence, and transmit pleadings and documents to opposing counsel, courthouse personnel, and clients for review and approval. My supervising attorneys do not give me specific instructions, as they know I am very familiar with the procedures and responsibilities of my job. I also assist my attorneys with basic research, document retrieval, document production, and even with their travel arrangements."

Patricia McEldowney works as a legal secretary for Henehan Donovan & Isaacson, Ltd., in Chicago, Illinois. Her firm specializes in probate, corporate, and real estate law. She has worked in the field for 21 years. "Upon my arrival at work, I see that the machines are turned on, unload the dishwasher (it is a small law firm), and get files in order for the day. The secretaries share in answering the phones. The day usually consists of letters taken in shorthand, preparing court forms, and photo-

Advice for Aspiring Legal Secretaries

Patricia Infanti, a legal secretary since 1977, offers the following advice to high school students who are considering a career as a legal secretary:

The most important advice I would give is not to discount the challenges and variety of the legal secretarial profession. What I do is an integral part of the law firm, and my attorneys would not be able to accomplish all that they do without me. So many young people believe that being a secretary is less than being a paralegal. But that is not the case. In fact, every day is different, with its own situations and challenges. I have become quite adept in finding solutions to keep my attorneys' practices running smoothly. I am the practice manager who coordinates the efforts of other departments to get my attorneys' work completed correctly and in a timely manner.

copying. There are days that I go to the Daley Center (which houses the Circuit Court of Cook County in Illinois) to file documents, place matters on court calendars, and order certified copies of documents, or I file materials with the Cook County Assessor's Office and/or Cook County Board of Review. I love being downtown with all the hustle and bustle." McEldowney says that the best part of her job is the fact that she is constantly learning and attaining "a deeper knowledge regarding probating estates, real estate transactions, and trust documents."

DO I HAVE WHAT IT TAKES TO BE A LEGAL SECRETARY?

To be successful as a legal secretary, you should be knowledgeable about legal terminology and court structures and practices. The ability to prioritize and balance different tasks is also necessary for the job. Legal secretaries must be organized and focused to handle their varying responsibilities. "When I entered the field, what was most surprising to me," says Patricia Infanti, "were the amount of details that were part of the legal profession. I had to learn how to prepare documents in conformance with various judges' preferences and how to work well with court staff so that I could get things done promptly and properly. At one time I considered continuing my education to become an attorney. However, I realized that my strengths were in my organizational skills and my ability to remember details and incorporate them into my work."

HOW DO I BECOME A LEGAL SECRETARY?
Education

High School

Because a legal secretary must be able to communicate the attorney's ideas in written and oral form, it's important to get a firm grounding in English (especially writing), spelling, typing, and public speaking. Computers are used in most law offices, so be sure to gain computer experience while in high school. Patricia Infanti advises students to learn basic and advanced applications in Microsoft Word, Outlook, Excel, and Power-Point. Government and political science courses, as well as classes that give you experience conducting research, will also be useful.

Participating in law-related clubs and activities are also good ways to learn more about this career. "When I was in high school," says Julie Abernathy, "I took an Office Education Administration class and actually became active in a school club where I was a state delegate. During my course of studies, we learned more about the difference in office education from a medical, legal, and executive standpoint. The legal field was very interesting to me. In fact, I participated in a local chapter's Day in Court program, where we toured the local county courthouse and jail. That visit sealed my love for law."

"Participating in any club or in student government (especially as secretary) would provide students with an excellent learning experience that would prepare them for the legal services profession," says Infanti. "Participating in the English club or the school newspaper would help with language skills. Also, students should participate in ethics seminars or programs if those are available."

Postsecondary Training

Many legal secretaries receive their training via established one- or two-year legal secretary programs. These programs are offered by vocational, business, and junior colleges. You could also obtain a four-year degree to get a more well-rounded education. Courses taken should focus on specific skills and knowledge needed by a legal secretary, such as computer, keyboarding, English, legal writing, editing, researching, and communication skills. NALS also offers basic and advanced legal secretary training courses.

After graduating from high school, Julie Abernathy attended a local junior college in Waco, Texas, and specialized in its legal secretarial training courses. "I took four semesters of shorthand, transcription classes, English classes (including written communication), psychology, computers, accounting/bookkeeping, and office procedures," she recalls. "Upon graduation with an associate's degree in applied science, I immediately obtained a job at a local law firm. The school had a placement office which sent me on my first job interview, and thus my first job offer and new career."

As businesses continue to expand worldwide, employers are increasingly looking for candidates with bachelor's degrees and professional certifications.

Certification or Licensing

NALS offers two general legal secretary certifications. After some preliminary office training, you can take an examination to receive the accredited legal

Lingo to Learn

affidavit A written or printed declaration or statement of facts, made voluntarily and confirmed by the oath of the person making it.

appeal In civil practice, the complaint to a superior court of an injustice done or error committed by a lower one, whose judgment or decisions the court above is called upon to correct or reverse.

brief A written document; a condensed statement of some large document, or of a series of papers, facts and circumstances, or propositions.

contract A promissory agreement between two or more persons that creates, modifies, or terminates a legal relation.

deposition The testimony of a witness taken not in open court, but during an investigation, and reproduced in writing, with the intention of being used in court proceedings.

discovery In a general sense, the disclosure or coming to light of what was previously hidden; the acquisition or knowledge of facts. In a legal sense, this refers to the required disclosure of facts or documents before a trial begins.

pleading A formal allegation of the respective claims and defenses by parties involved in litigation.

subpoena Formal papers that cause a witness to appear and give testimony.

secretary designation. This certification is for legal secretaries with education, but little to no experience. Legal secretaries with three years of experience can become certified as a professional legal secretary (PLS). The PLS certification designates a legal secretary with exceptional skills and experience.

Other specific legal secretary certifications are offered by Legal Secretaries International. You can become board certified in civil litigation, probate, real estate, business law, criminal law, or intellectual property. Applicants must have a minimum of five years of law experience and pass an examination.

Internships and Volunteerships

Your school's career services office or legal secretary program head will be able to provide you with information about internships and volunteer opportunities. "I would encourage high school students to participate in office internships through school-to-work programs," advises Infanti. "These will provide valuable office experience."

WHO WILL HIRE ME?

The majority of the approximately 275,000 legal secretaries employed in the United States work for law offices or law firms. Other legal secretaries are employed by government agencies at the state and national level. More law firms and offices are located in Washington, D.C., and in larger metropolitan areas, so these regions provide more opportunities. However, most law offices and firms are now online. The Internet enables workers to send information easily from the law office to the courtroom, so offices are not forced to be located close to the courts. Legal secretaries are in demand anywhere lawyers practice.

Many legal secretaries get their first job through the career services offices of their college or vocational school. Patricia McEldowney attended Southwest School of Business in Chicago. "The school placed me with Henehan Donovan & Isaacson, Ltd., and I have been there ever since except for the 10 years when I lived out of state. And when I moved back to town, I was asked to return."

After graduating from college, Patricia Infanti learned about an opening for a legal secretary via a coworker at her job at the time. "I called for an interview and took a substantial cut in pay (I was an assistant department manager in a retail store) in order to get my foot in the door," she recalls. "It was difficult even then to get a job without experience so I knew I needed to learn quickly. I did not know what to expect upon entering the legal field. My education prepared me for work in a business office. Consequently, I had to quickly learn all of the legal aspects of a law office. I was fortunate that the office manager/legal secretary was actually looking for someone with no legal knowledge who she could train to do things her way. This consummate professional taught me everything—from what it means to be a legal secretary, to court procedures, to law office accounting, to how to work with court personnel, other legal secretaries, and clients. She taught me all I needed to know about this service-oriented profession. I have never regretted my decision to move into the legal field."

Still other legal secretaries start by working part time, gaining experience toward a first full-time position. Some legal secretaries may work as a "floater," a secretary who is not assigned to any particular lawyer, but fills in for absent secretaries and handles overflow. Working as a floater will expose you to a wide variety of legal practices, which will help you decide the area in which you want to specialize. Don't forget to contact the local law offices in your area and let them know you are available; often direct contact now can lead to a job later.

WHERE CAN I GO FROM HERE?

Experienced legal secretaries are often promoted to oversee less experienced legal secretaries. Some firms have *senior legal secretaries*, who are given more responsibility and less supervision duties. Senior legal secretaries may be responsible for drafting letters and documents and passing them on to lawyers for revision or signature. Legal secretaries may continue their education and become paralegals or lawyers. Many of the skills legal secretaries obtain can be transferred to almost any other office setting.

WHAT ARE THE SALARY RANGES?

The median annual salary for legal secretaries was approximately $50,250 in

2008, according to the U.S. Department of Labor. Earnings ranged from less than $29,670 to more than $95,990. An attorney's rank in the firm will also affect the salary of his or her legal secretary; secretaries who work for a partner will earn higher salaries than those who work for an associate. Legal secretaries who are certified generally receive higher pay than those who have not received certification.

Most law firms provide employees with sick days, vacation days, and holidays. Health insurance, 401(k) plans, and profit sharing may be offered as well. "My firm provides a wonderful variety of medical benefit plans, a 401(k) plan, dental and life insurance, and is very generous with vacation, sick days, and firm-closed holidays," says Patricia Infanti. Some law firms offer in-house training or pay for off-site classes to increase their secretaries' skills.

WHAT IS THE JOB OUTLOOK?

Employment for legal secretaries will grow about as fast as the average for all careers through 2016, according to the *Occupational Outlook Handbook*. The legal services industry as a whole is growing, which will create demand for legal secretaries. An increased need for lawyers in such areas as intellectual property will leave lawyers in need of assistance with their caseloads. Legal secretaries with strong research skills, as well as certification, will have plentiful job opportunities, especially in large metropolitan areas.

Technological advances in recent years have revolutionized traditional secretarial tasks such as typing or keeping correspondence. The use of email, scanners, and the Internet will make secretaries more productive in coming years. The downside to these advancements is a possible decrease in demand: Fewer workers are needed to do the same workload. For the legal profession, however, advances in technology have only expanded the responsibilities for secretaries.

"The future of legal professionals who support attorneys is very exciting," says Julie Abernathy. "One of the things you need to be is flexible and learn to go with the flow when it comes to new technology and working with different generations of staff and attorneys. It's truly amazing to look back on the past 35 years and see where my job has changed significantly from when I started. The role of legal secretaries may change throughout the years, but it will never phase out. I can only imagine what my job will be like in the next 10 to 15 years, and I am looking forward to learning new things."

Paralegals

"I made the decision to enter the paralegal field when I was in high school," says
Deborah Nelson, a paralegal since 1990. "I
was very inquisitive and always wanted to
debate the issues. My guidance counselor
told me of the paralegal field, and I was
instantly sold. The more I explored the
field, the more I realized that the paralegal is the heart of the case. My inquisitive
nature made this job perfect for me as I
truly enjoy putting the pieces of the litigation puzzle together."

WHAT DOES A PARALEGAL DO?

Paralegals, also known as *legal assistants*,
research laws, investigate facts, prepare

documents, and, in general, do background work for lawyers, who review
their work and assume legal responsibility for the projects. Only lawyers are
licensed to actually practice law. That
is, although a majority of paralegals are
officially trained in key aspects of the law,
they are not lawyers, and as such cannot
set legal fees, give legal advice, or present
cases in court.

The types of material that paralegals
research are statutes, recorded judicial
decisions, legal articles, treaties, constitutions, and legal codes. These in turn
are used to prepare documents—briefs,
pleadings, appeals, wills, contracts, initial
and amended articles of incorporation,
stock certificates and other securities,

buy-sell agreements, closing papers and binders, deeds, trust instruments, and so on—for review, approval, and use by attorneys. Research also aids in making discoveries that will be used to structure a case. Paralegals have to position and articulate their findings in written and verbal form to the supervising attorney.

Other activities include filing pleadings with court clerks, preparing affidavits of documents and maintaining document files, and delivering or directing the delivery of subpoenas to witnesses and parties to action.

What a paralegal does on any given day depends on his or her specialty or the area of law in which he or she works; paralegal specialties are thus as varied as legal specialties.

A paralegal may work for a law firm, corporation, government agency, community legal service, or for a private practice in the area of litigation, which could cover any number of business practices. They may specialize in bankruptcy, corporate law, criminal law, labor law, patent/copyright law, real estate law, or medical malpractice. The most varied functions can be found among paralegal generalists who work for small general law firms where they may do any number of the above-mentioned tasks, from research on judicial decisions to preparing a contract. Conversely, working in a medium to large law firm, government agency, or corporation that offers more specialization, such as labor law, a paralegal's duties and responsibilities may also be highly specialized, to the degree that he or she only works on cases dealing with, say, employee benefits.

Paralegals who work for governmental agencies analyze legal material for internal use, maintain reference files, conduct research for attorneys, collect and analyze evidence for agency hearings, and prepare informative or explanatory material on the law, agency regulations, and agency policy for general use by the agency and the public. Paralegals in community legal service basically assist with providing legal aid to the poor by filing forms, conducting research, and preparing documents.

Paralegals who work for a corporation are less frequently involved with litigation and research than with preparing and filing annual financial reports, maintaining corporate minute books and resolutions, and reviewing governmental regulations to ensure that the corporation is operating within the law.

Paralegals have the added prestige of directing the tasks of other paralegals or legal secretaries who help them with projects. Paralegals who coordinate the work of other paralegals are known as *paralegal administrators* and are usually found in larger law firms or corporations that employ five or more paralegals.

Paralegals often work in pleasant and comfortable offices. Much of their work is performed in a law library. Some paralegals work out of their homes in special employment situations. When investigation is called for, paralegals may travel to gather information. Most paralegals work a 40-hour week, although long hours are sometimes required to meet court-imposed deadlines. Longer hours—sometimes as much as 90 hours per week—are usually the normal routine for paralegals starting out in law offices and firms.

Many of the paralegal's duties involve routine tasks, so they must have a great deal of patience. However, paralegals may be given increasingly difficult assignments over time. Paralegals are often unsupervised, especially as they gain experience and a reputation for quality work.

WHAT IS IT LIKE TO BE A PARALEGAL?

Deborah Nelson has worked in the practice areas of employment, products liability, and warranty litigation—primarily in law departments of corporations rather than law firms. She currently works as the litigation manager for Genmar Holdings, Inc. in Minneapolis, Minnesota. A typical day for Deborah involves "overseeing the day-to-day management of all litigation claims and lawsuits, including management of a litigation database; communication with outside counsel, experts, and witnesses; gathering case documents; communication with various corporate employees; investigating and responding to customer claim letters; reviewing discovery responses, answers, and correspondence; and communicating with customers, business leaders, and outside counsel."

When Deborah arrives at work, her first task is to review the litigation database calendar to determine what deadlines must be met that day or specific projects that must begin. "Once the tasks are identified," she says, "I begin working on individual tasks. Since all of our litigation is handled by outside coun-

To Be a Successful Paralegal, You Should...

- be ethical

- be logical

- have an inquisitive nature

- have excellent communication skills, both verbal and written

- be willing to continue to learn throughout your career

- be persistent when gathering information and accomplishing tasks

- have strong research skills

- have good time-management skills

- be organized and flexible

- be able to work effectively and efficiently in a high-pressure work environment

- pay attention to details

- be able to structure and balance your own schedule

sel, I am tasked with the responsibility of case coordination. As such I act as a liaison between outside counsel and the company, witnesses (expert and lay), and my managing attorney. On any given day, I may be reviewing draft discovery responses, gathering documents, conducting investigations, drafting responses to customer and/or agency claims and drafting agreements, all while maintaining constant communication with my managing attorney."

The Benefits of Association Membership

The editors of *What Can I Do Now? Law* asked Deborah Nelson, a paralegal since 1990, to detail the benefits of association membership:

The greatest benefit of an association membership is networking. The Minnesota Paralegal Association [in which she is a member] offers a great networking resource. Membership includes not only working paralegals, but also vendors in the legal arena. Building a network of resources will only make your career stronger and more successful. I consider myself a perfect example of why networking is so important. I secured my first paralegal job as a direct result of networking with a vendor at an association event while I was a student. I also met my mentor there and have been able to maintain a relationship with her since 1990.

In addition to her general litigation management duties, Deborah must also be aware of budgetary issues, including case reserves, review and approval of outside counsel invoices, and time management. She handles these tasks on a daily basis.

John Goudie, a paralegal since 1987, works as a regulatory analyst for Assurant Health, a leading provider of health insurance. He has practiced in the areas of civil personal injury, workers' compensation, insurance defense, and corporate insurance regulation. He also has served in several leadership positions, including

president, for the Paralegal Association of Wisconsin; serves on the Board of Directors of the American Alliance of Paralegals; and sits on the Advisory Council for the Paralegal Program at Milwaukee Area Technical College. "I had always had an interest in the rightness and wrongness of the law, but did not have the desire to be an attorney," John says. "When the paralegal profession began to develop, I was studying other educational pursuits. Due to the economy at the time, that career did not develop. I then decided one day that the paralegal profession seemed like a good career path for me, as this satisfied my desire to work in the legal field."

John says that he has had three distinctly different positions in the paralegal field, with each having a different "typical" day. "When I worked in personal injury litigation," he explains, "my day consisted of managing case files; requesting, organizing, and summarizing medical and employment records; filing documents with the court; interviewing witnesses; reviewing accident site investigations; working with hired expert witnesses to be certain they have all of the documentation they need to form their opinions; preparing cases for trial; researching legal issues; writing research memorandums for the attorneys I worked with; and assisting attorneys in trial.

"For a period of 14 years, I managed the workers' compensation practice in a personal injury firm I worked for. I hold a license to appear before the Division of Worker's Compensation in Wisconsin. In that capacity, I was responsible for all aspects of our clients' claims relating to workers' compensation injuries, including intake with the client; obtaining, organizing and filing documents with the agency; negotiating settlements of injury claims; and appearing as the employees' legal representative at formal hearings before the administrative agency.

"Presently, I work in the corporate legal department for an insurance company, and my position involves monitoring, reviewing, and researching state and federal laws as they pertain to privacy, security, and compliance. Additionally, I perform legal research on issues affecting the insurance industry, I sit in on meetings for project development teams where there may be a component of the project that involves a policy holder's privacy and security to offer our department's input on those issues. Our department is responsible for the corporation's compliance with the state and federal privacy laws."

DO I HAVE WHAT IT TAKES TO BE A PARALEGAL?

Communication skills, both verbal and written, are vital to working as a paralegal. "A good deal of this profession involves contact with people," says John Goudie, "whether it be clients, attorneys, medical personnel, courthouse personnel, etc. Your ability to communicate with people is critical." Paralegals must be able to turn research into reports that a lawyer or corporate executive can use. They must also be able to think logically and learn new laws and regulations quickly. "Always be willing to undertake new tasks and responsibilities and express a willing-

ness to learn and expand your knowledge base," advises John. "Be inquisitive and persistent." Research skills, computer skills, people skills, and organizational skills are other necessities. "A primary component of this position, irrespective of the area of practice, is organization," says John.

Deborah Nelson believes that the most important personal and professional qualities for paralegals include "excellent organization and time management skills, strong ethics, and the ability to evaluate, analyze, and apply all facts and evidence, including those that may negatively affect your case."

No matter what type of law or what sorts of issues are involved, a tremendous amount of responsibility weighs on the shoulders of the attorneys and paralegals working on a case. Paralegals working on real estate deals, for example, must prepare, copy, notarize and file documents before a specific, unchangeable deadline. At stake could be millions of dollars, an individual's civil rights, or the reputation of a law firm or corporation, not to mention justice. Because of the high stakes, paralegals work under a great deal of pressure. Impatient attorneys, last-minute changes that mean staying late, or rush deliveries to the offices of city officials to have documents filed, for example, require a person with the ability to think and act quickly, while also remaining calm enough to prevent careless errors. Being assertive and not easily intimidated also helps when dealing with everyone from cantankerous senior partners to slow-moving county clerks.

HOW DO I BECOME A PARALEGAL?

Education

High School

The most important skill for all paralegals, regardless of their specialty, is the ability to read and analyze what is often complex information. Paralegals must also be efficient in researching, investigating, and summarizing information. High school courses that exercise language skills are thus of primary importance, so English, literature, expository writing, speech, and logic classes are necessary. Standard high school courses in mathematics, science, and computer science, and electives in subjects like shop and drafting, can help develop investigative and problem-solving skills, accuracy, and attention to detail.

Extracurricular activities that could strengthen both the communication and fact-finding skills of a potential paralegal are memberships in the drama club and the speech and debate teams. Extemporaneous speaking and debating both require the ability to research and document topics and theories, as well as to articulate those ideas in well-reasoned arguments.

You should also take foreign languages, especially Spanish and Latin. Because legal terminology is used constantly, word origins and vocabulary should be a focus.

Postsecondary Training

Requirements for paralegals vary by employer. Some paralegals start out as legal secretaries or clerical workers and are gradually given more training and responsibility. The majority, however, choose formal training and education programs.

John Goudie attended a comprehensive 15-week/240-hour paralegal certificate program at a college in Wisconsin in 1987. "Prequalifications for this program were that one needed to possess a bachelor's degree and be at least 25 years of age," he recalls. "As such, most of my classmates were, as I was, embarking on their second or third careers. A good deal of credit was given for 'life' experience. Although an internship was part of the course, obtaining an internship was the individual's responsibility, and they were few and far between at the time. For those of us who did not obtain an internship, we were provided with additional classroom instruction by experts in other fields of the law."

Formal training programs usually range from one to three years and are offered in a variety of educational settings: four-year colleges and universities, law schools, community and junior colleges, business schools, proprietary schools, and paralegal associations. Admission requirements vary, but good grades in high school and college are always an asset. There are approximately 1,000 paralegal programs, about 260 of which have been approved by the American Bar Association. The National Federation of Paralegal Associations reports that 84 percent of all paralegals receive formal paralegal education.

Some paralegal programs require a bachelor's degree for admission; others do not require any college education. In either case, those who have a college degree usually have an edge over those who do not. Because of the number of specialties available in the paralegal field, a bachelor's degree in almost any subject would be beneficial. For example, many health science majors find the areas of personal injury or medical malpractice compatible with their education. A science major might work in patents and copyrights, while a business or liberal arts major might be comfortable as a paralegal generalist. Basically, successful fulfillment of the standard college requirements in all academic categories is important. Science and mathematics, especially statistics, will further sharpen reasoning ability, analytical skills, and problem solving.

Certification or Licensing

Paralegals are not required to be licensed or certified. Instead, when lawyers employ paralegals, they often follow guidelines designed to protect the public from the practice of law by unqualified persons.

Paralegals may, however, opt to be certified. To do so, they may take and pass an extensive two-day test conducted by the National Association of Legal Assistants (NALA) Certifying Board. Paralegals who pass the test may use the title certified legal assistant (CLA) after their names. CLAs who prefer to be referred to as "certified paralegals" can use the certified paralegal designation. The NALA also offers an advanced certified paralegal designation to experienced paralegals who complete education requirements. Several specialized courses are available, including Contracts Management/Contracts Administration, Discovery, Social Security Disability, and Trial Practice. The National Association of Legal Secretaries (NALS) offers a basic and an advanced certification for legal professionals and the professional paralegal certification for paralegals. Contact the association for more information.

In 1994 the National Federation of Paralegal Associations established the Paralegal Advanced Competency Exam as a means for paralegals who fill education and experience requirements to acquire professional recognition. Paralegals who pass this exam and maintain the continuing education requirement may use the designation registered paralegal.

The American Alliance of Paralegals offers the American Alliance certified paralegal designation to applicants who have at least five years of experience as a paralegal and meet educational criteria.

Internships and Volunteerships

Many beginning paralegals become oriented in the field through internships, either during their training or afterward. To receive pay during an internship is ideal, but there are also unpaid internships. They key is to find an internship—whether it offers pay or not—that provides you with a good introduction to the field and valuable networking contacts.

You can also offer yourself as a volunteer to the law offices in town. Ask your guidance counselor to help you set up a volunteer/internship agreement with a lawyer.

WHO WILL HIRE ME?

Paralegals and legal assistants hold approximately 238,000 jobs in the United

States. The majority (70 percent) work for lawyers in law offices or in law firms. Other paralegals work for the government, namely the Federal Trade Commission, Justice Department, Treasury Department, Internal Revenue Service, Department of the Interior, and many other agencies and offices.

Paralegals also work in the business community. Anywhere legal matters are part of the day-to-day work, paralegals are usually handling them. Paralegals fit in well in the business world because many smaller corporations must deal with legal regulations but don't necessarily need an attorney or a team of lawyers.

Paralegals in business can be found all over the country. Larger cities employ more paralegals who focus on the legal side of the profession, and government paralegals will find the most opportunities in state capitals and Washington, D.C.

Although some law firms promote legal secretaries to paralegal status, most employers prefer to hire individuals who have completed paralegal programs. To have the best opportunity at getting a quality job in the paralegal field, you should attend a paralegal school. In addition to providing a solid background in paralegal studies, most schools help graduates find jobs. Even though the job market for paralegals is expected to grow rapidly over the next 10 years, those with the best credentials will get the best jobs. John Goudie landed his first job through his educational program. "I was very fortunate," he recalls, "that the director of our program at the time knew of an attorney who had a substantial practice in personal injury and medical malpractice,

and the director referred me to him for an interview. I had several years of work experience in the medical field in both a hospital setting and in emergency work. The attorney who hired me was most interested in my ability to review medical records and summarize the records for him. That was the criteria upon which I was hired."

The National Federation of Paralegal Associations recommends using job banks that are sponsored by paralegal associations across the country. For paralegal associations that may be able to help, see the organizations listed in Look to the Pros in Section 4 of this book. Many jobs for paralegals are posted on the Internet as well.

Deborah Nelson encourages paralegal students to carefully consider their strengths and weaknesses as they evaluate what area of law they hope to work in. "Most importantly," she advises, "don't be afraid to work your first few years as a temporary paralegal through an employment agency. This will allow you the opportunity to explore all areas of the law and find the one that best fits your skill strengths and your interest."

WHERE CAN I GO FROM HERE?

There are no formal advancement paths for paralegals. There are, however, some possibilities for advancement, as large firms are beginning to establish career programs for paralegals.

For example, a person may be promoted from a paralegal to a head legal assistant who supervises others. In addition, a paralegal may specialize in one area of law, such as environmental, real estate, or medical malpractice. Many paralegals also advance by moving from small to large firms.

For the experienced paralegal, a freelance business providing services to a client list of attorneys is another option. Rather than work for one firm, these freelance paralegals often contract their services to many lawyers. Just like any other small business owner, freelance paralegals, or consultants, should consult an attorney or accountant and put together a business plan. Is there a demand for freelance paralegal services in your area? Should you be incorporated, form a partnership, or remain a sole proprietor? Will you purchase professional liability insurance? Will you lease an office space and equipment or work from home? Will you have to hire personnel? What about your billing and fee structure? Networking? And most importantly, how will you finance your business? Many paralegal associations offer help in setting up a freelance business.

Some paralegals with bachelor's degrees enroll in law school to train to become lawyers.

Paralegals can also move horizontally by taking their specialized knowledge of the law into another field, such as insurance, occupational health, or law enforcement.

WHAT ARE THE SALARY RANGES?

Salaries vary greatly for paralegals. The size and location of the firm and the education and experience of the employee are

> ## Advancement Possibilities
>
> *Attorneys* perform a variety of legal services for clients, including doing legal research, filing deeds and other official documents, drawing up wills and prenuptial agreements, writing briefs, and presenting arguments in civil and criminal courts of law.
>
> *Legal administrators* manage the day-to-day business of running a law firm. A separate board of attorneys exists to monitor and run the law firm, but a legal administrator might sit on this board, sharing the details of day-to-day office expenses and expenditures, such as delivery costs and billable hours for paralegals.
>
> *Paralegal administrators* supervise other paralegals, helping them with assignments when necessary and coordinating with attorneys the delegation of case loads, so that no one paralegal is getting too few or too many assignments. A paralegal administrator might also function as both the liaison between the paralegals and attorneys and the spokesperson for the paralegals whenever a particular issue or concern arises that requires arbitration or discussion.

some factors that determine the annual earnings of paralegals.

The U.S. Department of Labor reports that paralegals and legal assistants had median annual earnings of $46,120 in 2008. The highest-paid 10 percent earned more than $73,450, while the lowest-paid 10 percent earned less than $29,260. According to the USDL, paralegals and legal assistants earned the following mean annual salaries in 2008 by industry: federal government, $60,340; insurance carriers, $53,310; legal services, $47,380; and employment services, $53,970.

Benefits for paralegals depend on the employer; however, they usually include such items as health insurance, retirement or 401(k) plans, and paid vacation days.

WHAT IS THE JOB OUTLOOK?

Employment for paralegals is expected to grow much faster than the average for all occupations through 2016, according to the U.S. Department of Labor. One reason for the expected rapid growth in the profession is the financial benefit of employing paralegals. The paralegal, whose duties fall between those of the legal secretary and those of the attorney, helps make the delivery of legal services more cost effective to clients. Additionally, as the population becomes more sophisticated about the legal options open to them, the need will increase for para-

legals to assist in the delivery of services provided by private law firms and in the benefits areas of corporations, insurance and real estate companies, title insurance firms, and banks and trusts. Prepaid legal services targeted to large corporations for employee benefits and mass marketed to the general public will also produce jobs for paralegals. An increased awareness of community legal services and advocacy will provide jobs, and greater attention to social, criminal, and family counseling arising from the court system will add to the bank of jobs for paralegals.

The growth of this occupation, to some extent, is also dependent on the economy. Businesses are less likely to pursue litigation cases when profit margins are down, thus limiting the need for new hires.

"I believe paralegals are vital to the legal industry and that the industry is strong and will continue to be strong," says Deborah Nelson. "However, given the current economic times it may be tough for inexperienced paralegals to get their foot in the door. A paralegal's education (i.e., bachelor's degree vs. no degree) will give a paralegal an advantage; more importantly, students should make certain their degree is approved by the American Bar Association (ABA) since many employers require an ABA-approved degree."

Prosecutors

SUMMARY

Definition
Prosecutors are lawyers who conduct criminal and civil proceedings on behalf of the government.

Alternative Job Titles
Assistant city attorneys
Assistant district attorneys
Assistant prosecuting attorneys
Assistant state attorneys
Assistant U.S. attorneys
City attorneys
District attorneys
Prosecuting attorneys
States attorneys
U.S. attorneys

Salary Range
$45,675 to $65,000 to $127,604

Educational Requirements
Law degree

Certification or Licensing
Required by all states

Employment Outlook
More slowly than the average

High School Subjects
English (writing/literature)
Government
Law
Speech

Personal Interests
Current events
Law
Writing

"I am told that I voiced my desire to be an attorney at a young age," says Terry Parker, district attorney for Allegany County in New York. "A family friend was an attorney and I remember asking him what he did and, given my age, he explained to me that attorneys 'helped people.' I was drawn to prosecution because it was a field where you could do a great deal of good for people who truly needed it. It truly is the best job in the world."

WHAT DOES A PROSECUTOR DO?

Prosecutors conduct criminal and civil proceedings on behalf of the government. They have a variety of job titles based on what level of government they are employed by and their responsibilities. At the city level, prosecutors are often known as *assistant city attorneys* and *city attorneys*. Prosecutors who work at the county level are known as *assistant district attorneys, assistant prosecuting attorneys, prosecuting attorneys*, and *district attorneys*. At the state level, prosecutors are known as *assistant state attorneys* and *states attorneys*. Federal prosecutors are known as *assistant U.S. attorneys* or *U.S. attorneys*. Some prosecutors are elected (for example, district attorneys) and others (such as U.S. attorneys) are appointed by government officials.

A prosecutor's approach will differ according to each case. Once assigned to a case, prosecutors familiarize themselves with the details of the case. They put considerable time and thought into preparing a case against the defendant. They review all evidence regarding the alleged crime, conduct a formal investigation, and interview witnesses who were present at the time of the crime. Prosecutors may also interview police officers or criminalists for more details. They may confer with social workers, physicians, or others for background information on the defendant or the nature of the crime. Police officers or investigators may be asked to uncover additional evidence against the defendant.

To Be a Successful Prosecutor, You Should...

- have excellent communication skills
- be able to handle pressure
- have good leadership skills
- be able to think on your feet
- have integrity
- be highly ethical
- be determined
- have exceptional trial and legal skills
- have strong management skills

At the defendant's first court appearance, known as a first appearance, the prosecutor states the charges and recommends the bail amount. Set by the presiding judge, bail is a monetary amount the defendant must pay the court in order to be released from jail during the duration of the trial. Usually, the defendant pays a percentage of the set bail amount to a bond company, which then pays the full amount to the court in the event the defendant fails to appear for any future court appearances. Prosecutors may also recommend that some defendants be denied bail if they are considered a danger to the public or a flight risk.

The next step in states that do not use a grand jury to indict is the preliminary hearing, in which the prosecutor presents evidence that helps the judge determine if probable cause exists and if the defendant charged is the person who committed the crime.

After this, an arraignment is scheduled. The prosecutor meets with the defendant and his or her attorneys to discuss the charges. He or she presents all evidence and charges against the defendant. At this time, a plea bargain—the act of a defendant being charged for the lesser of multiple crimes in exchange for an admission of guilt—may be discussed. Most criminal prosecutions in the United States, about 90 percent, are resolved through some form of plea bargain.

Sometimes, defendants refuse to plead guilty, or the alleged crime is too serious to strike a plea bargain. In such cases prosecutors are challenged to prove "beyond a reasonable doubt" that the defendant is guilty of the crime. Prosecutors must often appear before a judge numerous times to defend the validity of the charge or challenge special requests from the defense (such as moving the case to another location)—even before the case is officially brought to trial.

Once at trial, prosecutors begin by making an opening statement that provides the judge or jury with an official account of the alleged crime. They present evidence, call witnesses or specialists to give testimony, and cross examine witnesses and challenge any evidence presented by the defense. If the defendant is convicted, the judge decides on the severity of the sentence, though prosecutors may make a recommendation.

Prosecutors have a considerable amount of authority, and they must take care to use this power wisely. Besides plea bargains, they have the authority to grant immunity to certain witnesses who may otherwise be reluctant to give testimony. They also decide when, where, and how to charge those accused of a crime.

The workplace for prosecutors can be as varied as the type of cases assigned. Their offices are comfortable and well lit, but prosecutors only spend a fraction of their time there. They often conduct research at law libraries, interview police officers and criminal investigators at police stations, meet with social workers and other specialists, and travel to the scene of an alleged crime. They also spend a great deal of time at courthouses meeting with the defense and the judge and participating in the actual trial. They also must manage office staff, prepare budgets and reports, attend community meetings, and sit on community boards. Long, stressful workdays and heavy caseloads are common for prosecutors.

WHAT IS IT LIKE TO BE A PROSECUTOR?

Terry Parker has been a prosecutor for 25 years. He joined the Allegany County District Attorney's Office in 1984 as an assistant district attorney, and after a few years he became the chief assistant. In 1997, Terry was elected to the office of district attorney. "As district attorney I wear many 'hats,'" he says. "I serve as an advocate, an investigator, a legal scholar, adviser to police agencies, chief law enforcement officer of the county, coordinator of criminal justice agencies, and administrator. Add to that a trial prosecutor, since I still regularly try felony cases.

"From a practical standpoint, I work long days in an office and in courtrooms, receive telephone calls from police agencies at all hours of the day and night, and go to the scene of any major crimes. I convene and manage a grand jury that investigates crimes and any allegations of corruption. I speak to community groups about topics connected to the law and the criminal justice system, and sit on the boards of various community organizations connected to advancing the public good, protecting children and vulnerable people, and fighting the spread of criminal behavior. With a lot of help from my assistants, our office handles approximately 3,000 cases per year (in 2008)."

Nola Tedesco Foulston is the district attorney of the 18th Judicial District of Kansas. "I believe in public service," she says. "I believe in prosecution and that this aspect of the criminal justice system is an important function. The prosecution is one of the gatekeepers for assuring the constitutional rights of all, including both victims and defendants. Our office has been called the 'gold standard' in prosecution in this state. We are the largest prosecution office, with 55 attorneys and a complementary staff. Wichita and its environs have a population base of approximately 500,000."

Nola says that her interest in public law began at an early age. "After college (where I had double majored in English and communications), I went on to study at Kansas University for my master's degree in fine arts. I then worked as an investigator with the State Civil Rights Commission in 1973—not long after the civil rights laws had passed and were being implemented. This bolstered my desire to attend law school, and I was accepted and started at Washburn University School of Law in Kansas in 1974. Our class had about 10 women in a total class of more than 200. Graduating in 1976, I accepted my first job as an assistant district attorney (DA) in Wichita. I was thrilled to be in public service and to work as a prosecutor. I spent four years as an assistant DA, prosecuting sex offenses. I then left this office to join the private bar in 1981 and in 1988, a number of colleagues, including many law enforcement officers and community leaders, encouraged me to run for the position of district attorney. A woman had never held this position. I was successful because of my prior diverse experience in criminal and civil law and because I was a trial attorney with credible credentials. I have held this office since 1988 (five four-year terms)."

Asked to detail what she likes most about her career, Nola responds: "I have the opportunity to make policy and enact procedures that fairly administer this office within the confines of the justice system. I continue to enjoy the ability to work in the public sector and to work toward the protection of our community by our contributions. I am able to still engage in trial practice as well as strengthen the administration of this office and its work with law enforcement and the courts. I enjoy continuing my legal education by studying new laws and cases and ensuring their proper application in this jurisdiction."

Gerald Mollen has been district attorney for Broome County, New York, since 1987, and has been a prosecutor since 1980. He was elected to his sixth four-year term in 2007. "I wanted to become a prosecutor since before law school," he says. "The job seemed to offer everything I desired from a career: challenging intellectual work; the opportunity to do good for people—whether it be victims, the community, or persons accused of crime; the opportunity to provide a decent, if not wealthy, lifestyle for my family; and the opportunity to match what I viewed to be my strengths (good communication skills, an ability to get along with people, and integrity) to the daily duties of the job.

"Being a prosecutor has allowed me to work with other lawyers and professionals from many walks of life to do good work prosecuting wrongdoers and protecting victims of crime, while at the same time improving community response in such areas as family violence, sexual assault, elder abuse, drug trafficking, gang violence, and violent crime."

When asked to name what he likes least about his job, Gerald cites his duties as an administrator. "This involves preparing budgets and reports and supervising a wide range of different personalities," he explains. "Not every person employed in an office of any size shares the same values and dedication that the best possess."

DO I HAVE WHAT IT TAKES TO BE A PROSECUTOR?

Besides having a keen knowledge of the law, prosecutors must have other skills. They must be good communicators—in court while presenting their case to the judge and jury, and out of court while interviewing witnesses and conducting interrogations and interacting with coworkers. Attention to detail is also important, especially because criminal cases may be won or lost due to the smallest factual detail. Prosecutors must also be able to work under the pressure of cases that at times may be physically and emotionally draining.

Nola Tedesco Foulston believes that the most important professional skills for district attorneys are "integrity, professional and personal ethics, exceptional trial and legal skills, and administrative

The Pros and Cons of Being a District Attorney

Terry Parker, district attorney for Allegany County, New York, tells what he likes most and least about his career:

What I like most is two-fold: The ability to know the whole story behind cases and make the decisions that will affect the course of an investigation and criminal case with the goal of "doing the right thing," and the ability to divert people who have a chance of redemption into treatment or situations other than prison if it is warranted.

As far as what I like the least, it is the "administrator" part of the job, and the paperwork, red tape, and wasted time spent in trying to make sure all the "t's" get crossed and "i's" dotted.

and executive skills, including personnel management, budget management, and office administration." She also believes that district attorneys should have "credible legal experience that includes practice in both the criminal and civil areas of practice."

In terms of personal qualities, Nola feels that a sense of balance in life is important since this career can be highly stressful. "Staying calm is an art to be appreciated and practiced daily," she says. "Frustration is often felt and must be channeled into appropriate action. Additionally, a district attorney must have the ability to deal personally and professionally with diverse members of the community and have a keen understanding of the laws that govern media contact, including pretrial publicity. Anyone who anticipates being in this role must govern their personal lives accordingly—they cannot live a double life. In brief, you must not have any skeletons in the closet. We have seen elected officials pilloried (as they should be) for their failures to pay taxes

Rewarding Experiences

The editors of *What Can I Do Now? Law* asked district attorneys Gerald Mollen and Terry Parker to detail some of their most rewarding experiences in the field.

Gerald Mollen, district attorney for Broome County (NY):

I have had many rewarding experiences as a prosecutor. To choose one is difficult, but to illustrate the kind of powerful experience that a prosecutor can have, I will describe one. In July of 2001 police found a 14-year-old girl and her mother lying dead on a basement floor, holding hands and each shot multiple times in the back and head. The investigation soon focused on the girl's brother-in-law, who lived in Baltimore and had been scheduled to go on trial the week after the murders for allegedly sexually abusing the young girl. Police soon arrested the brother-in-law and a friend of his in Baltimore for committing these heinous murders. My chief assistant and I handled the subsequent prosecutions of the two men, resulting in two guilty verdicts after jury trials and sentences against each man of life without possibility of parole. We became very close to the surviving members of the victims' family and felt tremendous relief and satisfaction that we were able to at least bring to the family a sense that justice had been served—though one still always feels sadness at the end of such cases because the victims cannot be brought back.

Terry Parker, district attorney for Allegany County (NY):

I have some background in the sciences, so the advent of DNA as a tool in criminal cases is very interesting to me. I prosecuted a homicide case where at the scene we had the deceased, who had been dead for a couple days, and no one had seen or heard anything to give us a lead. The only evidence we had was a bloody kitchen knife wrapped in a towel left by the door (apparently dropped by the defendant). DNA testing led us to the suspect, and additional investigation let us put together a successful case to convict him of murder.

One of the most personally rewarding parts of my job involves past crime victims, and I have two illustrations. There was a crime victims' ceremony a few years ago in which several friends and family members of homicide victims came forward to thank me for my help during the most difficult time of their lives. They still keep in touch with me. But the top has to be a young victim in a sexual abuse trial I prosecuted, who, years later, still keeps in touch with me, invites me to her school events (which I attend if I can), and who tells me she wants to be a prosecutor when she grows up so she can help people like I helped her. You see, I believed in her when a lot of people did not and she has never forgotten that.

and engaging in reckless conduct (drug abuse, extramarital affairs, etc.) that could make them suspect and likely to engage in reckless conduct in their official position. Because the position of district attorney is one within the public trust, elected officials must be able to assure that their position will not be compromised."

Prosecutors should also be mindful of prosecutorial discretion—the knowledge and judgment of when and to what extent to pursue a criminal charge. Successful prosecutors know when to prosecute for the fullest extent for a crime, accept a plea bargain, or drop a case in the interest of the community they serve.

HOW DO I BECOME A PROSECUTOR?

Education

High School

If you plan to become a lawyer and then a prosecutor, take courses such as government, history, and social studies. Speech and English courses will also be especially useful. "Like a carpenter uses saws and rulers and a mechanic uses wrenches, a lawyer uses the English language," says Terry Parker. "Be proficient in the language so as to be able to explain, persuade, and convince juries and judges. The journalist and speechwriter William Safire once wrote that there is one word in the English language, and only one, which is perfect for any given situation. Secondly, be fully aware that entering this career is a long process, and that it will take several years to reach the goal of becoming a law-

yer and a prosecutor. Keep your eyes on that goal and it will happen!"

"For high school students considering prosecution as a career," says Gerald Mollen, "I would recommend, first, working to acquire the most important skills necessary for any lawyer—being able to read well and widely, and being able to communicate well both verbally and in writing. Secondly, I would recommend exposing yourself to as wide a range of experiences as possible. A prosecutor must deal openly and honestly with people of all races, ethnicities, socioeconomic classes, and occupations. Broad experience is perhaps the best background for an excellent prosecutor."

Postsecondary Training

A law degree and admission to the bar of the state where you wish to practice is required in order to work as a prosecutor. While in law school, any classes related to criminal law will be helpful to your career.

Most employers prefer candidates with at least two years of practice in criminal and civil law. Trial experience is a must. In addition to their work, many attorneys gain experience via pro bono work, volunteer opportunities, and community service.

Certification or Licensing

To work as a prosecutor, you must have a law degree and be admitted to the bar of the state where you plan to practice. To be admitted to the bar, you must graduate from an ABA-approved law school and pass a written examination.

Internships and Volunteerships

As an undergraduate student, try to participate in an internship at a courthouse, law firm, or other legal employer. Your career services office or prelaw (or other major) program may also require you to participate in an internship as part of its curricula. While in law school, it is a good idea to participate in a judicial clerkship. A clerkship with a judge who oversees criminal or civil proceeding will provide you with a behind-the-scenes look at the court system and the issues judges and lawyers deal with every day. Nola Tedesco Foulston encourages law students to participate in a clerkship so they "have an idea of the diverse areas of legal practice, including criminal law." The American Bar Association (ABA) provides information on clerkships at its Web site, http://www.abanet.org.

Volunteer positions at a courthouse, prosecutor's office, or law firm will also provide a helpful introduction to the field.

WHO WILL HIRE ME?

Prosecutors are government employees at the local, state, or federal level. Local and state prosecutor's offices seek experienced attorneys, but may consider new graduates with extensive clerkship or internship experience. The District of Columbia's Office of the Attorney General, for example, has positions available for those completing honors programs at D.C. law schools or clerkships at the local or federal level. The U.S. Department of Justice seeks experienced attorneys, especially those with extensive courtroom experience. Some positions also demand specialized experience or knowledge. For example, the U.S. Department of Justice's intellectual property division may require its attorneys to have expertise in computers or information technology. Visit http://www.usdoj.gov/oarm and http://www.usdoj.gov/usao for more information on employment with the U.S. Department of Justice.

Before employment, prospective hires must undergo drug testing and extensive background checks. "Individuals with a criminal history are generally not eligible for prosecution practice," says Nola Tedesco Foulston. "In our office, all applicants are subjected to background checks and drug screening. This demonstrates the importance of keeping on the straight and narrow, because what you do today will reflect on your entire life." Additionally, prosecutors often must be U.S. citizens.

WHERE CAN I GO FROM HERE?

Assistant prosecutors may advance by becoming supervising prosecutors. All prosecutors may seek to advance by earning higher pay, taking on more complex or demanding cases, or by achieving recognition from professional associations or the public. Some prosecutors go on to become judges, FBI agents, politicians, and law professors. Others pursue lucrative and rewarding careers as lawyers in the private sector.

WHAT ARE THE SALARY RANGES?

According to the *2008 Public Sector and Public Interest Attorney Salary Report* from the National Association for Law Placement, entry-level prosecutors at the local level earned median annual salaries of $45,675. Those employed for five years earned $60,000, while those with 11 to 15 years on the job made $77,500. The association reports the following median salaries for state prosecuting attorneys in 2008 by level of experience: entry-level, $50,000; five years, $62,780; and 11 to 15 years, $80,830.

The U.S. Attorney's Offices use an Administratively Determined pay schedule, which is based on the amount of experience an individual has and other qualifications. Information on this pay schedule is unavailable, but prosecuting attorneys at the federal level typically earn salaries that are equivalent to the GS-11 to GS-15 categories on the General Schedule scale (another pay scale that is used for government workers). In 2009 government employees at these levels earned base salaries that ranged from $49,544 to $127,604.

Prosecutors typically receive such benefits as vacation days, sick leave, health and life insurance, and a savings and pension program. Some prosecutors receive reimbursement for law school or continuing education.

WHAT IS THE JOB OUTLOOK?

The employment outlook for prosecutors is expected to remain stable during the next decade. Most positions open as a result of existing prosecutors leaving the field. Opportunities will be best at the local level, where there is more turnover. Prosecutors with experience overseeing large jurisdictions will have the best employment prospects.

Public Defenders

SUMMARY

Definition
Public defenders represent individuals who are unable to afford an attorney.

Alternative Job Titles
District defenders
Indigent lawyers

Salary Range
$47,435 to $60,000 to $75,000+

Educational Requirements
Law degree

Certification or Licensing
Required

Employment Outlook
About as fast as the average

High School Subjects
English (writing/literature)
Government
Law
Sociology
Speech

Personal Interests
Current events
Law
Writing

"Every day is exciting and exhausting at the same time," says Travis Stearns, a public defender and deputy director of the Washington Defender Association. "Most people expect that the most rewarding experience of your career is when you walk out of a trial having won your case. For me, the most rewarding experiences are when you know that you have helped your clients successfully navigate their cases. This can mean trial, but it can also mean helping them turn their lives around and stopping the cycle of returning to the courts. I want to see my clients leave the justice system ready to handle their lives, and I hope that they are able to stay out of it in the future. The greatest success is to help someone stay out of the system, and I am most rewarded when I know that I have helped someone do that."

WHAT DOES A PUBLIC DEFENDER DO?

Lawyers practicing public defense, sometimes referred to as indigent law, represent those unable to afford private counsel. Such lawyers are termed *public defenders* or *indigent lawyers*. Their clients include those charged with a variety of offenses, misdemeanors, or felony crimes. They may also represent the developmentally disabled, the mentally ill, and those appearing before family court, many of who are juveniles. They may also represent clients continuing on to appeals court.

Public defenders are assigned cases according to the jurisdiction of their workplace—local, state, or federal public defender offices. They often begin a new case with a one-on-one consultation with the client to determine the nature of the charge. Public defenders then conduct research on a case by interviewing the defendant and other witnesses, conducting background checks, consulting with the prosecuting attorneys, and preparing briefs. They often consult with the police department, social workers, and criminal investigators who may be able to provide additional information about the case. Public defenders usually work without the help of support staff, so they spend a great deal of time doing their own investigative work and filing legal documents.

To start, public defenders may advise their client to make a plea bargain, or choose to proceed to trial. If the case goes to trial before a judge or jury, public defenders prepare their client for the proceedings and ready them for any questioning or cross examination that may take place. They will also write their brief, notify and prepare key witnesses, and collect any pertinent information or documents. If their client is found guilty, public defenders may, depending on the state and severity of the crime, be retained to appeal the verdict.

Public defenders may also be employed as attorneys for nonprofit organizations. In such cases, they may provide other services such as community intervention, family counseling, education, and social service support.

A public defender's work environment varies from case to case. Misdemeanor cases usually begin with a lawyer–client consultation at the public defender's office. If the client is charged with a criminal case and is in police custody, the public defender may have to travel to the appropriate jail or detention center for consultation. Public defenders spend a great deal of time in the court system

To Be a Successful Public Defender, You Should...

- have a desire to help others, especially the underserved

- be very knowledgeable about the law

- be committed to pursuing justice for your clients

- have strong interpersonal skills

- be aggressive and confident when dealing with lawyers and judges

- be compassionate and patient when working with clients

- be highly organized

- be able to think on your feet

- be able to work under pressure

- have excellent communication skills

appearing before judges and juries on behalf of their clients.

Long hours may be required to conduct research and write briefs, consult with clients and prosecuting attorneys, or compile needed documents. There is often a high level of stress in this occupation, as public defenders try to juggle multiple cases during limited time frames and with limited resources.

WHAT IS IT LIKE TO BE A PUBLIC DEFENDER?

Travis Stearns has worked as an attorney for nearly 20 years, almost all of them as a public defender. "I work for the Washington Defender Association," he says, "which is an organization dedicated to training lawyers and advocating on behalf of their clients. Before working here, I was a public defender in New York City and Bellingham, Washington. I became a public defender because I believe in the right of all persons to be fairly represented when they are accused of a crime. I don't believe that money should ever be a barrier to effective representation."

Travis says that life as a public defender is very fast paced. "You are in court almost every day and try a lot of cases," he explains. "You manage a large caseload and get exposed to a lot of issues. Every day, the first thing that you do is review your calendar for your court appearances. You then meet with your clients and attend court hearings. You may need to go to the jail to meet with incarcerated clients, go out to crime scenes to conduct investigations, and meet with experts to discuss potential trial strategies. Of course, when you are in the middle of a trial, you don't do much other than try your case."

Karie Comstock is the district defender for District 26 of the Missouri Public Defender System. She has worked in the field for seven years. "When I went to law school, I was not sure what kind of law I wanted to practice," she recalls. "I didn't know any attorneys and had no legal experience. I actually thought I would be interested in contracts and estates and trusts law. Then I discovered during class how boring those fields actually were—too much like algebra or calculus. Who wants to go to work every day wondering about shifting and

---

Quote

"If you worry about whether the people you represent are innocent or guilty, this is not the right career for you. The question to be asked is whether the law, in prosecuting a person, has respected the individual's constitutional and legal rights. If we let law enforcement trample the rights of those believed to have committed a crime, then it is only a matter of time until anyone can be wrongly accused and persecuted in the name of 'justice.'"

—Karie Comstock, district defender, Missouri Public Defender System

springing executory interests and the rule against perpetuity? Then I got my first legal job between my first and second year of law school. My job was as a summer intern for the National Criminal Defense College at my law school (Walter F. George School of Law). I was able to meet, interact with, and learn from some of the best criminal defense attorneys in the country. These weren't stiff people who argued over the definition of the word *is* and tried to construe sentences to save a $10,000 contract. They were real attorneys who represented the socially obscure and the nationally infamous. They had a true passion for their job, and the most awesome war stories. I knew then that I wanted to be a criminal defense attorney."

DO I HAVE WHAT IT TAKES TO BE A PUBLIC DEFENDER?

The most important quality to have as a public defender is the desire to help others, especially the underserved. Public defenders should possess strong knowledge of the law and be committed to pursuing justice. They should also have strong interpersonal skills. They need to be aggressive and confident when dealing with lawyers and judges, but compassionate and patient when working with clients.

"You need to have empathy for your clients, a belief in the constitution, and an understanding that a state that does not defend the poor is one that fails for all of us," says Travis Stearns. "A society

> ### Related Jobs
>
> - human services workers
> - judges
> - patient advocates
> - social workers

is judged by how we treat the dispossessed. A strong public defender system affirms the belief that we will take care of indigent persons and make sure that they are fairly treated. We do not want a system where the rich walk away from their troubles and the rest go to jail. A strong public defender system ensures justice for all persons."

HOW DO I BECOME A PUBLIC DEFENDER?
Education

High School

A high school diploma, a college degree, and three years of law school are minimum requirements for a law degree. In high school take courses in government, history, social studies, economics, English, speech, psychology, and sociology to prepare for college.

"There is no straight path to public interest law," says Travis Stearns, "but you should take classes that concentrate on writing and analysis. I was active in the debate team and played sports, both of which taught me how to think and be part of a team, which are important qualities to have in legal advocacy."

Postsecondary Training

In order to become a public defender you must have a law degree and be admitted to the bar of the state in which you wish to practice. Currently, 200 law schools in the United States are approved by the American Bar Association. Most law schools require that applicants take the Law School Admission Test (LSAT), where prospective law students are tested on their critical thinking, writing, and reasoning abilities.

While in law school, take classes in criminal procedure and evidence, as well as any classes that provide experience in oral advocacy, trial advocacy, and moot court. While classroom work is important, valuable experience in these areas can also be gained through clinics, internships, and volunteer opportunities. A degree of juris doctor (J.D.) or bachelor of laws (LL.B.) is usually granted upon graduation from law school.

Certification or Licensing

Lawyers must be admitted to the bar of their state before they can practice. Bar applicants must have graduated from an approved law school and pass a written examination. In a few states, graduates of law schools within the state are excused from these written examinations. After lawyers have been admitted to the bar in one state, they can practice in another state without taking a written examination if the states have reciprocity agreements; however, they will be required

> ### Other Jobs in Law
>
> Here are a few additional career opportunities in the legal field that are not covered in detail in this book:
>
> - crash reconstruction consultant
> - criminologist
> - forensic psychologist
> - human resources manager (law firm)
> - information broker
> - law school career counselor
> - law school dean
> - legal search consultant
> - legal technology consultant
> - legislative assistant
> - marketing manager (law firm)
> - private investigator

to meet certain state standards of good character and legal experience and pay any applicable fees.

Internships and Volunteerships

The career services office at the college where you pursue your undergraduate and law degrees will be able to provide information on internships, which provide an excellent way to gain experience in the field and make valuable contacts. Many private public defense organizations offer internships. For example, the Legal Aid Society offers internships to undergraduate and law students, as well as volunteer opportunities.

"When you are in college, volunteer in the public defender's office as an investigator," advises Travis Stearns. "This will give you an opportunity to see how things work and whether it is the place for you."

"Contact your local public defender's office," advises Karie Comstock, "and ask if you can volunteer or help in their office. Contact a local criminal defense-centered practice. See if they need someone to help prepare cases for trial. Get your foot in the door so you can see and hear what really goes on in a criminal defense practice."

WHO WILL HIRE ME?

Public defenders work at the local, state, and federal level. As employees of the government of a county or state, they work out of a designated public defender's office, often handling 100 or more cases at a time. Those working at the federal level handle about 30 to 50 cases at a time. Though federal public defenders are responsible for fewer clients at a time, their cases are often more complex.

Public defenders can also find employment at nonprofit agencies, such as the Legal Aid Society. These holistic or community-based agencies offer legal repre-

---

The Law School Class of 2008: A Statistical Profile

- 43,587 students were awarded law degrees.

- Men made up 52.9 percent of graduates.

- 22 percent of graduates were minorities.

- 89.9 percent reported finding employment after graduation.

- Employment by sector: private practice, 56.2 percent; business, 13.4 percent; government, 10.6 percent; judicial clerk, 9.6 percent; public interest, 5.4 percent; academic, 2.3 percent; and unknown, 1.2 percent.

- Size of firm: solo, 2.8 percent; 2–10 employees, 31.3 percent; 11–25 employees, 9.1 percent; 26–50 employees, 5.7 percent; 51–100 employees, 5.5 percent; 101–250 employees, 8.2 percent; 251–500 employees, 8.8 percent; 501+ employees, 23.0 percent; and unknown size, 5.5 percent.

- Source of job lead: fall on-campus interviewing program, 22.6 percent; self-initiated/letter, 22.3 percent; referral, 15.4 percent; job posting, 14.0 percent; other, 7.7 percent; return to prior job, 6.5 percent; job fair/consortia, 2.7 percent; started own practice, 2.7 percent; commercial Internet site, 2.6 percent; temporary agency, 1.7 percent; and spring on-campus interviewing program, 1.6 percent.

Source: NALP—The Association For Legal Career Professionals

Public Defender Spotlight: Scott Thompson

Scott Thompson is the district defender for Area 51 of the Missouri Public Defender System. He discussed his career with the editors of *What Can I Do Now? Law*.

Q. Can you please tell us about yourself and your professional background? What made you want to enter this career?

A. I am a district defender for an office of the Missouri State Public Defender handling appeals and post-conviction cases for indigent persons convicted of crimes in state court. My route to becoming a criminal defense lawyer was a little out of the ordinary. My grandfather and uncle were lawyers, but I never thought of law as a career while growing up. However, my grandfather always impressed me with his thoughtfulness and the reasoned way he approached any problem.

   I went to college with the idea of becoming a veterinarian. Although I liked science, I also enjoyed history, philosophy, and art studies as well. When I graduated from college in 1988, I did not go to veterinary school, but instead went to work as a research assistant in the area of molecular biology for a local medical school. Because I enjoyed debating topics of the day in the laboratory, my coworkers suggested I should go to law school. Maybe they were trying to get rid of me, but I took them up on it. In law school, I really took an interest in criminal law because it seemed to be an area of law that people feel most passionate about. Because I like helping people and working with other people who want to stand up for the underdog, working for the public defender was a natural fit.

Q. What are the most important personal and professional qualities for public defenders?

A. The most important personal qualities an aspiring public defender should possess are the strong desire to help people and a persistent attitude. Working on behalf of a client accused or convicted of a crime can be hard work if you don't have a commitment to protecting your clients' rights as you would your own. Being a public defender does not make you many friends; judges, prosecutors, and sometimes your own client may get mad at you. Additionally, public defenders don't often make as much money as their colleagues in the private sector, even though public defenders have the same law license and training as any other lawyer. So you have to have a strong desire to help folks who may have no one else in their corner. You must be persistent in standing up for your clients' rights. Sometimes you may be pressured to just move cases along and take shortcuts. But you have to persist in treating your clients as the people they are, not as "cases." If the prosecutor and the judge don't like seeing you, you're probably doing a good job. We joke sometimes that the public defender's office attracts lawyers who have "a problem with authority."

   All lawyers should possess certain professional skills. Lawyers are principally problem solvers, so finding creative solutions to tough problems is an important skill. But problems are only half solved if an advocate cannot get his or her ideas across. Lawyers must be effective communicators, in written form and in person. Writing and speaking in a clear, understandable way are marks of a capable attorney. Public defenders also have to be able to absorb and integrate facts quickly because in one day they may be dealing with police, witnesses, experts, judges, prosecutors, and clients. Making sure a client understands the legal system even when there are language, cultural, and educational differences is a must. To that end, public defenders (and all lawyers) need to be attentive listeners.

Q. What has been one of your most rewarding experiences while working in this field?

A. One of the most rewarding experiences I had as a public defender was trying the case of a man accused of burglary. My client had been convicted and sent to prison for burglarizing a house. His conviction was overturned on appeal after two years, and I was assigned to retry his case in circuit court. He was granted the new trial because the original judge did not give the jury the option of considering if he was guilty of the lesser offense of trespassing in this abandoned house. I was nervous because my client was a crusty "jailhouse lawyer" and I did not want to jeopardize his chances now that he had a new trial. But the evidence and the witnesses fell into place and I told the jury in closing argument that although they could see a crime had been committed, they should only convict my client of trespassing, the thing he really did wrong. The jury did return a verdict for trespassing, and my client was released that afternoon. I saw my client that afternoon when I left the courthouse; he was sitting on the steps of the jail. He gruffly said, "Scott, you did okay." In a way it was a public defender outcome, not necessarily getting someone "off the hook," but making sure justice was done.

Q. What is the employment outlook for public defenders?

A. The employment outlook for public defenders varies by state. Some states, like Missouri, have a statewide system where there may be frequent openings. Other areas of the country have different systems organized by county. Still other courts appoint private attorneys or have more or less designated defenders paid for by the court. As far as public defender systems organized in cities, counties, or states are concerned, job openings and compensation may be affected by budgets; in tight budgets, fewer public defenders may have to do more work. To be honest, public defenders often make less than their colleagues in private law firms, but there are advantages to public service that bridge the money gap. Public defenders can often qualify for student loan forgiveness. Public defenders get to spend their time practicing law and not drumming up business. Finally, most new lawyers in the private sector have to spend years working as an associate before they see the inside of a courtroom; public defenders get to try cases very soon after law school.

The Pros and Cons of Being a Public Defender

The editors of *What Can I Do Now? Law* asked Karie Comstock, a public defender for the Missouri Public Defender System, to detail what she likes most and least about working in the field:

The best thing about the job is taking a case from initial interview through trial, and standing next to your client when the jury comes back with a "not guilty." I can ride that high for weeks. Other good things: Seeing someone you helped have their name in the paper for graduating from high school/college, instead of for committing a new offense. And helping those who cannot speak for themselves. The worst part is standing next to your client after a trial when the jury comes back with a "guilty" verdict. I just go home and cry. Then I start all over with the next person who needs my help, and try to assist them in getting the best possible outcome. Other bad things about the job: Clients who think public defenders aren't "real lawyers" and being called a "public pretender" due to our overload of cases, which often doesn't leave us with enough time to spend with each individual.

sentation and other services including social service and education.

The National Association of Criminal Defense Lawyers and the National Legal Aid and Defender Association offer job listings for public defenders at their Web sites. See the "Look to the Pros" chapter in Section 4 for contact information for these organizations.

WHERE CAN I GO FROM HERE?

Attorneys working as public defenders have an edge over those in other specialties in that they have the opportunity to gain litigation and courtroom experience almost from the start of their careers. Many use this experience in public defense as a background to pursue other options, including teaching, private practice, or government office. Others find the work both challenging and rewarding, and choose to devote their entire careers to public defense—enjoying the work atmosphere and camaraderie with their coworkers. They either continue to work as public defenders or seek promotion or election to the position of chief public defender. "A public defender's office is a great place to work," says Travis Stearns. "You have a lot of support from your colleagues. You get to defend the constitution and be in the courtroom every day. You also have a lot of work, so you have to be able to work under stress and learn how to think on your feet."

WHAT ARE THE SALARY RANGES?

If high income is a motivator, then this career may not be for you, as public defenders typically earn the lowest salaries compared to those practicing in other areas of the law. According to the *2008 Public Sector and Public Interest Attorney Salary Report* from the National Association for Law Placement, entry-level public defenders earned median annual salaries of $47,435. Those employed for five years earned $60,000, while those with 11 to 15 years on the job made $75,000.

Benefits for public defenders depend on the employer; however, they usually include such items as health insurance, retirement or 401(k) plans, and paid vacation days.

WHAT IS THE JOB OUTLOOK?

Public defenders will continue to be in steady demand over the next decade. Most opportunities will be available as a result of public defenders retiring or leaving the field for other reasons.

SECTION 3

Do It Yourself

So you're thinking about a career in law—good choice! Not only is law an exciting, rewarding, and highly respected field, it also holds many varied opportunities for employment. The typical path to a legal career is law school or at least some postsecondary training, but you don't have wait until high school graduation to get started. There are many law-related activities for people in your age group. Read on for some suggestions.

❏ START READING

Looking for detailed information about law? One great place to start is your high school or local library, where you can find a variety of books and periodicals about law specialties (such as environmental, maritime, and entertainment law), mock trial competitions, famous lawyers and judges (such as Clarence Darrow, Thurgood Marshall, and Sandra Day O'Connor), the history of law in countries throughout the world, landmark cases, the U.S. court system, and almost any other law-related topic you can think of. For a great list of books and periodicals about law, check out "Read a Book" in Section 4.

❏ JOIN AN ASSOCIATION

Although most law associations require members to be lawyers or in law school, there are a few associations that offer membership to high school students or people with a general interest in the field. For example, the National Legal Aid and Defender Association offers a membership option for private citizens who share its goals, while the National Association of Legal Assistants has a membership category for those "who endorse the legal assistant concept." The National Paralegal Association has a pre-student membership category for young people who are considering a career as a paralegal. Membership benefits include the chance to participate in association-sponsored competitions, seminars, and conferences; subscriptions to magazines; and mentoring and networking opportunities. Visit "Look to the Pros" in Section 4 for more information on associations that offer student membership.

❏ VISIT LEGAL ASSOCIATIONS ON THE INTERNET

Law association Web sites are great places to visit if you are interested in a career in law. For example, the American Bar Association's Web site (http://www.abanet.org) provides a wealth of information about law school education, career options, legal topics, internships, and other resources. This is just one example of a professional association for students who are interested in law. See "Look to the Pros" in Section 4, What Can I Do Right Now?, for a comprehensive list of law-related associations.

❏ WATCH MOVIES ABOUT THE LAW INDUSTRY

You can learn more about law by heading to your local video store or adding some DVDs to your Netflix queue! Hollywood has had a long-standing fascination with lawyers, creating some memorable movies about the legal industry and its movers and shakers. We give the thumbs up to the following flicks—oh, and don't forget the popcorn.

To Kill a Mockingbird (1962). Gregory Peck is Atticus Finch, a small town lawyer appointed to defend a black man accused of rape in 1930s Alabama. In the end, integrity and justice win over racial bias and injustice. Not only will this movie make you want to cry; it will make you want to become a lawyer.

Erin Brockovich (2000). Julia Roberts plays a feisty law clerk turned law investigator who helps uncover an industrial giant's poisonous waste cover-up that is affecting the health of nearby communities. Based on a true story, *Erin Brockovich* proves legal cases are won not only because of the work of attorneys, but also by the research and investigative work of other members of the legal team.

Legally Blonde (2001). Follow Elle (Reese Witherspoon) as she creatively gains admission to Harvard Law School, survives her first-year law classes, and interns with a top law firm tasked with providing the defense in a high-profile murder trial. Somewhere among the pink designer clothes, purse dogs, and many trips to the nail salon, Elle develops confidence, a competitive nature, and legal savvy.

Looking for more law movies? If so, try *Young Mr. Lincoln* (1939), *Twelve Angry Men* (1957), *Anatomy of a Murder* (1959), *Judgment at Nuremberg* (1961), *A Few Good Men* (1992), *Amistad* (1997), and *The Insider* (1999).

❏ TAKE HIGH SCHOOL CLASSES THAT FOCUS ON LAW

Tailor your academic schedule by taking classes that will help prepare you for a career in the legal profession. Good choices include English, law, political science, U.S. history, and any other classes that require extensive writing and critical thinking skills. Take speech or communication courses to help you develop your oral communication skills. You can also enroll in classes that will give you background in a particular field of law that you think you might want to specialize in. For example, taking physics and other science classes will help you prepare for a career as a patent lawyer. Taking biology and earth science will give you a good preparatory background if you decide to study environmental law.

You also can take U.S. Government & Politics, an Advanced Placement course (http://www.collegeboard.com/student/testing/ap/subjects.html). This college-level class covers the institutions of national government (Congress, the presidency, and the federal courts), the constitutional underpinnings of our government, political beliefs and behaviors, political parties and interest groups, public policy, and civil liberties and civil rights.

Consult with your school counselors when determining your next semester's academic schedule. Tell them about your career goals so they can help steer you in the right academic direction.

❏ PARTICIPATE IN A SPEECH OR DEBATE COMPETITION

Attorneys are known for their excellent rhetorical abilities. Hone your speaking skills by joining your school's speech club or debate team. Participating in a debate or speech competition will help you to develop your ability to think critically, perform research, write effectively, and communicate persuasively—important skills you will use every day in the legal profession. Some school clubs participate in regional and national competitions, where they compete against teams from high schools throughout the nation. Besides winning bragging rights, participants compete for awards and academic scholarships.

If your school does not have such clubs in place, then start them. Consult with your principal and student representative for help with guidelines, find a teacher willing to sponsor the groups, recruit new members by advertising in the school paper, and off you go.

❏ VISIT A LAW MUSEUM

Did you know there is a national law museum? Sponsored by the American Bar Association, the Museum of Law (http://www.abanet.org/museum) offers exhibits and programming that focus on the role of the law and the legal profession in the United States as well as throughout the world. A recent exhibit, *Famous Trials in American History: Cases that Shaped and Shocked the Nation*, included landmark cases that have helped improve or, in some cases, detracted from the way the public views the justice system. Featured cases in this exhibit include *U.S. v. Nixon* and the infamous O. J. Simpson murder trial.

At the ABA Museum of Law, you'll be able to view priceless law artifacts and documents such as those used by John Quincy Adams (a lawyer and the sixth president of the United States); news footage of the Lindbergh baby kidnapping trial; and courtroom sketches of infamous figures such as the Chicago mob kingpin Al Capone and the child killers Leopold and Loeb.

The Museum of Law is located at ABA headquarters in Chicago, Illinois. It is open to the public. The best part? Admission is free!

❏ RUN FOR STUDENT GOVERNMENT

If you want to become a lawyer one day, you should consider running for student office. Student body presidents have some of the same responsibilities as attorneys. For example, as president you may act as a liaison between your fellow students and faculty. You may bring "cases" of student discontent regarding dress code, school activities, and even the poor quality of the cafeteria food, to the attention of school officials. In order to make desired changes, you'll investigate all complaints, gather evidence to back your case, present your main points, argue to modify existing laws/rules, and make suggestions for compromise. By doing this, you will not only give your classmates a voice in the daily life of your school, you will also earn a wealth of experience.

❑ STAGE A MOCK TRIAL AT YOUR SCHOOL OR IN YOUR NEIGHBORHOOD

Is there a long-running argument in your neighborhood? For example, you can create a mock trial for Mike vs. Mark: the case of the damaged Wii. Take the initiative and get a feel for what a court trial is like by staging a trial to resolve this dispute. Your friends can serve as attorneys to prosecute and defend, jury members to render a verdict, and law investigators or clerks to gather the facts of the case. You will also need to find a mock judge and mock court reporter for the trial. Regardless of who wins, have fun with this exercise of due process.

❑ TOUR THE SUPREME COURT

If you were always curious about the happenings inside the highest court of our land, get in line for a tour of the Supreme Court in Washington, D.C. Before you enter the "temple of justice" you'll pass two famous statues—"Justice, the Guardian of Liberty" on the east pediment, and "Equal Justice Under the Law" on the west. You can attend public lectures, view portraits of all justices, and watch a film about the function of the Supreme Court. If you are lucky enough to visit while court is in session, you may be able to attend an oral argument. During oral arguments, attorneys for each side of the case make presentations to the court and field questions as posed by the justices. Make sure that you arrive early to snag a spot, as seating is limited and assigned on a first-come basis. For more information on visiting the U.S. Supreme Court, visit http://www.supremecourtus.gov/visiting/visiting.html.

If you can't travel to Washington, D.C., contact your local courthouse to see if it offers tours or other activities.

❑ ATTEND A SUMMER CAMP

If you are interested in law, public service, public policy, politics, or government, you should consider attending a summer camp specifically designed to fuel this passion. One example of such a program is the St. Albans School of Public Service. Held on the grounds of St. Albans School in Washington, D.C., this four-week summer program immerses students in the exploration of government, public service, and politics. Your activities include simulation exercises in courtroom proceedings, trying cases, and debating key public policy issues. You'll also have the chance to participate in conversations with members of Congress, visit with a sitting Supreme Court Justice, attend dinners with ambassadors, and rub shoulders with other legal professionals. You may be even invited to a Q&A session with a Pulitzer Prize-winning investigative reporter

Don't worry, there's also time for leisure. You'll have the opportunity to explore the best the Washington-area has to offer, including tours of national monuments and museums and trips to the U.S. Naval Academy and Mount Vernon (George Washington's residence). You can also take time out for dining and shopping.

High school seniors with strong academic backgrounds, interest in government or public policy, and a desire to interact with like-minded students should apply. The competition for the coveted 35 slots is fierce, but it's an experience of a lifetime. For more information, visit http://www.stalbansschool.org/home/content.asp?section=SPS.

The St. Albans School of Public Service is just one example of a summer program for students who are interested in law. See "Get Involved" in Section 4 for a comprehensive list of law-related summer programs.

❑ LAND A PART-TIME JOB AT A LAW FIRM

Most law firms hire law students to fill many of their part-time positions. As a result, it may be difficult to land a job in the legal profession due to your age and lack of experience. However, some firms believe in reaching out to the future generation of lawyers and other legal professionals, even if they are still in high school. For example, Porter & Hedges LLP, one of the 10 largest law firms in Houston, partners with Communities in School, a community-based organization dedicated to helping kids succeed in school and life. It offers part-time employment to area high school students. Positions range from receptionist to assistant file clerk. While they aren't exactly starring roles in a courtroom drama, these part-time jobs give students exposure to the legal profession while adding a few dollars toward their college savings account.

Another plus: Part-time jobs are a great networking tool.

❑ GET AN INTERNSHIP

One of the best ways to acquire valuable, hands-on experience in the law field is to work as an intern, either after school, on the weekends, or during the summer. It's important to note that most internships go to students in college or law school, but there are some opportunities available for high school students. When searching for an internship, start with the obvious places. Ask your school counselors or history or government teachers if they know of any law firms or other law organizations in your area that offer internships or might be interested in having another pair of eyes, ears, and hands to help with projects. Contact adults you, your parents, or teachers know who are lawyers, paralegals, or court reporters. As an intern, you won't be trying cases or using a stenograph machine in a courtroom to record testimony; instead, you will be answering phones, filing documents, and performing other basic office tasks.

Some internships are paid; others do not offer compensation. Most importantly, an internship will provide you with the opportunity to work with law professionals and observe the inner workings of law firms and other legal employers. An internship will also provide you with a chance to build your professional network, which will help you when you start looking for a full-time job.

❏ CONDUCT AN INFORMATION INTERVIEW OR JOB SHADOW A LEGAL PROFESSIONAL

What better way is there to learn about the legal biz than by talking to someone already in the field? Perhaps a family member or friend works as an attorney or paralegal. If not, you can contact a local law firm or courthouse to request an interview with a lawyer, judge, legal secretary, or other legal professional. Legal associations are also great sources of information and they are often more than willing to provide interview contacts.

Once your appointment is set, prepare a list of questions to ask, including: What are good classes to prepare for this career? Do you find your job rewarding? What is a typical day like? Where do you see yourself, career-wise, in 10 years? Would you recommend your career to others? Bring along a notebook to jot notes, or even a tape recorder, if the interviewee agrees. Note that depending on how busy the individual is or his or her job location, you may not be granted a face-to-face interview. In such cases, telephone interviews work just as well. Keep within your time frame; if your interviewee gives you 20 minutes, stick to it. And don't forget to send a thank-you note.

Job shadowing is another great way to investigate a profession. Job shadowing involves following and observing a worker (such as a paralegal or lawyer) on the job. If you don't have any contacts in the industry, ask your high school counselor for help. Counselors usually maintain a list of area employers that are open to job shadowing.

It's a good idea to conduct research before your appointment. Read up on the industry, or visit the firm's Web site to get background information on the type of law it practices and other details. Dress professionally to make a good impression: Wear a business suit, or a simple dress; definitely no jeans, shorts, or skimpy tank tops. You'll follow your guide through his or her workday. Perhaps you'll go to a law library to do some case research, to the courthouse to file legal papers, or sit in during a mid-day meeting or briefing. Take notes during the activities, and jot down any questions you may have. Through shadowing, you'll get a true feeling for the industry and its pace and activities. As with any interviews, don't forget to send a thank-you note to the individual for providing this learning experience. Perhaps he or she will remember you when it comes time to hire part-time summer help.

❏ VOLUNTEER WITH YOUR LOCAL CONGRESSMAN

Contact your local congressman and volunteer your time as a *page.* Pages serve members of Congress, running messages across Capitol Hill in Washington, D.C. The length of a page's service varies from one summer to one year. Students that are at least 16 years old are eligible to apply. Contact your state's senator or representative for an application. Similar opportunities are available in state legislatures.

If you can't find a position as a page, check the Web sites of your local or national senator or congressperson for volunteer opportunities. Opportunities are often plentiful during election cycles. Any duties assigned to you will be commensurate with your age and work experience—so get ready to hand out lawn campaign signs or stuff envelopes for an upcoming mailing. You have to start somewhere, right?

SECTION 4

What Can I Do Right Now?

Get Involved: A Directory of Camps, Programs, Competitions, and Other Opportunities

Now that you've read about some of the different careers available in the field of law, you may be anxious to experience this line of work for yourself to find out what it's really like. Or perhaps you already feel certain that this is the career path for you and want to get started right away. Whichever is the case, this section is for you. There are plenty of things you can do right now to learn about law careers while gaining valuable experience. Just as important, you'll get to meet new friends and see new places, too.

In the following pages you will find programs designed to pique your interest in law and start preparing you for a career. You already know that this field is complex, and that to work in it you need a solid education. Since the first step toward a law career will be gaining that education, we've found more than 50 programs/activities offered by 56 organizations that will start you on your way. Some are special introductory sessions, others are actual college courses—one of them may be right for you. Take time to read over the listings and see how each compares to your situation: how committed you are to a career in law, how much of your money and free time you're willing to devote to it, and how the program will help you after high school. These listings are divided into categories, with the type of program listed right after its name or the name of the sponsoring organization.

❏ THE CATEGORIES
Camps

When you see an activity that is classified as a camp, don't automatically start packing your tent and mosquito repellent. Where academic study is involved, the term "camp" often simply means a residential program that includes both educational and recreational activities. It's sometimes hard to differentiate between such camps and other study programs, but if the sponsoring organization calls it a camp, so do we! For an extended list of camps (such as those that focus on debate or leadership), visit http://www. kidscamps.com or http://find.acacamps. org/finding_a_camp.php.

College Courses/Summer Study

These terms are linked because most college courses offered to students your age must take place in the summer, when you are out of school. At the same time, many summer study programs are sponsored by colleges and universities that want to attract future students and provide them with a head start in higher education. Summer study of almost any type is a good idea because it keeps your mind and your study skills sharp over the long vacation. Summer study at a college offers a number of additional benefits, including giving you the tools to make a well-informed decision about your future academic career. Study options, including some impressive college and university programs, account for most of the listings in this section—primarily because higher education is so crucial to many law careers.

Competitions

Competitions are fairly self-explanatory, but you should know that there are only a few listed in this book because many legal-oriented competitions are offered at the local level (and are too numerous to list in this book). What this means, however, is that if you are interested in entering a competition, you shouldn't have much trouble finding one yourself. Your school counselor or government teacher can help you start searching in your area. In your own city or county, you should be able to find civic groups or government agencies that sponsor essay contests, mock trials, debate teams, and other competitions related to your interest in the law.

Conferences

Conferences for high school students are usually difficult to track down because most are for professionals in the field who gather to share new information and ideas with each other. Don't be discouraged, though. A number of professional organizations with student branches invite those student members to their conferences and plan special events for them. Some student branches even run their own conferences. This is an option worth pursuing because conferences focus on some of the most current information available and also provide you with the chance to meet professionals who can answer your questions and even offer advice.

Employment and Internship Opportunities

As you may already know from experience, employment opportunities for teenagers can be very limited. This is particularly true in law professions, where many positions require workers to have college degrees in addition to experience. There are a few jobs in the field for high school students, but you may just have to earn your money by working at a mall or restaurant and get your law experience in an unpaid position elsewhere. Bear in mind that, if you do a good enough job and the group you work for has the funding, this summer's volunteer position could be next summer's job.

Basically, an internship combines the responsibilities of a job (strict schedules, pressing duties, and usually written evaluations by your supervisor) with the uncertainties of a volunteer position (no wages [or only very seldom], no fringe benefits, no guarantee of future employment). That may not sound very enticing, but completing an internship is a great way to prove your maturity, your commitment to a career in law, and your knowledge and skills to colleges, potential employers, and yourself. Some internships here are just formalized volunteer positions; others offer unique responsibilities and opportunities. Choose the kind that works best for you.

Field Experience

This is something of a catchall category for activities that don't exactly fit the other descriptions. But anything called a field experience in this book is always a good opportunity to get out and explore the work of legal professionals.

Membership

When an organization is in this category, it simply means that you are welcome to pay your dues and become a card-carrying member. Formally joining any organization brings the benefits of meeting others who share your interests, finding opportunities to get involved, and keeping up with current events. Depending on how active you are, the contacts you make and the experiences you gain may help when the time comes to apply to colleges or look for a job.

In some organizations, you pay a special student rate and receive benefits similar to regular members. Many organizations, however, are now starting student branches with their own benefits and publications. As in any field, make sure you understand exactly what the benefits of membership are before you join.

Finally, don't let membership dues discourage you from making contact with these organizations. Some charge college students dues as low as $20 because they know that students are perpetually short of funds. When the annual dues are higher, think of the money as an investment in your future and then consider if it is too much to pay.

Seminars

Like conferences, seminars are often classes or informative gatherings for those already working in the field, and are generally sponsored by professional organizations. This means that there aren't all that many seminars for young people. But, like conferences, they are often open to affiliated student members. Check with various organizations to see what kind of seminars they offer and if there is some way you can attend.

Volunteer Programs

Volunteerism is now enjoying great popularity, particularly among young people. Whether you're volunteering to meet your school's community service requirements or simply to help others and support a worthy cause, you can use the experience to explore law careers. Working in a law office or for a legal association is just one type of volunteer activity that a young person like you might be able to do. Depending on your needs and interests, volunteering can be a long- or short-term commitment, perhaps part time during the school year or full time during the summer. This is an option that is flexible and broad enough for almost everyone. Although there are tens of thousands of volunteer opportunities at law firms and associations, none are listed in this section. Why? Because these opportunities are usually so localized that listing them here would only be helpful to a very small number of readers. The best way to find a volunteer opportunity in your town is to contact a local law firm or legal advocacy organization to see what opportunities are available.

❏ PROGRAM DESCRIPTIONS

Once you've started to look at the individual listings themselves, you'll find that they contain a lot of information. Naturally, there is a general description of each program, but wherever possible we also have included the following details.

Application Information

Each listing notes how far in advance you'll need to apply for the program or position, but the simple rule is to apply as far in advance as possible. This ensures that you won't miss out on a great opportunity simply because other people got there ahead of you. It also means that you will get a timely decision on your application, so if you are not accepted you'll still have some time to apply elsewhere. As for the things that make up your application—essays, recommendations, etc.—we've tried to tell you what's involved, but be sure to contact the program about specific requirements before you submit anything.

Background Information

This includes such information as the date the program or organization was established, the name of the organization that is sponsoring it financially, and the faculty and staff who will be there for you. This can help you—and your family—gauge the quality and reliability of the program.

Classes and Activities

Classes and activities change from year to year, depending on popularity, availability of instructors, and many other factors. Nevertheless, colleges and universities quite consistently offer the same or similar classes, even in their summer sessions. Courses like Introduction to Law and Mock Trial 101, for example, are simply indispensable. So you can look through the listings and see which programs offer foundational courses like these and which offer courses on more variable topics. As for activities, we note when you have access to recreational facilities on campus, and it's usually a given that special social and cultural activities will be arranged for most programs.

Contact Information

Wherever possible, we have given the title of the person whom you should contact instead of the name because people change jobs so frequently. If no title is given and you are telephoning an organization, simply tell the person who answers the phone the name of the program that interests you and he or she will forward your call. If you are writing, include the line "Attention: Summer Study Program" (or whatever is appropriate after "Attention") somewhere on the envelope. This will help to ensure that your letter goes to the person in charge of that program.

Credit

Where academic programs are concerned, we sometimes note that high school or college credit is available to those who have completed them. This means that the program can count toward your high school diploma or a future college degree just like a regular course. Obviously, this can be very useful, but it's important to note that rules about accepting such credit vary from school to school. Before you commit to a program offering high school credit, check with your guidance counselor to see if it is acceptable to your school. As for programs offering college credit, check with your chosen college (if you have one) to see if they will accept it.

Eligibility and Qualifications

The main eligibility requirement to be concerned about is age or grade in school. A term frequently used in relation to grade level is "rising," as in "rising senior"(someone who will be a senior when the next school year begins). This is especially important where summer programs are concerned. A number of university-based programs make admissions decisions partly in consideration of GPA, class rank, and standardized test scores. This is mentioned in the listings, but you must contact the program for specific numbers. If you are worried that your GPA or your ACT scores, for example, aren't good enough, don't let them stop you from applying to programs that consider such things in the admissions process. Often, a fine essay or even an example of your dedication and eagerness can compensate for statistical weaknesses.

Facilities

We tell you where you'll be living, studying, eating, and having fun during these programs, but there isn't enough room to go into all the details. Some of those details can be important: what is and isn't accessible for people with disabilities, whether the site of a summer program has air-conditioning, and how modern the laboratory and computers are. You can expect most program brochures and application materials to address these concerns, but if you still have questions about the facilities, just call the program's administration and ask.

Financial Details

While a few of the programs listed here are fully underwritten by collegiate and corporate sponsors, most of them rely on you for at least some of their funding. 2009 prices and fees are given here, but you should bear in mind that costs rise slightly almost every year. You and your parents must take costs into consideration when choosing a program. We always try to note where financial aid is available, but really, most programs will do their best to ensure that a shortage of funds does not prevent you from taking part.

Residential vs. Commuter Options

Simply put, some programs prefer that participating students live with other participants and staff members, others do not, and still others leave the decision entirely to the students themselves. As a rule, residential programs are suitable for young people who live out of town or even out of state, as well as for local residents. They generally provide a better overview of college life than programs in which you're only on campus for a few hours a day, and they're a way to test how well you cope with living away from home. Commuter programs may be viable only if you live near the program site or if you can stay with relatives who do. Bear in mind that for residential programs especially, the travel between your home and the location of the activity is almost always your responsibility and can significantly increase the cost of participation.

❏ FINALLY . . .

Ultimately, there are three important things to bear in mind concerning all of the programs listed in this volume. The first is that things change. Staff members come and go, funding is added or withdrawn, supply and demand determine which programs continue and which terminate. Dates, times, and costs vary widely because of a number of factors. Because of this, the information we give you, although as current and detailed as possible, is just not enough on which to base your final decision. If you are interested in a program, you must contact the organization concerned to get the latest and most complete information available, or visit its Web site. This has the added benefit of putting you in touch with someone who can answer your individual questions and problems.

Another important point to keep in mind when considering these programs is that the people who run them provided the information printed here. The editors of this book haven't attended the programs and don't endorse them; we simply give you the information with which to begin your own research. And after all, we can't pass judgment because you're the only one who can decide which programs are right for you.

The final thing to bear in mind is that the programs listed here are just the tip of the iceberg. No book can possibly cover all of the opportunities that are available to you—partly because they are so numerous and are constantly coming and going, and partly because some are waiting to be discovered. For instance, you may be very interested in taking a college course but don't see the college that interests you in the listings. Call their admissions office. Even if they don't have a special program for high school students, they might be able to make some kind of arrangements for you to visit or sit in on a class. Use the ideas behind these listings and take the initiative to turn them into opportunities.

❏ THE PROGRAMS
American Association of Legal Nurse Consultants
Membership
The association offers sustaining membership to anyone with an interest in its goals and activities. Members receive the *Journal of Legal Nurse Consulting* and an e-newsletter, as well as networking opportunities and other resources.

American Association of Legal Nurse Consultants
401 North Michigan Avenue
Chicago, IL 60611-4255

877-402-2562
info@aalnc.org
http://www.aalnc.org

The American Bar Association Museum of Law

Field Experience

Explore the role of law and the legal profession by visiting the American Bar Association (ABA) Museum of Law, which the ABA touts as the only one of its kind in the nation. A recent exhibit, *America's Lawyer-Presidents*, focused on the legal careers of our nation's presidents. The exhibit included more than 250 illustrations, photos, documents, and artifacts. Other exhibits have included *America's Advocate: The Story of the ABA* and *Famous Trials in American History: Cases that Shaped and Shocked the Nation*. The museum is open Monday through Friday, and admission is free.

> **The American Bar Association Museum of Law**
> 321 North Clark Street
> Chicago, IL 60654-4714
> 312-988-6222
> http://www.abanet.org/museum

American Collegiate Adventures at American University

College Courses/Summer Study

American Collegiate Adventures (ACA) offers high school students the chance to experience and prepare for college during their summer vacation. Adventures, which last four weeks, are based at American University in Washington, D.C. Participants attend college-level courses (for enrichment or college credit) taught by university faculty during the week and visit other college campuses and recreation sites on weekends. Students live in comfortable en suite accommodations just down the hall from an ACA resident staff member. Enrichment courses vary but recently included Public Speaking/Debating, Introduction to Psychology, Criminal Justice & Forensics, and Washington Insiders: Behind the Scenes of U.S. Politics—perfect for those planning to pursue a degree in a law-related field. Courses for college credit included Criminal Justice & Forensics and Washington Insiders: Behind the Scenes of U.S. Politics. Tuition (which includes room and board) for the program is approximately $6,195. Contact American Collegiate Adventures for current course listings and application procedures.

> **American Collegiate Adventures**
> 1811 West North Avenue, Suite 201
> Chicago, IL 60622-1488
> 800-509-7867
> info@acasummer.com
> http://www.acasummer.com

American Collegiate Adventures at the University of Wisconsin

College Courses/Summer Study/Employment and Internship Opportunities

American Collegiate Adventures (ACA) offers high school students the chance to experience and prepare for college during their summer vacation. Adventures are based at the University of Wisconsin in Madison; they vary in length from two to six weeks. Participants attend college-level courses (for enrichment or college credit) taught by university faculty during the week and visit other regional colleges and recreation sites during weekends. All students live in comfortable en suite accommodations just down the hall from an ACA resident staff member. Enrichment courses vary but recently included Public Speaking/Debating, Introduction to Psychology, and Criminal Justice. Students in the six-week program can also participate in law- and government-related internships. Tuition (which includes room and board) for the two-week program is approximately $2,895; the three-week program, $4,395; the four-week program, $5,595; and the six-week program, $6,995. Contact American Collegiate Adventures for current course listings and application procedures.

American Collegiate Adventures

1811 West North Avenue, Suite 201
Chicago, IL 60622-1488
800-509-7867
info@acasummer.com
http://www.acasummer.com

American Collegiate Moot Court Association

Competitions

This organization's goal is to "build a system of top-quality undergraduate moot court competitions in America." It oversees regional and national moot court competitions, as well as a brief writing competition. Visit its Web site for more information.

American Collegiate Moot Court Association

http://falcon.fsc.edu/mootcourt

American Mock Trial Association

Competitions

The American Mock Trial Association is the governing body for intercollegiate mock trial competition. It sponsors regional- and national-level competitions for law school students, as well as mediation simulation tournaments. If you are about to start law school or are already attending, this is a great organization to contact about mock trial competitions at your school.

American Mock Trial Association

2700 Westown Parkway, Suite 220
West Des Moines, IA 50266-1411
515-283-0803
amta@dwx.com
http://www.collegemocktrial.org

Barrett Summer Scholars Program and Collegiate Scholars Program at Arizona State University

College Courses/Summer Study

Arizona State University offers two programs for students with an interest in law: the Barrett Summer Scholars Program and the Collegiate Scholars Program.

Students in the eighth or ninth grades can participate in the three-week Barrett Summer Scholars Program, in which students take a required humanities course and a Jury Trial elective course. In the elective course, participants learn about the law and the trial system via activities, lectures, speakers (such as former Supreme Court Justice Sandra Day O'Connor), participation in a mock trial in the school's high-tech courtroom, and field trips. Applicants must have a "test score in the 97th percentile or above on a state board approved test for the identification of gifted students in Arizona." Participants live in residence halls on campus and have access to recreational facilities. They are required to return home on weekends since there is no scheduled programming during this time. Cost for the program, which is typically held in June, is $1,500. The program fee covers tuition, a room in a residence hall, books for the course, three meals per day, and transportation and fees for field trips. Scholarships will be awarded based on financial need. The application deadline is typically in early March.

The Collegiate Scholars Program allows high school students to earn college credit during summer academic sessions. Students get the opportunity to explore careers and interact with college professors, as well as receive access to internships, mentoring programs, and research opportunities. Arizona high school seniors may apply, and they are evaluated for admission based on their "high school GPA and/or class rank, test scores, high school schedules, and involvement in other programs offering college credit." Some of the courses that will be of interest to students who would like to explore the field of law include Public Speaking, Introduction to Justice Studies, Introduction to Psychology, and The Justice System. Contact the Collegiate Scholars executive coordinator for information on program costs and other details.

Arizona State University
Barrett Summer Scholars Program
Mail Code 5420
522 North Central Avenue, Suite 247
Phoenix, AZ 85004-2165
602-496-4357
bss@asu.edu
http://promise.asu.edu/bss

Arizona State University
Collegiate Scholars Program
Attn: Executive Coordinator
480-965-2621
mark.duplissis@asu.edu
http://promise.asu.edu/csp

The Bill of Rights Institute's Constitutional Academy
College Courses/Summer Study

Rising high school juniors and seniors who are interested in learning more about American government, history, and personal liberty can participate in the Constitutional Academy, a six-week distance-learning program that culminates in a week-long residential program in Washington, D.C. Students who complete the program will earn three college credits from Ashland University. During the residential portion of the program, students explore the following topics: Principles of American Independence; A Constitutional Republic; Private Property and Citizenship, Self-Interest, and Leadership; The Judiciary, the Rule of Law, and Personal Liberty; and The Executive, The Rule of Law, and Security. They will also have the opportunity to study and work with historical documents in the National Archives, interact with teachers and scholars, visit historical sites (such as Mount

Vernon and Monticello), participate in a mock Supreme Court Case, sightsee in the Washington, D.C., area, and attend a semi-formal dinner and closing awards reception. Tuition for the academy is $1,495 (which includes six nights of lodging at Marymount University), meals, social activities, and transportation between the university and Ronald Reagan National Airport. Financial aid is available. Applicants must demonstrate leadership ability and have a GPA of at least 3.2 in all social studies classes. They also must submit a writing sample, a letter of recommendation, a completed application, and a $25 processing fee. The application deadline is typically in mid-April. Contact the institute for further details.

Bill of Rights Institute
Constitutional Academy
200 North Glebe Road, Suite 200
Arlington, VA 22203-3754
800-838-7870
http://www.constacademy.org

Challenge Program at St. Vincent College

College Courses/Summer Study

The Challenge Program is just what its name implies. Challenge gives gifted, creative, and talented students in grades nine through 12 the opportunity to explore new and stimulating subjects that most high schools just can't cover. If you qualify for this program and are highly motivated, you will spend one week in July on the campus of St. Vincent College taking courses such as Mock Trial and the Justice System and Debate With Me. Should you choose, you may live on campus, meeting and socializing with other students who share your ambitions and interests. Resident students pay about $600 for the week, while commuter students pay closer to $500. A limited amount of financial aid is available. For more information about Challenge and details of this year's course offerings, contact the program coordinator. A similar Challenge program is available for students in the sixth through ninth grades; it is usually held one week before the high school session.

Challenge Program at St. Vincent College
c/o Program Coordinator
300 Fraser Purchase Road
Latrobe, PA 15650-2690
724-532-6600
challenge@stvincent.edu
http://www.stvincent.edu/challenge_
   home

College Experience Program at Southern Methodist University (SMU)

College Courses/Summer Study

Gifted and highly motivated high school students who have completed the 10th or 11th grades can participate in SMU's College Experience Program. The five-week residential program allows students to experience college-level instruction and earn up to six college credits. Students take two courses (such as Congress and Legislative Process or Business Ethics) from SMU's summer school schedule. Applicants must submit an academic transcript, recommendations, an essay, and PSAT, SAT, or ACT scores. Tuition for the program is approximately $2,470. An additional $1,600 for room and board and a nonrefundable registration fee of $35 are also required. Contact SMU for more information.

Southern Methodist University

Summer Programs
PO Box 750383
Dallas, TX 75275-0383
214-768-0123
gifted@smu.edu
http://www.smu.edu/continuing_
   education/youth

Cooperative Education Program at the U.S. Department of State

Employment and Internship Opportunities

The Cooperative Education (Co-Op) Program, also known as the Student Career Experience Program, integrates and coordinates academic studies with on-the-job experience. To participate in this program, you must be a U.S. citizen, at least 16 years of age, enrolled in your school's cooperative education program, in good academic standing, and pass a background check. Co-op opportunities are available to high school through graduate students; most positions are in Washington, D.C., but some past participants have been placed in other cities. This program offers great employment flexibility, with full- and part-time work options available. Contact your school's co-op coordinator (probably your guidance counselor) or the U.S. Department of State's Co-Op Program coordinator for more information; you can also sign up at the department's Web site to receive email updates regarding the program.

U.S. Department of State

Attn: Co-Op Program Coordinator
Office of Recruitment
2401 E Street, NW, Suite 518H
Washington, DC 20522-0001
http://www.careers.state.gov/
   students/programs.html

Diversity Committee of the Memphis Bar Association High School Summer Law Intern Program

Employment and Internship Opportunities

The High School Summer Law Intern Program introduces rising high school juniors and seniors from minority backgrounds to the practice of law and encourages them to enter the field. Interns work at least 15 hours per week for a month-long period performing clerical work and shadowing attorneys as they go to court and participate in business negotiations. Students who complete the program receive a $500 stipend. Students also "participate in group activities, such as meeting the judges and learning about undergraduate and graduate admissions." The application deadline is typically in March. Contact the Diversity Committee for more information.

Memphis Bar Association

Diversity Committee
High School Summer Law Intern
   Program
80 Monroe Avenue, Suite 220
Memphis, TN 38103-2441
901-527-3573
http://www.memphisbar.org/
   displaycommon.cfm?an=1&subartic
   lenbr=91

Early Experience Program at the University of Denver

College Courses/Summer Study

The University of Denver invites academically gifted high school students interested in law and other subjects to apply for its Early Experience Program, which involves participating in university-level classes during the school year and especially during the summer. This is a commuter-only program. Interested students must submit a completed application (with essay), official high school transcript, standardized test results (PACT/ACT/PSAT/SAT), a letter of recommendation from a counselor or teacher, and have a minimum GPA of 3.0. Tuition is approximately $1,850 per four-credit class. Contact the Early Experience Program coordinator for more information.

University of Denver
Center for Innovative and Talented
  Youth Early Experience Program
Attn: Coordinator
1981 South University Boulevard
Denver, CO 80208-0001
303-871-3408
city@du.edu
http://www.du.edu/city/programs/
  year-round-programs/early-
  experience-program

Exploration Summer Programs

College Courses/Summer Study

Exploration Summer Programs (ESP) has been offering academic summer enrichment programs to students for more than three decades. Rising high school sophomores, juniors, and seniors can participate

in ESP's Senior Program at Yale University. Two three-week residential and day sessions are available, and they are typically held in June, July, and August. Participants can choose from more than 80 courses in law (such as May It Please the Court-Mock Trial, Make Your Point-Debate, and Liberty and Justice for All?—Law, Controversy, + The Constitution) and other areas of study. All courses and seminars are ungraded and not-for-credit. In addition to academics, students participate in extracurricular activities such as tours, sports, concerts, weekend recreational trips, college trips, and discussions of current events and other issues. Basic tuition for the Residential Senior Program is approximately $4,555 for one session and $8,390 for two sessions. Day session tuition ranges from approximately $2,100 for one session to $3,820 for two sessions. A limited number of need-based partial and full scholarships are available. Programs are also available for students in grades four through nine. Contact ESP for more information.

Exploration Summer Programs
932 Washington Street
PO Box 368
Norwood, MA 02062-3412
781-762-7400
http://www.explo.org

Explore-A-College at Earlham College

College Courses/Summer Study

Rising freshmen, sophomores, and juniors can participate in Explore-A-College, a two-week college experience program that offers 10 classes. Students take one class for college credit and learn how to develop their time management, research, and discussion skills. Students interested in law can take Philosophy & Law: Retrying Socrates, which re-examines the famous trial of the ancient Greek philosopher Socrates. They reassess the verdict by reading Plato's *Euthyphro*, *Apology*, and *Crito*; discussing the trial of Sir Thomas More as depicted in *A Man for All Seasons*; and reviewing contemporary cases involving religious beliefs. Classes are typically held in late June. The application deadline is June 1. Students stay in residence halls on campus. Tuition is $1,600 (which includes room and board). Very limited financial aid is available. Contact the program director for more information.

Earlham College
Explore-A-College
Attn: Program Director
801 National Road West
Richmond, IN 47374-4095
800-327-5426
http://www.earlham.edu/~eac

High School Summer Scholars Program at Washington University in St. Louis

College Courses/Summer Study

Rising sophomores and juniors can earn up to seven units of college credit by participating in the High School Summer Scholars Program. Two five-week sessions are available. More than 60 college courses, including American Politics (which covers the U.S. political and legal systems), are available. Students spend 16-20 hours each week in class; during the rest of the time, they do homework, participate in planned social activities, and explore the campus and the St. Louis area. Applicants must have a B+ average and have a combined SAT score of at least 1800, a combined PSAT score of 180, or an ACT or PLAN composite score of at least 25. Tuition for the program is about $5,935, which includes the classes, housing in a campus residence hall, three meals per day, and access to student health services. Financial aid is available. The average award is $2,300, and 80 percent of students receive financial aid. Contact the program director for more information, including details on application deadlines.

Washington University in St. Louis
High School Summer Scholars Program
Attn: Program Director
One Brookings Drive
Campus Box 1145, January Hall, Room 100
St. Louis, MO 63130-4862
866-209-0691
mhussung@artsci.wustl.edu
http://ucollege.wustl.edu/programs/highschool

Hispanic National Bar Association Future Latino Leaders Law Camp

Camps/College Courses/Summer Study

Latino high school students who are interested in learning more about legal careers can participate in the Future Latino Leaders Law Camp, a week-long residential camp held each July in Washington, D.C. Students attend classes on the legal profession; visit various government offices and buildings, where they meet Latino judges, lawyers, and other government officials; attend workshops on college and law school admissions; and participate in a leadership workshop and mock trial competition. Students stay in dorms on the campus of Georgetown University. Applicants must be rising sophomores, juniors, or seniors, or be recent graduates; considering a career in law; be U.S. citizens, legal permanent residents, or legal U.S. visitors with a valid visa and passport; and interested in community service and honing their leadership skills. They must also have a GPA of at least 2.3, although students with a GPA that is lower than 2.3 should still apply and include a short explanation of why their grades were low (family illness, etc.). Applicants must submit an essay, letters of recommendation, and a completed application. There is no fee for the program, except a $50 registration fee (waivers of this fee can be requested). Contact the executive director of the program for more information.

Hispanic National Bar Association

c/o Future Latino Leaders
   Law Camp
Attn: Executive Director
1900 K Street, NW, Suite 100
Washington, DC 20006-1110
202-496-7206
ccarrasco@hnbf.org
http://www.hnbf.org/page.aspx?id=12
   5&AspxAutoDetectCookieSupport=1

Honors College Summer Scholars Program at Hofstra University
College Courses/Summer Study

Rising high school juniors and seniors can take part in the Honors College Summer Scholars Program at Hofstra University. The four-week program allows students to explore college life, learn about careers, and earn three transferable college credits. Students choose from one of three courses: Political Science, Forensic Science, and Drama. Students who are interested in law might want to take Political Science. A recent Political Science course focused on the first 100 days of the Obama Administration. (President Obama, like many U.S. presidents, has a law degree.)

Class sessions are held on Monday, Tuesday, Thursday, and Friday from 10 A.M. to noon. After a break for lunch, students might attend a lecture, take a field trip, or participate in a guided discussion. On Wednesdays, students explore career paths in their field of interest by taking field trips, where they meet Hofstra alumni who are employed as law professionals and politicians, among other professions. Classes are taught by Hofstra professors. Students also participate in cultural and recreational activities and attend seminars and workshops that educate them about the college admission process, financial aid, and career development. Program participants live in the Honors College residence hall, which has a "courtyard, double and single occupancy rooms, lounges, cable TV, Internet access, washer/dryers, and common area bathrooms." There are a variety of opportunities available for students on evenings and weekends, such as movies, karaoke, comedy skits, dessert socials, trips to New York City, sporting events, and other attractions. The cost of the program is $5,800 (which includes tuition, excursions, residence hall accommodations, and meals Monday through Friday). Additionally, Hofstra advises students to bring approximately $500 to "cover incidental expenses and meals on their own during weekends and excursions." Books and course supplies cost about $170. Financial aid is not available. The application deadline is typically April 15.

Hofstra University
Summer Scholars Admission Office
100 Hofstra University
Hempstead, NY 11549-1000
516-463-6600
http://www.hofstra.edu/Academics/
 Colleges/HUHC/summerscholars

Insight at the University of Chicago
College Courses/Summer Study

Rising sophomores, juniors, and seniors who are interested in learning more about the legal system can take American Law and Litigation, a three-week course for college credit that is offered in at least one of two summer sessions. Participants study the process by which laws are made, investigate landmark cases, and learn how the law is interpreted and reinterpreted. They also learn courtroom skills and "will be expected to perform a direct examination, a cross-examination, and either an opening statement or closing argument" during the course's culminating mock

trial. A field trip to the federal court in Chicago is also scheduled. Residential tuition for the program is approximately $4,265 (which includes a residential program fee). The cost for nonresidential participants is $2,670. Both residential and nonresidential participants must pay an additional student health service fee of $185.

University of Chicago
Summer Session Office
1427 East 60th Street, 2nd Floor
Chicago, IL 60637-2902
773-834-3792
summerhs@uchicago.edu
https://summer.uchicago.edu

Intern Exchange International
Employment and Internship Opportunities

High school students ages 16 to 18 (including graduating seniors) who are interested in gaining real-life experience in law can participate in a month-long summer internship in the United Kingdom. Participants work as interns with barristers and solicitors, known as judges and lawyers, respectively, in the United States. The cost of the program is approximately $7,335 plus airfare; this fee includes tuition, housing (students live in residence halls at the University of London), breakfast and dinner daily, housekeeping service, linens and towels, special dinner events, weekend trips and excursions, group activities including scheduled theatre outings, and a Tube Pass. Contact Intern Exchange International for more information.

Intern Exchange International
2606 Bridgewood Circle
Boca Raton, FL 33434-4118
561-477-2434
info@internexchange.com
http://www.internexchange.com

Internship Connection
Employment and Internship Opportunities

Internship Connection provides summer or "gap year" internships to high school and college students in Boston, New York City, and Washington, D.C. For students interested in law, internships are available in law offices and other settings. As part of the program, participants learn how to create a resume, participate in a job interview, and develop communication and personal skills that are key to success in the professional world. They also get the chance to make valuable contacts during their internships that may help them land a job once they complete college. The program fee for interns is $2,500 in each city. Contact Internship Connection for more information.

Internship Connection
17 Countryside Road
Newton, MA 02459-2915
617-796-9283
carole@internshipconnection.com
http://www.internshipconnection.
  com

Just the Beginning Foundation
Camps/Field Experience

The Just the Beginning Foundation (JTBF) offers programs that introduce middle school and high school students—especially those from diverse backgrounds—to legal concepts and careers in the field.

Middle school students can attend the foundation's week-long Middle School Law Camp, where they participate in exercises that will help them develop "basic legal reasoning, case analysis, negotiations, and oral advocacy skills." Participants also "visit a local federal court to observe proceedings, participate in a scripted mock trial, and meet with judges and other legal professionals." The camp has been held in several different locations around the United States; contact the foundation for details on camp location, costs, and other information. Additionally, the foundation offers educational programs and e-mentoring with older students and/or legal professionals during the year.

The following programs are available for high school students: Mentoring Program, College Admissions Workshop, Extern Program, School Year Programming, and the Summer Legal Institute. In the Mentoring Program, young people receive support and mentoring from past JTBF scholars. The College Admissions Workshop provides participants with advice on a variety of admission-related topics. In the Extern Program, students are placed with federal judges. They "work two to three hours a day, three days a week with the participating judges and learn filing systems, write basic inner office memos, and learn about the inner workings of a courtroom—all through the lens of working in the judges' chambers." They also participate in a mock trial competition.

Students who participate in the six-week School Year Programming get help preparing for the ACT from law students and legal professionals. They also learn more about law careers by participating in "writing workshops, negotiation simulations, and field trips to law firms and organizations like the Equal Employment Opportunity Commission."

The Summer Legal Institute is the foundation's most popular program. Rising high school sophomores, juniors, and seniors learn about law and related professions by participating in a five- to 10-day program, which "consists of classroom lectures on substantive information, logic and critical thinking exercises, writing and oral advocacy in mock trial environments, panel discussions of judges and attorneys, and field trips to area law firms, government offices, and courthouses." Participants also get tips on preparing for college, obtaining financial aid, and achieving success in college. Institutes are held in Chicago, Illinois; Jackson, Mississippi; Minneapolis/St. Paul. Minnesota; Seattle, Washington; and Washington, D.C. Programs may be offered in other cities in the future. (An Advanced Summer Legal Institute is available to students who have already participated in the basic institute and want to explore law careers in more detail.) Contact the program director for more information about the foundation's programs.

Just the Beginning Foundation
Attn: Program Director
233 South Wacker Drive, Suite 6600
Chicago, IL 60606-6360
312-258-4868

http://www.jtbf.org/index.php?submenu=HighSchoolPrograms&src=gendocs&ref=HighSchoolPrograms&category=Programs

Law Camp at Lipscomb University
Camps/College Courses/Summer Study

High school students can participate in Lipscomb University's one-week residential Law Camp. "Campers" get the opportunity to participate in a mock trial; network with lawyers, lobbyists, corporate executives, and elected officials; explore health care, sports and entertainment law, social justice issues, the legislative process, and the court system; and attend recreational and social activities. Students stay in residence halls on campus. Tuition for the camp is $400 (which includes room, board, and course materials). The registration deadline is typically in early June. Contact the Institute for Law, Justice & Society for more information.

Lipscomb University
Institute for Law, Justice & Society
One University Park Drive
Nashville, TN 37204-3951
800-333-4358, ext. 2500
beth.morrow@lipscomb.edu
http://ljs.lipscomb.edu/page.asp?SID=185&Page=5429

Learning for Life Exploring Program
Field Experience

The Exploring Program is a career exploration program that allows young people to work closely with community organizations to learn life skills and explore careers. Opportunities are available in law/government and other fields. Each program has five areas of emphasis: Career Opportunities, Citizenship, Leadership Experience, Life Skills, and Character Education. As a participant in the law/government program, you will work closely with legal professionals and participate in a mock trial competition.

To be eligible to participate in this program, you must have completed the eighth grade and be 14 years old *or* younger than 21.

To find a Learning for Life office in your area (there are more than 300 throughout the United States), contact the Learning for Life Exploring Program.

Learning for Life Exploring Program

1325 West Walnut Hill Lane
PO Box 152079
Irving, TX 75015-2079
972-580-2433
http://www.learningforlife.org/
  exploring/lawandgovt

Legal Eagle Law Camp for Middle and High School Students at North Carolina Central University

Camps

Rising seventh through 12th graders are eligible to attend the Legal Eagle Law Camp, which provides an introduction to the field of law. Students participate in a mock trial, visit a courthouse, learn about legal research at the university's law library, and receive advice on preparing for and excelling in law school. They also work closely with law professors and stu-

dents and attend presentations by local judges and attorneys. The five-day camp runs from 9:00 A.M. to 4:00 P.M. daily. It is typically held in June. The cost of the program is $110 (lunch is not provided); scholarships are available.

North Carolina Central University

Legal Eagle Law Camp
PO Box 1967
Durham, NC 27702-1967
919-560-3816
http://web.nccu.edu/law/clinic/law_
  camp.html

Michigan Supreme Court Historical Society Learning Center Law Day and Exploring Careers in the Law

Field Experience

The Michigan Supreme Court Learning Center sponsors two activities for students who are interested in Law: Law Day and Exploring Careers in the Law.

Law Day is held each spring. Students learn about the law and careers in the field through field trips, presentations by law professionals, and other activities. There is no charge for the program. Organizations in approximately 20 states offer Law Day-related programs for elementary, middle, and high school students. Visit the American Bar Association's Web site (http://www.abanet.org) for more information on activities in your state.

Exploring Careers in the Law is a week-long learning opportunity that is offered each summer to rising seventh through 12th graders. Rising seventh through ninth graders learn about law careers by participating in a variety of tours and activities, including watching court proceedings and meeting lawyers, judges, and other legal professionals. Tenth through 12th graders serve as attorneys, justices, and other court workers in a mock trial. Legal professionals help them prepare for the trial. Both sessions are held in the Michigan Hall of Justice in Lansing, Mich. Tuition for this commuter program is $75. Applications are typically due in mid May.

Michigan Supreme Court Historical Society Learning Center Fund

925 West Ottawa Street
Lansing, MI 48915-1741
517-373-5027
http://courts.michigan.gov/plc/
　resources/programs.htm

Mock Trial Institute at the University of California—Los Angeles

College Courses/Summer Study

The University of California—Los Angeles (UCLA) offers a week-long Mock Trial Institute each June for high school students who are interested in learning more about our nation's legal system. The program, which is not for credit, offers residential and commuter options. Participants learn more about the law and courtroom procedures from the national champion UCLA Mock Trial Team coach and team members. They also attend seminars that teach them about careers in law; take field trips to the UCLA law school, a federal courthouse, and a crime lab; and attend sessions that teach them how to participate in mock trial competitions. Residential tuition (which includes two meals daily) for the institute is $1,235; the nonresidential fee is $825. Financial aid is available to California residents. Contact UCLA for more information.

University of California—Los Angeles

Summer Sessions and Special
　Programs
Mock Trial Institute
405 Hilgard Avenue
1332 Murphy Hall
Los Angeles, CA 90025-9000
310-825-4101
info@summer.ucla.edu
http://www.summer.ucla.edu/
　HighSchool/overview.htm

National Association of Criminal Defense Lawyers

Membership

This organization provides membership options for law students and "allied non-lawyers." Membership benefits include a subscription to *The Champion*, access to listervs, networking opportunities, and discounts on products.

National Association of Criminal Defense Lawyers

1660 L Street, NW, 12th Floor
Washington, DC 20036-5603
202-872-8600
assist@nacdl.org
http://www.nacdl.org

National Association of Legal Assistants

Membership

The association offers a membership category for those "who endorse the legal assistant concept." Members receive career information, access to networking opportunities, a subscription to *FACTS & FINDINGS,* and other resources.

National Association of Legal Assistants

1516 South Boston Avenue,
  Suite 200
Tulsa, OK 74119-4013
918-587-6828
nalanet@nala.org
http://www.nala.org

National Bar Association Crump Law Camp

Camps/College Courses/Summer Study

Rising high school freshmen, sophomores, and juniors can participate in the Crump Law Camp, a two-week residential camp that encourages young people of color to consider careers in the legal field. (The National Bar Association is the largest national association of African-American lawyers and judges.) The camp is typically held in July. Students stay in residence halls on the campus of Howard University in Washington, D.C. Applicants must be between 14 and 17 years old. They must submit a one-page statement detailing why they want to attend the camp, a letter of recommendation, a copy of their last report card, and a completed application. The amount of tuition a participant pays is based on his or her family income; tuition is free for students from families that have an income of $35,000 or less. Tuition includes housing, meals, class materials, field trips, and transportation to and from Washington,

D.C. A nonrefundable application fee of $30 is required. The application deadline is typically in mid-April. Contact the association for more information.

National Bar Association

Crump Law Camp
PO Box 11048
Washington, DC 20008-0248
301-249-8355
http://www.nationalbar.org/lawcamp

National High School Mock Trial Championship

Competitions

The first national mock trial championship was held in 1984. Each year, teams of high school students from more than 40 U.S. states, Guam, South Korea, the Commonwealth of Northern Marianna Islands, and other countries compete for the opportunity to be chosen as the best of the best. According to the program's Web site, "participation in a performance-based, hands-on program of this nature provides students with a practical knowledge about how our legal system operates and who the major players are in that system." For more information on this competition, visit the organization's Web site.

National High School Mock Trial Championship

http://www.nationalmocktrial.org

National Legal Aid and Defender Association (NLADA)

Membership

This organization offers membership for law students and private citizens who share its goals. Members receive a subscription to *Cornerstone* magazine and other resources.

National Legal Aid and Defender Association

1140 Connecticut Avenue, NW, Suite 900
Washington, DC 20036-4019
202-452-0620
info@nlada.org
http://www.nlada.org

National Paralegal Association

Membership

The association offers a pre-student membership category for young people who are considering a career as a paralegal.

National Paralegal Association

PO Box 406
Solebury, PA 18963-0406
215-297-8333
admin@nationalparalegal.org
http://www.nationalparalegal.org

National Student Leadership Conference

College Courses/Summer Study

The National Student Leadership Conference (NSLC) offers a 10-day Law & Advocacy Program for high-achieving high school students. College credit is awarded upon completion of the program, which is available in four sessions each summer. Participants experience life on a college campus, develop leadership skills, explore law careers, and meet judges and politicians (past speakers include Senators Hillary Clinton, Evan Bayh, Chuck Hagel, and U.S. Supreme Court Justices Anthony Kennedy, San-

dra Day O'Connor, and David Souter). A typical day includes classes/lectures, off-campus tours and briefings, guest speakers, leadership exercises/workshops, and social activities. Applicants are nominated by their school counselors and teachers or identified as prospective candidates from national talent identification surveys such as the College Board Student Search Service and the ACT EOS. Participants must have a B average. Tuition for the program is $2,395 (which covers course materials, on-campus meals, housing, and social activities). Financial aid is available. Students are responsible for transportation to and from the program. In 2009, the Law & Advocacy Program was held at American University in Washington, D.C., but the program location may change. Contact the NSLC for more information.

National Student Leadership Conference

414 North Orleans Street, Suite LL8
Chicago, IL 60654-1887
800-994-6752
info@nslcleaders.org
http://www.nslcleaders.org

National Verbatim Reporters Association

Membership

The association offers a membership option for individuals with an interest in the voice writing profession who are not verbatim reporters. Members receive discounts on association products and services, a personal home page, a subscription to *The Verbatim Record*, and other resources.

National Verbatim Reporters Association

207 Third Avenue
Hattiesburg, MS 39401-3868
601-582-4345
nvra@nvra.com
http://www.nvra.org

National Youth Leadership Forum on Law and Crime Scene Investigation

Field Experience

High-achieving high school and college students who are interested in law and criminal justice careers can participate in the National Youth Leadership Forum on Law and Crime Scene Investigation. Rising ninth through 11th graders are eligible for the forum. Summer and fall sessions are available. Participants work closely with "nationally-recognized legal professionals, analyze different types of evidence, and explore the process of forensic crime solving . . . and take an active role in a simulated trial and go behind the scenes at some of the most prominent law firms, universities, and legal sites in Washington, D.C., such as the U.S. Supreme Court." Each session is divided into the following main study areas: Welcome to the Field of Law, From Crime Scene to Trial, Becoming a Lawyer: Legal Education, and A Closer Look at the Legal System. Visit the forum's Web site to see a schedule of breakout sessions. Students must be nominated by academic advisors or organizations; they can also be admitted through an application process. All participants must "demonstrate strong academic abilities, leadership, and an interest in the career field being studied." Tuition for the session is $1,585 (which

includes accommodations, breakfasts and dinners, supervisory personnel, program materials, instruction, all forum activities, and private motor coach transportation during the program). Financial aid is available. Transportation to and from Washington, D.C., is not included. The forum recommends that participants also bring $8 to $10 per day for lunches and other incidentals. Contact the forum for more information.

National Youth Leadership Forum on Law and Crime Scene Investigation

Office of Admissions
1919 Gallows Road, Suite 700
Vienna, VA 22182-4007
703-584-9403
law_adm@nylf.org
http://www.nylf.com/law

Nursing Camp at Briar Cliff University

Camps

Rising high school juniors and seniors who are considering a career in nursing (including legal nurse consulting), can learn more about the field by attending Briar Cliff University's summer nursing camp. Attendees participate in clinical experiences, learn first aid and CPR, job shadow actual nurses, and work closely with Briar Cliff nursing faculty and graduates. Specialty areas of study include emergency room, hospital (medical-surgical), intensive care, labor and delivery, nursery, operating room, pediatrics, and public health. Students who successfully complete the camp earn one hour of college credit. Nursing Camp is held for four days in late June and/or early

July. Participants live in a residence hall. Tuition is approximately $250 and covers three nights of lodging, all meals from Monday lunch through Thursday lunch, and transportation to clinical experiences and recreational activities. Visit the program's Web site for more information.

Briar Cliff University

Nursing Camp
Chairperson, Department of Nursing
3303 Rebecca Street
Sioux City, IA 51104-2324
800-662-3303, ext. 1662
rick.petersen@briarcliff.edu
http://www.briarcliff.edu/
   departments/nursing/new_nursing/
   camp.aspx

Nursing Camp at Seattle Pacific University

Camps

Rising high school juniors and seniors who are considering a career in nursing can attend the Nursing Camp at Seattle Pacific University, a week-long camp where young people can explore nursing careers and make new friends in the process. Participants can watch nurses in action, become certified in CPR, learn to take a person's blood pressure and pulse, and talk with nursing faculty and recent graduates about the field. Specialty areas include pediatrics, public health, and operating room. Students live in residence halls while attending the camp, which is held in early August. Tuition is approximately $750, and includes lodging, all meals from Sunday dinner through Saturday lunch, and transportation to hospital clinicals and recreation activities. Some

financial aid is available. Visit the camp's Web site for more information.

Seattle Pacific University

Nursing Camp
School of Health Sciences
3307 Third Avenue West, Suite 106
Seattle, WA 98119-1922
206-281-2233
nursingcamp@spu.edu
http://www.spu.edu/depts/hsc/
   nursingcamp

Pre-College Courses at Brown University

College Courses/Summer Study

High school students in the Pre-College Courses Program at Brown can take one or more interesting college-level courses. Classes, which last anywhere from one to four weeks, are held Monday through Friday. More than 200 classes are available. Students spend three hours per day in class, and the rest of the time studying, interacting with professors and fellow students, and participating in cultural and social activities. Students with an interest in law will find a wealth of fascinating courses, including How the Legal System Works: Anatomy of a Case (three-week course), Do You Think You Want To Be A Lawyer? (one week), U.S. Congress (three weeks), Freedom and Responsibility (two weeks), and Swearing on the Bible: The U.S. Supreme Court and Religion (one week). There are also classes that help you develop your communication or study skills or better prepare for the college admissions process, including Cracking the AP Code (one week), Putting Ideas into Words (one week), Persuasive Communication (one week), Writing the Academic Essay (three weeks), and Writing the College Admissions Essay (one week). Program participants live in residence halls that are within walking distance of classes and other activities. Students who are interested in taking Pre-College Courses must have intellectual curiosity, be emotionally mature, and have a strong academic record. The following tuition rates are charged for Pre-College Courses: one week residential ($2,153), one week commuter ($1,652); two week residential ($3,265), two week commuter ($2,255); three week residential ($4,702), three week commuter ($3,200); four week residential ($5,454), four week commuter ($3,449). Housing and meals are included in the residential tuition. A limited amount of financial aid is available. Contact the Office of Summer & Continuing Studies for more information.

Brown University

Office of Summer & Continuing
  Studies
42 Charlesfield Street, Box T
Providence, RI 02912-9063
401-863-7900
http://brown.edu/scs/pre-college/
  pre-college-courses.php

Pre-College Programs at the University of California—Santa Barbara

College Courses/Summer Study

The University of California—Santa Barbara offers two six-week programs for high school students who are interested in law: Early Start and Academic & Enrichment. In the Early Start Program, students take two college-level courses to help them explore career options and prepare for college study. Students interested in law can take Intro to Law & Society or Social Legal Research Methods. Applicants must have completed the 10th, 11th, or 12th grades and have a GPA of at least 3.3 to be eligible for the program.

Students in the Academic & Enrichment Program take one for-credit course and one noncredit, skills-based enrichment course. Applicants must have completed the 10th, 11th, or 12th grades and have a GPA of at least 3.15 to be eligible for the program. A typical 1+1 pairing for students interested in law might consist of Crime Scene Investigation (noncredit) and Introduction to Law and Society (credit).

Students in both programs live in Santa Cruz Residence Hall, which is located near the Pacific Ocean. The rooms feature high-speed Internet access. Other amenities in the residence halls and on campus include a recreation center, a pool table, video games, a multi-station computer center, and laundry room. The cost for either program is approximately $6,770 (which includes tuition, housing, three daily meals, and extracurricular activities). A nonrefundable application fee of $95 is also required.

University of California—Santa Barbara

c/o Summer Discovery
1326 Old Northern Boulevard
Roslyn, NY 11576-2244
805-893-2377
http://www.summer.ucsb.edu/
  precollegeprograms.html
http://www.summerdiscovery.com

Precollege Program at New York University

College Courses/Summer Study

Rising high school juniors and seniors in the New York metropolitan area who are interested in law and other fields can participate in New York University's Precollege Program. During this commuter program, students take one or two courses for college credit (for up to eight credits) and get a feel for college life. (A noncredit writing workshop is also available.) One law-related class is Law and Society, which "explores law and legal institutions from a sociological perspective; examines how courts, lawyers, police, and prosecutors work within legal institutions . . . and provides an excellent introduction to the law as a social system and as a profession." Other applicable courses include Criminology, Introduction to Psychology and Its Applications, Philosophy of Law, Logic, and various foreign language courses. Tuition is approximately $4,665 for each four-credit course. Financial aid is available. The application deadline is typically in April. Contact the Precollege Program for more information.

New York University
Precollege Program
110 East 14th Street, Lower Level
New York, NY 10003-4170
212-998-2292
http://www.nyu.edu/summer

Residential Institutes at Wright State University (WSU)

College Courses/Summer Study

Rising sophomores, juniors, and seniors can participate in WSU's Residential Institutes, one-week residential programs that cover a variety of academic fields, including law. In the Law and Politics Program, students learn about the constitution, laws, the Supreme Court, legal and trial procedures, and "investigate political and legal issues that may affect their lives as well as the lives of others." Students stay on campus in rooms that have an air conditioner, refrigerator, and microwave, and eat meals in the university dining hall. Tuition for the program is about $550. The application deadline is typically two weeks before the beginning of the program. Contact the Office of Pre-College Programs for more information.

Wright State University
Office of Pre-College Programs
3640 Colonel Glenn Highway
Dayton, OH 45435-0001
937-775-3135
precollege@wright.edu
http://www.wright.edu/academics/
   precollege

School of Public Service at St. Albans School

College Courses/Summer Study

The School of Public Service at St. Albans is a four-week summer program for rising high school seniors from across the United States and Europe who are interested in learning more about government, politics, and public service. (St. Albans School educates boys in grades 4 through 12, but the School of Public Service is coeducational.) Students who are accepted into the program "use the case study method (the teaching method used in graduate programs in law, business, and public policy) to discuss and dissect public policy issues." Recent topics discussed include "the debate over climate change, the role of the media in modern political campaigns, and the experience of Army General David Petraeus in trying to construct a working government in the city of Mosul, Iraq." Students take part in simulations in which they get to play a member of Congress in their first-term or a lawyer or judge in a courtroom. They also take an economics mini-course and a course in public speaking, a key skill for success in law and government careers. Field trips to the U.S. Supreme Court, the offices of the *Washington Post*, the White House, and other law-related locales provide students with a chance to interact with professionals in the field. Students in the program, which usually starts in June, live on campus at St. Albans School on the grounds of the Washington National Cathedral; a commuter option is also available. Applicants must have a strong academic record; be interested in government, public policy, and public service; and have a desire to learn and interact with others who share their interests. Residential tuition is $4,800, and the program fee for day students is $4,000. Financial aid is available. The majority of students apply between January 1 and March 31; students who apply after March 31 must pay a $25 application fee. Contact the School of Public Service for more information.

St. Albans School
School of Public Service
Mount St. Alban
Washington, DC 20016-5005

202-537-5286
sps@cathedral.org
http://www.stalbansschool.org/
   home/content.asp?section=SPS

Secondary School Program at Harvard University
College Courses/Summer Study

High school students who have completed their sophomore, junior, or senior years may apply to Harvard's Secondary School Program. The program is held for six weeks each summer, and participants earn college credit. Students who live on campus take either two four-credit courses or one eight-credit course. Commuting students may take two concurrent four-credit courses or one eight-credit course. Recent law-related courses included Law and Psychology, International Law, and Congress: Policy, Parties, and Institutions. In addition to academics, students can participate in extracurricular activities such as intramural sports, a trivia bowl, a talent show, and dances. Tuition for the program ranges from $2,475 (per four-unit course) to $4,950 (per eight-unit course). A non-refundable registration fee ($50), health insurance ($165), and room and board ($4,250) are extra. Contact the program for more information.

In addition to the aforementioned on-site offerings, Harvard also offers selected online classes (such as Intellectual Property) to students who can't make it to campus.

Harvard University
Secondary School Program
51 Brattle Street

Cambridge, MA 02138-3722
617-495-3192
ssp@dcemail.harvard.edu
http://www.summer.harvard.
  edu/2009/programs/ssp

Stay-in-School Program at the U.S. Department of State
Employment and Internship Opportunities

The Stay-in-School Program, also known as the Student Temporary Employment Program, is designed for students who require financial assistance to continue their education. (Note: students with a disability do not need to demonstrate financial need to participate in this program.) In this program, you may work in technical, clerical, or administrative positions part time during the school year or full time during the holidays and summer vacation. To be eligible for this program, you must be a U.S. citizen, be at least 16 years of age, pass a background check, and be enrolled in a high school, vocational, or undergraduate program. Most positions are in Washington, D.C., but some past participants have been placed in other cities. Contact your guidance counselor or state employment service to learn more about the financial criteria. Contact the program coordinator for more information; you can also sign up at the department's Web site to receive email updates regarding the program.

U.S. Department of State
Attn: Stay-in-School Program
  Coordinator
Office of Recruitment

2401 E Street, NW, Suite 518H
Washington, DC 20522-0001
http://www.careers.state.gov/
  students/programs.html

Summer @ Georgetown University for High School Students
College Courses/Summer Study

Georgetown University offers a week-long Law & Society seminar that allows students to "explore the social, political, economic, and cultural realities and impact of the nation's legal system." This noncredit seminar is held in August, and is open to rising sophomores, juniors, and seniors. Students learn about the legal system through classes, lectures, field trips to courtrooms and other places, and conversations with legal and policy professionals, professors, and law students. Residential and commuter options are available. Students who live on campus stay in air-conditioned residence halls. Access to laundry facilities is provided. In their off hours, students can attend dances, movie nights, ice cream socials, and other activities, as well as explore the campus and the Washington, D.C., area. The cost of the seminar is $1,575 for commuter students. Students who stay on campus pay approximately $1,800, which includes room and a meal plan. A nonrefundable application fee of $50 is also required. Financial aid is available. Contact the university for more information. Other seminars that may be of interest to students include International Relations, American Politics & Public Affairs, and Leadership & Ethics.

Summer Programs for High School Students

Georgetown University
Box 571006
Washington, DC 20057-1006
202-687-8700
scsspecialprograms@georgetown.
  edu
http://scs.georgetown.edu/
  departments/21/summer-programs-
  for-high-school-students

Summer Challenge Program at Boston University

College Courses/Summer Study

Rising high school sophomores, juniors, and seniors in the University's Summer Challenge Program learn about college life and take college classes in a noncredit setting. The program is offered in three sessions. Students choose two seminars (which feature lectures, group and individual work, project-based assignments, and field trips) from a total of 15 available programs, including Law, Persuasive Writing, Business: From the Ground Up, Mass Communication, International Politics, and Creative Writing. Students in the Law program learn about the U.S. court system; how to read, interpret, and brief a court opinion; legal vocabulary and procedures; and a how to engage in a mock trial. Students live in dorms on campus and participate in extracurricular activities and tours of local attractions. The cost of the program is approximately $3,070 (which includes tuition, a room charge, meals, and sponsored activities). Visit the university's Summer Programs Web site for more information.

Boston University Summer Challenge Program

755 Commonwealth Avenue,
  Room 105
Boston, MA 02215-1401
617-353-0556
buhssumr@bu.edu
http://www.bu.edu/summer/
  high-school-programs/summer-
  challenge/seminars.shtml

Summer Clerical Program at the U.S. Department of State

Employment and Internship Opportunities

The Summer Clerical Program allows young people to work in office support positions in which they gain work experience and a better understanding of how the State Department works. Participants work during the summer and over the holidays. Typical duties might include the following: answering telephones and performing other receptionist-related duties; filing and maintaining office files; typing and/or using a computer terminal to perform office functions; reviewing outgoing correspondence for correct format, grammar, punctuation, and typographical errors; and photocopying and assembling reports and briefings. To be eligible for this program, you must be a U.S. citizen, 16 years of age or older at the time of appointment, be enrolled or accepted for enrollment in a postsecondary program, and pass a background check. Most positions are in Washington, D.C., but some past participants have been placed in other cities. Applications are due by February 1 in the year in which you wish to begin work. Contact the Summer Clerical Program coordinator for more information; you can also sign up at the department's Web site to receive email updates regarding the program.

U.S. Department of State
Attn: Summer Clerical Program
  Coordinator
Office of Recruitment
2401 E Street, NW, Suite 518H
Washington, DC 20522-0001
http://www.careers.state.gov/
  students/programs.html

Summer College for High School Students at Cornell University
College Courses/Summer Study

As part of its Summer College for High School Students, Cornell University offers two three-week Exploration in Law and Politics Programs for high school students. High school students who have completed their sophomore, junior, or senior years can participate in the Freedom and Justice: Law in Theory and Practice Program. You'll discuss topics such as "Law, community, and wisdom in Greco-Roman thought; Plato's alternative to the rule of law; law and God in the Judeo-Christian tradition; liberal notions of rights, law, and the state; and inequality and the law, with a focus on gender, class, and race." You'll also participate in discussions with legal and governmental professionals such as mayors, district attorneys, judges, and lawyers. Students who have completed their junior or senior years can take Democracy and its Discontents: Politi-

cal Traditions in the United States. During this seminar, you'll "explore these 'truths,' and the evolution of democracy and dissent in America," and discuss the emancipation of slaves, women's rights, free-speech issues, civil rights, and other topics. You'll also participate in hands-on activities that will help you develop your research skills, as well as attend a session on the college admissions process. Cornell University awards letter grades and undergraduate credit for any course you complete. Residents live and eat on campus, and enjoy access to the university's recreational facilities and special activities. Applications are due in early May, although Cornell encourages students to apply well in advance of the deadline; those applying for financial aid must submit their applications in late April. Further information and details about the application procedure are available from the Summer College office.

Cornell University
Summer College for High School
  Students
B20 Day Hall
Ithaca, NY 14853-2801
607-255-6203
http://www.sce.cornell.edu/sc

Summer College for High School Students at Syracuse University
College Courses/Summer Study

The Syracuse University Summer College for High School Students features a Law Program for those who have just completed their sophomore, junior, or senior years. The Summer College lasts six weeks and offers a residential option so participants can experience campus life while still in high school. The program has several aims: to introduce you to the many possible majors and study areas within this general area; to help you match your aptitudes with possible careers; and to prepare you for college, both academically and socially. Students attend classes, listen to lectures, and take field trips to destinations that are related to their specific area of interest. All students are required to take two courses (one that is liberal-arts based) during the program, and they receive college credit if they successfully complete the courses. Students in the Law Program get the chance to participate in trial practice in a fully appointed courtroom. They either serve as a prosecutor or a defense attorney and "write and deliver a performance of an opening statement in the case, the direct examination of their own witness, cross examination of the opposing counsel's witness, and a closing argument." Admission is competitive and is based on recommendations, test scores, and transcripts. The total cost of the residential program is about $6,595; the commuter option costs about $4,995. Some scholarships are available. The application deadline is in mid May, or mid April for those seeking financial aid. For further information, contact the Summer College.

Syracuse University
Summer College for High School
  Students
700 University Avenue
Syracuse, NY 13244-2530
315-443-5000
sumcoll@syr.edu
http://summercollege.syr.edu/law.html

Summer Law Camp at the University of New Mexico
College Courses/Summer Study

Rising seventh and eighth graders can participate in the Summer Law Camp, a residential program that is held on the campus of the University of New Mexico. Two five-day sessions are typically available. Campers "engage in educational, recreation, leadership, team building, and community service activities." They meet with judges and lawyers, tour a federal courthouse, and participate in a mock trial. Applicants must be residents of New Mexico. They must also submit a handwritten essay, letters of recommendation, and academic transcripts. There is no cost for the camp. Applications are typically due in mid April. Contact the program coordinator for more information.

University of New Mexico
College Prep Program: Summer Law
  Camp
Attn: Program Coordinator
One University of New Mexico
MSC 02 1630
Albuquerque, NM 87131-0001
505-277-0401
http://specialprograms.unm.edu

Summer Program for High School Students at Columbia University
College Courses/Summer Study

Rising ninth through 12th graders who are interested in law and other fields can participate in Columbia University's weeklong Summer Program for High School Students. Freshman-Sophomore Division Courses include Introduction to Trial Advocacy and The Constitution Under Pressure: Civil Rights in War and Peace. Junior-Senior Division Courses include Constitutional Law, Leadership in Law, Trial Advocacy, and Legal Reasoning, Research, and Writing. A course on college preparation is also available. Courses are rigorous, but are not available for college credit. During the week, students take classes from 10:00 A.M. to 12:00 P.M.; break for lunch and activities from 12:00 to 2:30 P.M.; and return to class from 2:30 to 4:30 P.M. In the evenings and on weekends, residential students participate in a wide variety of extracurricular activities, including on-campus events (such as parties, a talent show, a scavenger hunt, an open mike night, and organized sports) and off-campus excursions in and around New York City (such as guided walking tours, films, museums, concerts, restaurants, beaches, and amusement parks). Participants also have access to university libraries, computer labs, a fitness center, a student activity center, and other facilities. Commuter students pay approximately $3,400 per session. Residential students pay $6,225, which includes housing and dining. Both commuter and residential students pay an additional fee of $135 for activities and health coverage. The university also suggests that residential students bring an additional $700 in spending money. Contact the School of Continuing Education for more information.

Columbia University
Summer Program for High School
   Students
School of Continuing Education
203 Lewisohn Hall
2970 Broadway, Mail Code 4119
New York, NY 10027-6902
212-854-9666
http://www.ce.columbia.edu/hs

Summer Scholars at the University of Richmond

College Courses/Summer Study

The Summer Scholars Program seeks to provide high school students with a "realistic, first-hand experience of college including the challenges and rewards that come with it, all while experiencing 'life on campus.'" Rising juniors and seniors are eligible to participate in this three-week, for-credit residential program. Approximately five courses are offered each summer, including one titled The Constitution, the Practice of Law, and You. Participants in this program learn how the Constitution is not just a piece of history, but a "living document" that is referred to daily by lawyers. Students participate in a hypothetical appellate court case that focuses on a constitutional issue and present arguments before actual judges and lawyers. Students also learn to hone their presentation skills by being filmed and critiqued, and they will have the opportunity to discuss law careers and prelaw undergraduate programs at the university with students and professors. Applicants must have a competitive grade point average and enjoy intellectual stimulation and academic challenges.

Program participants stay in air-conditioned residence halls and have access to study lounges, vending machines, and laundry facilities. The cost of the program is $4,200 (which includes tuition, textbooks and classroom supplies, residence hall lodging, a meal plan, and extracurricular activities). Financial assistance is available. Students also receive access to on-campus facilities such as the library, computer labs, and a sports center. The application deadline is typically in early May. Contact the director of summer programs for more information.

University of Richmond
School of Continuing Studies
Director of Summer Programs
28 Westhampton Way
Richmond, VA 23173-0001
804-289-8382
dkitchen@richmond.edu
http://summer.richmond.edu/
  scholars

Summer Scholars Institute at Pace University
College Courses/Summer Study

Rising high school juniors and seniors can participate in Pace University's Summer Scholars Institute, a two-week program that allows them to take college-level courses and get a taste of college life. Each major features two classes—one in the morning and one in the afternoon. In the evenings, students participate in activities that help them learn how to write better college essays and applications, as well as explore the culture of New York City. Students in the Legal Studies at Home and Abroad major take two interesting classes. Civil Rights in American History examines the history of civil rights in the United States and covers such topics as education, desegregation, Jim Crow, voting rights, affirmative action, and gender equality. Human Rights in the 21st Century explores human rights issues in the United States and the world. Recent topics covered in the class included "the unlawful detention of immigrants, homelessness, the responses to Hurricane Katrina and 9/11, international crimes such as genocides, the trafficking of people and blood diamonds, child soldiering, terrorism, and the role of human rights in foreign policy." The cost of the program is $1,000 for commuters (which includes one meal per day and social events) and $2,000 for residents (which includes room, two meals per day, and social events). Financial aid is available. Applications are typically due in mid June.

Pace University
Summer Scholars Institute
Attn: Program Coordinator
Pforzheimer Honors College
W207E Pace Plaza
New York, NY 10038
212-346-1192
summerscholar@pace.edu
http://www.pace.edu/page.cfm?doc_
  id=17156

Summer Scholars Pre-College Programs at George Washington University
College Courses/Summer Study

Rising high school sophomores, juniors, and seniors who are interested in exploring law and other subjects can take 10-day mini courses, which are held twice each summer. Students in the Law and Evidence: Inside Criminal Law mini course will "analyze, examine, and participate in case studies, legal processes, and trial procedures" via classroom lectures, guest speakers, and on-site visits to the U.S. Capitol, federal courthouses, and other law-related locales. Students live in air-conditioned residence halls that have mini-fridges, microwaves, and telephones. A commuter option is also available. Wireless Internet is available throughout the campus. Students also have access to a community lounge, kitchen, library, athletic facilities, and laundry facilities. The residential rate for the program is about $2,600; the commuter rate is $1,950. A $40 application fee is also required. The application deadline for this noncredit program is typically in late April.

George Washington University
Summer Scholars Pre-College
  Programs
2100 Foxhall Road
Washington, DC 20007-1150
202-242-6802
scholars@gwu.edu
http://www.summerscholars.gwu.edu

Summer Scholars Program at Furman University

College Courses/Summer Study

Rising juniors and seniors with strong academic skills who are interested in law careers can take A Mock Trial: Did Blitz News Network Defame Drew Walton?, a one-week residential course that introduces students to trial practice techniques via this hypothetical case. (Note: Rising sophomores may be admitted under special considerations.) Participants learn "proper courtroom etiquette, direct and cross examination tactics, the structure of opening statements and closing arguments, federal rules of evidence, and other matters related to trial advocacy in a civil matter." They will be divided into defense and plaintiff trial teams, and the case will be tried in a federal courtroom at the end of the class. Students stay in residence halls and have access to the campus library and athletic facilities. Tuition for the one-week program is $800 (which includes room, board, activities, and fields trips). Applications are typically due in June. Contact the Office of Enrollment for more information.

Furman University
Office of Enrollment
3300 Poinsett Highway
Greenville, SC 29613-0002
864-294-2054
mary.hearne@furman.edu
http://www.furman.edu/camps
andconferences/camps.htm

Summer Scholars Program at the University of Notre Dame

College Courses/Summer Study

The Summer Scholars Program consists of more than 10 two-week classes for rising junior or senior high school students, including a pre-law track: Jurisprudence, Justice, and the American Legal System. Students receive introductions to constitutional, civil, criminal, corporate, and tort law; court systems; civil procedure; and legal careers. The capstone of the class is preparation for and participation in a mock trial in which students take on various courtroom roles, such as judge, lawyer, and jury member. Tours of the university's law school and library, the St. Joseph County Courthouse, the South Bend Federal Courthouse, and the federal courthouse in Chicago are also scheduled. The application deadline for the program is typically in early March. Tuition for this residential program is $2,500 (which includes room/board and meals), plus a $45 application fee. A limited amount of financial aid is available. Contact the Office of Pre-College Programs for more information.

University of Notre Dame

Office of Pre-College Programs
202 Brownson Hall
Notre Dame, IN 46556-5601
574-631-0990
precoll@nd.edu
http://precollege.nd.edu/
    summer-scholars

Summer Study at Pennsylvania State University

College Courses/Summer Study

High school students who are interested in law and other fields can apply to participate in the following Summer Study programs: the College Credit Program and the Summer Enrichment Program. The six-and-a-half-week College Credit Program begins in late June and recently offered the following law-related classes: Criminology and Introduction to the American Criminal Justice System. Students typically choose one college credit course (for three or four credits) and either an enrichment class/workshop (such as Law & The Justice System) or The Kaplan SAT or ACT prep class. Students who have completed the 10th, 11th, and 12th grades are eligible to apply. The noncredit Summer Enrichment Program offers three-and-a-half week and two-week options and recently featured law-related classes such as Debate and Law & The Justice System. Students who have completed the 9th, 10th, and 11th grades are eligible for the program. Tuition for the College Credit Program is approximately $6,995, while tuition for the noncredit Enrichment Program is approximately $4,495 (three-and-a-half-week program) and $2,495 (two-week program). Limited financial aid is available. Contact the Summer Study Program for more information.

Pennsylvania State University

Summer Study Program
900 Walt Whitman Road
Melville, NY 11747-2293
800-666-2556
info@summerstudy.com
http://www.summerstudy.com/
    pennstate

U.S. Supreme Court

Field Experience

One great way to learn about the legal system and the professionals who work in it is to take a tour of the Supreme Court, the highest-level court in the United States. The Supreme Court is located in Washington, D.C, and is open for tours on Monday through Friday. A variety of educational programs are available, including exhibits, a film about the court, and courtroom lectures (held on days when the court is not in session). Additionally, visitors can actually attend the court while it is in session. During the first Monday in October through mid May, visitors can listen to oral arguments in which attorneys from each side make a presentation to the court and may be asked questions by the justices. From mid May until the end of June they can listen to the release of orders and opinions from the court. Visit the Supreme Court's Web site for more information on tours.

You don't have to go to Washington, D.C., to tour a courtroom, though. Courthouses are located in communities of all sizes, and many offer tours or allow visitors to attend judicial proceedings. Contact your local courthouse for more information about opportunities near you.

U.S. Supreme Court
One First Street, NE
Washington, DC 20543-0002
202-479-3211
http://www.supremecourtus.gov/
   visiting/visiting.html

Young Scholars Program at the University of Maryland
College Courses/Summer Study
Participants in the three-week Young Scholars Program spend July exploring the field of law and taking a college-level course. College credit is awarded to students who satisfactorily complete the course. Students who take the Mock Trials/Trial Advocacy course learn how to prepare and present a case to a jury or judge, how to examine witnesses, and how to deliver oral arguments. Program participants live in the residence halls at the University of Maryland and take their meals on campus or in selected College Park restaurants. To apply, you must be a rising high school junior or senior and submit an application form, an essay, two letters of recommendation, a current transcript, and an application and enrollment fee of $205 by mid May. Admissions decisions are based primarily on the recommendations, the applicant's academic record (they must have a GPA of 3.0 or higher), and overall academic ability. Residential tuition for the program is about $2,785; tuition for commuters is approximately $1,665. For further details and an application form, contact the Office of Extended Studies.

University of Maryland
Office of Extended Studies
Student Services
0132 Main Administration Building
College Park, MD 20742-5000
301-405-7762
http://www.summer.umd.edu/s/ysp

Read a Book

When it comes to finding out about law, don't overlook a book. (You're reading one now, after all.) What follows is a short, annotated list of books and periodicals related to law. The books range from fiction and personal accounts to biographies of the greats and career-oriented publications. Don't be afraid to check out the professional journals, either. The legalese may be way above your head right now, but if you take the time to become familiar with one or two, you're bound to pick up some of what is important to law professionals, not to mention begin to feel like a part of their world, which is what you're interested in, right?

We've tried to include recent materials as well as old favorites. Always check for the most recent editions, and, if you find an author or topic you like, ask your librarian to help you find more. Keep reading good books and periodicals!

❑ BOOKS

American Association of Legal Nurse Consultants. *Legal Terminology Primer for the Legal Nurse Consultant.* Chicago: American Association of Legal Nurse Consultants, 2003. Provides an overview of basic legal terms encountered by legal nurse consultants.

Barron's Educational Series. *Barron's 2009 Guide to Law Schools.* 18th ed. Hauppauge, N.Y.: Barron's Educational Series, 2008. Provides an overview of more than 190 law schools that have been approved by the American Bar Association.

Bently, Lionel, and Brad Sherman. *Intellectual Property Law.* 3d ed. New York: Oxford University Press, 2008. Offers an overview of key intellectual property topics.

Blevins, Nancy, Renee Miller, JoAnn Pugh, and Elizabeth Riggs. *Developing an Independent Legal Nurse Consulting Practice.* Chicago: American Association of Legal Nurse Consultants, 2001. Provides tips on starting, promoting, and developing a legal nurse consulting business.

Bogira, Steve. *Courtroom 302: A Year Behind the Scenes in an American Criminal Courthouse.* New York: Vintage Books, 2006. A fascinating look into the day-to-day workings of a big-city courtroom through the experiences of judges, court officers, public defenders, prosecutors, and defendants.

Bouchoux, Deborah E. *Legal Research and Writing for Paralegals.* 5th ed. New York: Aspen Publishers, 2008. This useful guide will help paralegals and paralegal students research and write legal documents.

Cannon, K. Charles. *The Ultimate Guide to Your Legal Career: What Every Young Lawyer Must Know to Avoid the Mistakes and Maximize the Value of a Career in the Law.* Cambridge, Mass.: Da Capo Press, 2007. This book provides advice on acing law school and developing a career that will be rewarding and a good fit for your personality and skill set. Also covers career alternatives for lawyers, such as those in banking and government.

Charrow, Veda R., Myra K. Erhardt, and Robert P. Charrow. *Clear and Effective Legal Writing.* 4th ed. New York: Aspen Publishers, 2007. Offers comprehensive advice on writing legal memos and briefs.

Curll, Joyce Putnam. *The Best Law Schools' Admissions Secrets: The Essential Guide from Harvard's Former Admissions Dean.* Naperville, Ill.: Sourcebooks, 2008. This helpful guide provides advice on preparing your application, taking the Law School Admissions Test, and paying for law school.

Darrow, Clarence. *The Story Of My Life.* Cambridge, Mass.: Da Capo Press, 1996. This is an interesting autobiography from a criminal, corporate, and labor attorney who participated in some of the most important legal cases of the 20th century.

Davis, Kevin. *Defending the Damned: Inside Chicago's Cook County Public Defender's Office.* New York: Atria, 2007. Provides a gripping examina-

tion of the work of public defenders in the Murder Task Force of the Cook County [Illinois] Public Defender's Office.

Delsohn, Gary. *The Prosecutors: A Year in the Life of a District Attorney's Office.* New York: Dutton Adult, 2003. An inside look at the Sacramento court system and the district attorneys and assistant district attorneys who work there.

Ehrenfreund, Norbert. *You Be the Judge: 20 True Crimes and Cases to Solve.* Naperville, Ill.: Sphinx Publishing, 2008. Put yourself in the shoes of a juror or judge by reading about these actual cases and rendering a verdict.

Friedman, Jane M. *America's First Woman Lawyer: The Biography of Myra Bradwell.* Amherst, N.Y.: Prometheus Books, 1993. This book provides an evenhanded look at the sometimes controversial Bradwell, who was denied the right to practice law in Illinois in 1869 because of her gender, but went on to a long career as the editor and publisher of the *Chicago Legal News.*

Friedman, Lawrence M. *A History of American Law.* 3d ed. New York: Touchstone, 2005. A comprehensive history of the development of the legal system in the United States.

Furi-Perry, Ursula. *50 Legal Careers for Non-Lawyers.* Chicago: American Bar Association, 2008. Provides an overview of careers in law that do not require a law degree. Some of the careers covered include litigation paralegals, law firm administrators, pro bono coordinators, legal investigators, trial graphics and animation support specialists, legal researchers, and paralegal instructors.

Gallo, Nancy R. *Elder Law.* Florence, Ky.: Delmar Cengage Learning, 2008. Provides a detailed overview of this fast-growing legal specialty. Includes information on advance directives, guardianship and conservatorship issues, long-term care planning, physical and financial elder abuse, age discrimination, and other topics.

Harr, J. Scott, and Karen M. Hess. *Careers in Criminal Justice and Related Fields: From Internship to Promotion.* 6th ed. Belmont, Calif.: Wadsworth Publishing, 2009. Provides practical advice for students interested in pursuing careers in criminal justice.

Hatch, Scott, and Lisa Zimmer Hatch. *Paralegal Career For Dummies.* Hoboken, N.J.: For Dummies, 2006. Includes information on landing a job, finding the right law specialty, and thriving as a paralegal.

Haworth, Anita, and Lesley Cox. *The Paralegal's Handbook: A Complete Reference for All Your Daily Tasks.* New York: Kaplan Publishing, 2008. A detailed look at the ins and outs of being a paralegal.

Hemmingson, Michael, ed. *The Mammoth Book of Legal Thrillers.* Philadelphia: Running Press, 2001. An anthology of fictional stories about courtrooms, criminals, judges, and juries from past and present masters.

Irons, Peter. *A People's History of the Supreme Court: The Men and Women Whose Cases and Decisions Have Shaped Our Constitution.* Rev. ed. New York: Penguin Books, 2006. Provides an overview of our nation's highest court and the 100+ men and women who have served on it.

Ivey, Anna. *The Ivey Guide to Law School Admissions: Straight Advice on Essays, Resumes, Interviews, and More.* New York: Harvest Books, 2005. This book provides everything you need to know about getting into law school, and is written by the former dean of admissions at the University of Chicago Law School.

Iyer, Patricia, ed. *Legal Nurse Consulting: Principles & Practice.* 2d ed. Chicago: American Association of Legal Nurse Consultants, 2003. This reference to the growing field of legal nurse consulting details the many practice opportunities for legal nurse consultants.

Kaplan Publishing. *First Year Lawyer: Wisdom, Warnings, and What I Wish I'd Known in My First Year Out of Law School.* New York: Kaplan Publishing, 2008. Provides useful advice for new lawyers.

Kroger, John. *Convictions: A Prosecutor's Battles Against Mafia Killers, Drug Kingpins, and Enron Thieves.* New York: Farrar, Straus and Giroux, 2008. A former assistant U.S. attorney takes readers behind the scenes of some of the biggest federal court cases in recent history.

Lammert-Reeves, Ruth. *Get Into Law School: A Strategic Approach.* 4th ed. New York: Kaplan Publishing, 2008.

Provides tips on choosing a school, preparing your application, writing personal statements, obtaining recommendations, and paying for law school.

Learning Express Editors. *Paralegal Career Starter.* 3d ed. New York: Learning Express LLC, 2006. Provides advice for aspiring paralegals.

Leonard, Peggy C. *Building a Medical Vocabulary.* 7th ed. New York: Saunders, 2008. Excellent guide to the language of health care. Teaches the fundamental word parts that are used as the "building blocks" of more complicated terminology.

Long, Judy A. *Administrative Procedures for the Legal Professional.* Florence, Ky.: Delmar Cengage Learning, 2008. Provides an overview of law office administrative procedures for legal secretaries and paralegals. Includes information on management of law offices, working with attorneys, ethics, legal research, filing and records management, and communications.

———. *Office Procedures for the Legal Professional.* Florence, Ky.: Delmar Cengage Learning, 2005. Provides an overview of the law office and court system for legal secretaries and paralegals. Topics include trial procedures, criminal law, civil litigation, estate planning, ethics, family law, and contracts.

Miller, Richard Lawrence. *Lincoln and His World: The Early Years, Birth to Illinois Legislature.* Mechanicsburg, Pa.: Stackpole Books, 2006. Provides an enlightening look at Abraham Lincoln's early years—including those he spent as an attorney.

Morton, Joyce. *Legal Office Procedures.* 7th ed. Upper Saddle River, N.J.: Prentice Hall, 2006. This popular guide for legal administrative professionals provides an overview of the everyday workings of a law office and information on litigation procedures, law specialties, legal research, and landing a job in the field.

Munneke, Gary A. *Nonlegal Careers for Lawyers.* 5th ed. Chicago: American Bar Association, 2006. Provides information about career opportunities for lawyers outside the legal profession, including those in government, public service, and business and industry.

National Legal Aid & Defender Association. *Directory of Legal Aid and Defender Offices and Resources.* Washington, D.C.: National Legal Aid & Defender Association, 2007. Provides addresses and key contact information for more than 4,000 public defender and civil legal aid offices, support and resource centers, and sentencing advocates and mitigation specialists in the United States.

O'Brien, David M., ed. *Judges on Judging: Views from the Bench.* 3d ed. Washington, D.C.: CQ Press, 2008. State, federal, and Supreme Court judges discuss the role of the judiciary, the judicial process, constitutional and statutory interpretation, and other topics.

O'Connor, Sandra Day. *The Majesty of the Law: Reflections of a Supreme Court Justice.* New York: Random

House Trade Paperbacks, 2004. Justice O'Connor provides an overview of the evolution of the U.S. legal system and the Supreme Court's role in it.

Peterson's. *Peterson's Nursing Programs 2009.* 10th ed. Lawrenceville, N.J.: Peterson's, 2009. Profiles nearly 3,500 undergraduate, graduate, and post-doctoral programs at more than 700 institutions in the United States and Canada.

Princeton Review. *Best 174 Law Schools.* 2009 Edition. New York: The Princeton Review, 2008. This annual guide provides detailed information about the top law schools in the United States, Canada, and England. Also offers information on applying to and paying for law school.

Russo, Linda L., and George B. Blake. *Diary of a Court Reporter.* Philadelphia: Xlibris Corporation, 2008. Provides an inside look at four court trials and verdicts.

Sax, Robin. *Reaching the Bar: Stories of Women at All Stages of Their Law Careers.* New York: Kaplan Publishing, 2009. This book features profiles of women law students and clerks, associates, senior partners, judges, and professors.

Shanahan, Danny. *Innocent, Your Honor: A Book of Lawyer Cartoons.* New York: Harry N. Abrams, 2005. Presents more than 120 humorous cartoons from the renowned *New Yorker* cartoonist.

Swartz, Salli A., ed. *Careers in International Law.* 3d ed. Chicago: American Bar Association, 2008. Lawyers from a variety of backgrounds and practice areas discuss career opportunities and starting and developing an international law practice.

Swick, Sandra, and Corrine Grimes. *Barron's Nursing School Entrance Exams.* 3d ed. Hauppauge, N.Y.: Barron's Educational Series, 2007. Provides a great review for the exam and the road to becoming a legal nurse consultant. Provides subject reviews and a full-length model test.

Toobin, Jeffrey. *The Nine: Inside the Secret World of the Supreme Court.* Reprint ed. New York: Anchor, 2008. An in-depth examination of the inner workings of the Supreme Court.

Trachtman, Michael G. *The Supremes' Greatest Hits: The 34 Supreme Court Cases That Most Directly Affect Your Life.* New York: Sterling Publishing Company, 2006. Covers key cases such as the Dred Scott decision, *Miranda v. Arizona, Brown v. Board of Education, Roe v. Wade,* and *Bush v. Gore.*

Weishapple, Cynthia. *Introduction to Legal Nurse Consulting.* Florence, Ky.: Delmar Cengage Learning, 2000. Important resource for nurses considering a career in legal consulting. Includes career profiles and advice from successful legal nurse consultants.

Wright, Carol L. *The Ultimate Guide to Law School Admission: Insider Secrets for Getting a "Big Envelope" with Your Acceptance to Law School!* Center Valley, Pa.: Marriwell Publishing, 2008. Provides practical information about getting into and thriving in law school.

❏ PERIODICALS

@Law. Published quarterly by NALS (NALS Resource Center, 8159 East 41st Street, Tulsa, OK 74145-3313, 918-582-5188, http://www.nals.org/atlaw), this publication covers current legal issues for paralegals, legal secretaries, legal assistants, office administrators, and educators.

American Bar Association Journal. Published monthly by the American Bar Association (321 North Clark Street, 15th Floor, Chicago, IL 60654-4714, 800-285-2221). This popular resource provides comprehensive coverage of the legal industry. An online version (http://www.abajournal.com) features articles, blogs, and a variety of other resources.

The American Intellectual Property Law Association Quarterly Journal. Published by the American Intellectual Property Law Association (241 18th Street South, Suite 700, Arlington, VA 22202-3419, 703-415-0780, aipla@aipla.org, http://www.aipla.org/Content/NavigationMenu/Publications/Quarterly_Journ al1/Default800.htm), this journal offers the latest information on intellectual property law.

The American Lawyer. Published 12 times annually by Incisive Media (Subscription Department, 120 Broadway, New York, NY 10271-0002, 800-755-2773). Provides comprehensive coverage of the legal industry, including information on career trends, salary surveys, and rankings of law firms. Free limited access is available at http://www.law.com/jsp/tal/index.jsp.

Association of American Law Schools Newsletter. Published quarterly by the Association of American Law Schools (1201 Connecticut Avenue, NW, Suite 800, Washington, DC 20036-2717, 202-296-8851), this newsletter features information about association events and interviews with professionals in the field. Visit http://www.aals.org/services_newsletter.php to read selected issues and sample articles.

The Champion. Published 10 times annually by the National Association of Criminal Defense Lawyers (1660 L Street, NW, 12th Floor, Washington, DC 20036-5603, 202-872-8600), this magazine features information on the "latest developments in search and seizure laws, grand jury proceedings, the death penalty, federal sentencing guidelines, forfeiture, and white-collar crime." Visit http://www.nacdl.org to read sample articles.

The Circuit Rider. Published quarterly by the United States Court Reporters Association (133 U.S. Courthouse, 501 Broadway, Paducah, KY 42001-6856, http://www.uscra.org/circuit_rider.htm), this trade publication covers developments in the field of court reporting.

Cornerstone. Published three times annually by the National Legal Aid and Defender Association (1140 Connecticut Avenue, NW, Suite 900, Washington, DC 20036-4019, 202-452-0620, info@nlada.org, http://www.nlada.org), this publication features peer-written articles about equal-justice issues.

Criminal Justice. Published quarterly by the American Bar Association Section of Criminal Justice (321 North Clark Street, Chicago, IL 60654-4714, http://www.abanet.org). This trade magazine for prosecutors, judges, defense lawyers, and academics focuses on practice and policy issues.

The Disclosure. Published monthly by the National Association of Patent Practitioners (3356 Station Court, Lawrenceville, GA 30044-5674, 800-216-9588), this online publication features information for intellectual property professionals. Visit https://www.napp.org/disclosure to read sample issues.

EVoice. Published 12 times annually by the National Verbatim Reporters Association (207 Third Avenue, Hattiesburg, MS 39401-3868, 601-582-4345, nvra@nvra.org, http://www.nvra.org/displaycommon.cfm ?an=14), this online resource covers trends in the industry for aspiring and practicing verbatim reporters.

FACTS & FINDINGS. Published quarterly by the National Association for Legal Assistants (1516 South Boston, Suite 200, Tulsa, OK 74119-4013, 918-587-6828, nalanet@nala.org), this professional resource for legal assistants provides feature articles and columns on ethics, technology, and other topics. Visit http://www.nala.org/Facts_Findings.htm to read sample articles.

The Federal Lawyer. Published monthly by The Federal Bar Association (Attn: TFL Subscriptions, 1220 North Fillmore Street, Suite 444, Arlington, VA 22201-6501). This resource offers articles written by judges and lawyers, book reviews, and commentary on recent Supreme Court rulings. Visit http://www.fedbar.org/magazine.html to read sample articles.

Guild Practitioner. Published quarterly by the National Lawyers Guild (PO Box 46205, Los Angeles, CA 90046-0205, http://nlg.org/resources/publications.php). Features articles about law theory and practice.

Journal of Court Reporting. Published 10 times annually by the National Court Reporters Association (8224 Old Courthouse Road, Vienna, VA 22182-3808, 800-272-6272, http://ncraonline.org). Provides articles about the court reporting and captioning professions for members of the association.

Journal of Legal Education. Published quarterly by the Association of American Law Schools (and hosted by Southwestern Law School, 3050 Wilshire Boulevard, Los Angeles, CA 90010-1106, jle@swlaw.edu, http://www.swlaw.edu/jleweb/overview). Covers topics of interest to legal educators. Sections include The Content of Legal Education, Institutional Issues in Legal Education, Legal Education in Other Venues, and Book Reviews.

Journal of Legal Nurse Consulting. Published quarterly by the American Association of Legal Nurse Consultants (401 North Michigan Avenue, Chicago, IL 60611-4255, 877-402-2562, jlnc@aalnc.org, http://www.aalnc.org/edupro/journal.cfm). Offers a variety of articles about medical and legal issues, including managed care, medical and products liability issues, life care planning, and forensics, as well as business advice and networking tips.

Legal Assistant Today. Published six times annually by James Publishing (3505 Cadillac Avenue, Suite H, Costa Mesa, CA 92626-1461, 877-202-5196). This independent publication for paralegals provides salary data, how-to sections, software and hardware reviews, and industry news. Recent articles include "Writing paralegal resumes," "A look at graduate-level paralegal studies," and "Getting started as a paralegal." A paralegal education guide appears in the January/February issue. Read sample articles at http://www.legalassistanttoday.com.

Legal Management. Published 10 times annually by the Association of Legal Administrators (75 Tri-State International, Suite 222, Lincolnshire, IL 60069-4435, 847-267-1252), this professional resource for law firm managers, legal administrators, and managing partners features articles about human resources trends, technological innovations, leadership issues, and general business practices. Visit http://www.alanet.org/publications/legalmgmt.aspx to read sample articles.

The National Academy of Elder Law Attorneys News. Published six times annually by the National Academy of Elder Law Attorneys (1577 Spring Hill Road, Suite 220, Vienna, VA 22182-2223, 520-881-4005, ext. 115, sfobar@naela.com, http://www.naela.org/Pros_Publications.aspx?Internal=true). Offers information on elder law topics for professionals in the field.

The National Law Journal. Published by Incisive Media (877-256-2472, customercare@incisivemedia.com). Covers a wide range of topics for lawyers and other legal professionals. Recent articles included "In cold economy, some practice areas remain hot," "Major high court reforms proposed," and "Wanted: law school deans. Lots of them." Limited free access is available at http://www.law.com/jsp/nlj.

National Legal Aid & Defender Association Cornerstone. Published three times annually by the National Legal Aid & Defender Association (1140 Connecticut Avenue, NW, Suite 900, Washington, DC 20036-4019, 202-452-0620, info@nlada.org, http://www.nlada.org/News/News_Pubs). Provides peer-written articles about equal justice rights topics.

National Verbatim Reporters Association Verbatim Record. Published quarterly by the National Verbatim Reporters Association (207 Third Avenue, Hattiesburg, MS 39401-3868, 601-582-4345, nvra@nvra.org, http://www.nvra.org/displaycommon.cfm?an=14). This online resource provides information on career trends, association activities, certification, and technological innovations in the field.

The Prosecutor. Published six times annually by the National District Attorneys Association (44 Canal Center Plaza, Suite 110, Alexandria, VA

22314-1548, http://www.ndaa.org/publications/ndaa/toc_prosecutor.html). Features articles on developments in the field. Recent articles included "Tech tips: writing clearer with bullet points in three easy steps," "The few and the proud: prosecutors who vigorously pursue animal cruelty cases," and "Using DNA to solve high-volume property crimes in Denver."

Student Lawyer. Published September through May by the American Bar Association (321 North Clark Street, 15th Floor, Chicago, IL 60654-4714, 800-285-2221). Covers education- and career-related topics for Law Student Division members and others. Sample articles are available at http://www.abanet.org/lsd/stude ntlawyer.

The Young Lawyer. Published 11 times annually by the American Bar Association (321 North Clark Street, 15th Floor, Chicago, IL 60654-4714, 800-285-2221). A practice-oriented publication for lawyers under the age of 36 or those in practice for five years or less. General topics covered include ethics/professional conduct, skills training, technology, practice management, quality of life, careers/jobs, women and minorities, and marketing/rainmaking. Visit http://www.abanet.org/yld/home.html to read sample articles.

Surf the Web

You must use the Internet to do research, to find out, to explore. The Internet is the closest you'll get to what's happening now all around the world. This chapter gets you started with an annotated list of Web sites related to the field of law. Try a few. Follow the links. Maybe even venture as far as asking questions in a chat room. The more you read about and interact with law professionals, the better prepared you'll be when you're old enough to participate as a professional.

One caveat: You probably already know that URLs change all the time. If a Web address listed below is out of date, try searching the site's name or other keywords. Chances are, if an address is still out there, you'll find it. If it's not, maybe you'll find something better!

❑ THE LIST

About.com: Law School
http://lawschool.about.com

Everything you ever wanted to know about law school—from applying to law school and writing your personal statement to paying for school—is available on this appropriately named Web site. Some of the most useful sections include Preparing for Law School, Choosing a Law School, Law School Culture, Surviving Law School, and Bar Exam. You might also want to sign up to receive a free law school newsletter to keep abreast of developments in the field. In the Community Forum section, you can register to participate in conversations with others interested in learning about the field.

American Bar Association: Attorney By Attorney—Online Attorney Profiles Showcase
http://www.abanet.org/career
counsel/profile/profession.html

Visit this Web site to read profiles of more than 120 lawyers in approximately 60 legal specialties (such as criminal, equine, franchise, pediatric, and technology law). In the profiles, the attorneys provide advice to people interested in entering their field, detailing how they entered the field, their specialty, the pros and cons of their specialty, and core skills necessary for success. This is a useful site to visit if you want a quick overview of legal specialties and the lawyers who work in them.

American Bar Association: Career Counsel
http://www.abanet.org/careercounsel

This Web site provides job-search tools—ranging from podcasts (that cover communication skills and how to attract clients) and videos (that offer advice on creating a compelling resume), to a job board, career articles, and links to resources and associations for students and legal professionals.

American Bar Association: Glossary

http://www.abanet.org/publiced/ youth/sia/glossary.pdf

If you don't know the meaning of legal terms such as appellate and apportion, cross examination and conviction, or habeas corpus and hung jury, then you should check out this online glossary. More than 400 legal terms are defined in simple terminology in this useful resource.

American Bar Association: How Courts Work

http://www.abanet.org/publiced/ courts/home.html

You've probably watched dozens of court dramas or reality courtroom shows on TV, but do you really understand the inner workings of our nation's judicial system? If not, this Web site is a great place to start. It has four main sections: Courts and Legal Procedures (where you'll get the skinny on the role and structure of courts, the role of judges, the role of juries, grand juries, trial juries, and judicial independence), Steps in a Trial, The Human Side of Being a Judge (which features personal reflections from judges), and Mediation (a process in which two parties in a legal or other type of dispute state their grievances, negotiate, and come to a compromise).

American Bar Association Journal: *Blawg Directory*

http://abajournal.com/blawgs

This Web site provides links to thousands of law-related blogs (blawgs) written by legal professionals. Browse these blogs for education- and career-related news and opinions and to get a general feel for the industry.

American Bar Association (ABA): Legal Education & Student Resources

http://www.abanet.org/legaled.html

Everything you need to know about law degrees and the legal profession is available on this Web site, which is organized into helpful categories. For example, if you are interested in learning about law school, there is a section devoted to how to prepare for law education, a list of accredited schools, as well as a U.S. map that links to ABA-accredited law programs that offer resources (student organizations, clinical programs, etc.) for law students with disabilities. Other sections focus on careers and public education.

American Bar Association: National Directory of Law-Related Programs

http://publiced.abanet.org/lre/basic_ search.jspa

This Web site provides a directory of law-related resources including colleges and universities that offer law programs, law associations (such as the Kansas Bar Association, Learning Law and Democracy Foundation, and Street Law Inc.), and K-12 law programs. Contact information and a summary of the organization are provided for each listing. The directory is searchable by organization type, country, state, and other criteria.

American Bar Association: Pre-Law Toolkit
http://www.abanet.org/career counsel/prelaw

This Web site provides useful links to students who are contemplating a career in law. Sections include Should I Become a Lawyer?; Grade School and Junior High Pre-Law Resources; High School and University Pre-Law Resources; University Pre-Law Pages and Links; Legal Organizations Allowing Student Enrollment (college and law students only); Law.com Legal Dictionary; Law Career Fairs; Diversity-Related Issues; Financial Aid; Choosing A Law School; Application Process; Law School Prep Courses; Understanding Court Decisions; Featured Pre-Law Publications; and Just for School Counselors. There are also eTip Sheets that provide students with advice from lawyers on a wide variety of topics ranging from law exams and financial aid, to networking and internships, to breaking into international law.

American Intellectual Property Law Association: Map of Women's Bar Associations
http://www.aipla.org/html/women/ women-ip.html

This Web site provides a map of women's bar associations in the United States. For example, if you click on the state of New York on the map, you will find links to more than 30 women's bar associations, including the Association of Black Women Attorneys, the Central New York Women's Bar Association, Legal Momentum: Advancing Women's Rights, and the New York State Bar Association Committee on Women in the Law.

American Mock Trial Association
http://www.collegemocktrial.org

Mock trials are a great way for law students to hone their critical thinking and public speaking skills, as well as put their knowledge of the legal system and procedures to actual use. The American Mock Trial Association's Web site allows you to search and register for mock trials throughout the nation either as an individual or as part of a team. Winners' names and videos of their trials are posted online.

Careers in Court Reporting & Broadcast Captioning
http://www.bestfuture.com

This Web site, which is sponsored by the National Court Reporters Association, is a key destination for students interested in learning more about careers in the field. The About Reporting Careers section provides information on career specialties (such as judicial reporter, broadcast captioner, and CART provider) and features interviews with and videos of professionals in the field. Becoming a Reporter discusses the most important skills and attributes for court reporters (such as being good audio learners and the ability to thrive under pressure and deadlines) and provides links to court reporting education programs. The Frequently Asked Questions section offers answers to common questions about the field, such as What is broadcast captioning and how does that relate to court reporting?, How much money can a court reporter earn?, What sorts of questions should I ask a school that I'm thinking of attending?, and I'm interested in court reporting as a career possibility, but what effect will technology have on the future of the profession? Finally, How the Steno Machine Works provides an example of a reporter's stenotype notes with English translation.

Careers in Intellectual Property Law

http://www.aipla.org/Content/
NavigationMenu/Student_Center/
Careers_in_IP_Law/Careers_in_IP_
Law.htm

This online brochure was created under the direction of the Committee on Law Students of the Intellectual Property Law Section of the American Bar Association. It provides information for people who are interested in learning more about career opportunities in intellectual property law. Sections include The Four Main Types of Intellectual Property; Preparing to Practice Intellectual Property Law; Patent Law as a Specialty: Preparation; Patent Law as a Specialty: Practice; and Employment Arenas for Intellectual Property Lawyers.

DiscoverLaw.org

http://discoverlaw.org

DiscoverLaw helps motivate and mentor undergraduate students from diverse racial and ethnic backgrounds who are interested in pursuing a career in law. Click on the Student Resources section for Fields of Law, a list detailing the different law specialties available, including civil rights and intellectual property law. There is also a timeline available that suggests different tasks to accomplish on the road to law school. Students can get further inspiration from the experiences of minority law students. Stories are told in print or video format and cover the struggles, challenges, and successes of students throughout the country. If you have any questions regarding law school requirements, you'll certainly want to visit the LAW FAQs section. It provides answers to questions such as What undergraduate courses can help me prepare for law school?, Do law schools apply different admission criteria to minorities?, How long does it take to get a law degree?, and How easy is it to get a job after going to law school?

Getting Started in Legal Nurse Consulting

http://www.aalnc.org/images/pdfs/
GetStartWeb.pdf

This is an online version of a short guide on career planning for legal nurse consultants from the American Association of Legal Nurse Consultants. Although written in 1999, it still provides a wealth of information on this fast-growing legal specialty for those with a nursing degree and an interest in law. The most useful section, Getting Started, features information about practice settings (such as insurance companies, law firms, forensic nursing, and independent practice) and tips for landing a job.

Landmark Cases: Supreme Court

http://www.landmarkcases.org

This Web site provides lesson plans and analysis for groundbreaking Supreme Court cases, as well as legal issues such as federalism, separation of powers and checks and balances, equal protection of the laws, judicial review, and due process. Anyone who is interested in learning more about key Supreme Court cases and legal topics should visit this Web site.

Law.com

http://www.law.com

Law.com provides a wealth of information about career trends in the field. Articles are culled from more than 20 national and regional legal publications, including *The National Law Journal*, *The American Lawyer*, *New York Law Journal*, and *Legal Times*. There are also links to blogs, surveys and rankings, and job listings.

Law School Admission Council: Getting Started

http://www.lsac.org/About-LawSchool/getting-started.asp

Any questions you may have about a law career and how to get started will be answered by browsing this site. Click on the Thinking About Law School section to learn more about law school curricula, how to research different law schools, and the application process. The Applying to

Law School section provides an overview of the admissions process. The Financing Law School section presents articles and videos on financing options and a step-by-step guide to finding financial aid as well as repayment options after graduation. There is also information on special resources and programs for law students from diverse backgrounds.

Law School Admission Council: The LSAT

http://www.lsac.org/LSAT/The LSAT-menu.asp

Everything you need to know about the LSAT is on this site, which includes topics ranging from test scores and fees to the location of testing centers. The site even provides a detailed list of what to expect of the test—covering things you should do the night before the test (such as checking your online account to make sure your registration information is correct and detailing what materials you should bring—an admission ticket and identification) and providing a thorough explanation of test center regulations.

Law School Admission Council: Preparing for Law School

http://www.lsac.org/About-LawSchool/Preparing-for-Law-School.asp

How well has your undergraduate work prepared you for a career in law? While students enter law school with degrees from different academic areas, this site offers advice on what you can do now regardless of your educational background. One suggestion is to enroll in classes that teach core skills and values that are often possessed by successful law students. Some key areas include analytical thinking, writing, oral communication, and good research skills. This site also advises students to seek situations to help promote justice and service to others. Another tip includes finding a prelaw adviser to make sure you are on the right track in regard to your studies and community service.

NALP, National Association for Law Placement: Directory of Law Schools

http://www.nalplawschoolsonline.org

This Web site provides a database of law schools in the United States and Canada. It is searchable by law school name, city, region, number of students enrolled, fields of study, areas of practice, and other criteria. Each school entry features information on degree programs, the demographic makeup of students, available fields of study, admissions criteria, student organizations, grading policies, and much more. This is a great place to learn more about law schools.

NALP, National Association for Law Placement: Directory of Legal Employers

http://www.nalpdirectory.com

This Web site provides a searchable database of legal employers. You can find employers by employer type (corporate, government, law firm, and public interest), employer name, city, state/province/territory, country, office/firm size, practice areas, starting salaries, and other criteria. For each entry, information is provided on student employment, demographics, salaries, fringe benefits, and diversity recruitment and retention efforts. A list of colleges where the firm or organization plans to recruit new workers is also provided.

Peterson's Summer Camps and Programs

http://www.petersons.com/ summerop/code/ssector.asp

This Web site offers great information about academic- and career-focused summer programs. Finding a camp that suits your interests is easy enough at this site; just search Peterson's database by activity (Academics, Arts, Sports, Wilderness/Outdoors, Special Interests), geographic region, category (Day Programs in the U.S., Residential Programs in the U.S., Travel in the U.S. and to Other Countries, Special Needs Accommodations), keyword, or alphabetically. By conducting a keyword search using the word *law*, you'll find a list of links to more than 80 programs. Click on a specific program or camp for a quick overview. In some instances you'll get a more in-depth description, along with photographs, applications, and online brochures.

The Princeton Review: Law School

http://www.princetonreview.com/ law-school.aspx

This Web site will provide you with everything you need to know about law school. Sections include Law School Rankings, Prepare for Law School, and the LSAT. There are also articles on what it's like to be a first-year law student, a podcast about law-related topics, and information on financial aid. You can also take a free LSAT practice test at the site.

Supreme Court Historical Society

http://www.supremecourthistory.org

This Web site will provide you with everything you need to know about the Supreme Court. Interesting features include a justice timeline, biographies of current justices, court history quizzes, and information on how the courts work (including sections on court customs and traditions, oral arguments, the role of law clerks, modernization and technology, and visiting the court).

Supreme Court of the United States

http://www.supremecourtus.gov

The Supreme Court is the highest court in the United States. It was first assembled in 1790. You can visit its Web site to read about past and current justices, its history and traditions, landmark cases, tours, and a wealth of other information.

U.S. News & World Report: America's Graduate Schools: Law

http://grad-schools.usnews.rankingsandreviews.com/grad/law

Use this online service to search for law schools by national ranking or name. Free information is provided on tuition, enrollment, type (private or public), student/faculty ratio, and other categories, and a handy feature allows you to compare attributes of schools side-by-side to help narrow your choice. Note: In order to read all of the information about each school, you must either buy the print publication or pay for the Premium Online Edition.

Ask for Money

By the time most students get around to thinking about applying for scholarships, grants, and other financial aid, they have already extolled their personal, academic, and creative virtues to such lengths in essays and interviews for college applications that even their own grandmothers wouldn't recognize them. The thought of filling out yet another application fills students with dread. And why bother? Won't the same five or six kids who have been competing for academic honors for years walk away with all the really good scholarships?

The truth is that most of the scholarships available to high school and college students are being offered because an organization wants to promote interest in a particular field, encourage more students to become qualified to enter it, and finally, to help those students afford an education. Certainly, having a great grade point average is a valuable asset. More often than not, however, grade point averages aren't even mentioned; the focus is on the area of interest and what a student has done to distinguish himself or herself in that area. In fact, sometimes the only requirement is that the scholarship applicant must be studying in a particular area.

❑ GUIDELINES

When applying for scholarships there are a few simple guidelines that can help ease the process considerably.

Plan Ahead

The absolute worst thing you can do is wait until the last minute. For one thing, obtaining recommendations or other supporting data in time to meet an application deadline is incredibly difficult. For another, no one does his or her best thinking or writing under the gun. So get off to a good start by reviewing scholarship applications as early as possible—months, even a year, in advance. If the current scholarship information isn't available, ask for a copy of last year's version. Once you have the scholarship information or application in hand, give it a thorough read. Try to determine how your experience or situation best fits into the scholarship, or if it even fits at all. Don't waste your time applying for a scholarship in literature if you couldn't finish *Great Expectations*.

If possible, research the award or scholarship, including past recipients and, where applicable, the person in whose name the scholarship is offered. Often, scholarships are established to memorialize an individual who majored in law or a related field, for example, but in other cases, the scholarship is to memorialize the *work* of an individual. In those cases, try to get a feel for the spirit of the person's work. If you have any similar interests, experiences, or abilities, don't hesitate to mention them.

Talk to others who received the scholarship, or to students currently studying in the same area or field of interest in which the scholarship is offered, and try to gain insight into possible applications or work related to that field. Doing this sort of research will give you real answers to use when you're working on the essay asking why you want this scholarship—"I would benefit from receiving this scholarship because studying environmental law will help me become a better advocate for reducing the amount of toxic emissions from oil refineries into the air."

Take your time writing the essays. Make sure that you are answering the question or questions on the application and not merely restating facts about yourself. Don't be afraid to get creative; try to imagine what you would think of if you had to sift through hundreds of applications: What would you want to know about the candidate? What would convince you that someone was deserving of the scholarship? Work through several drafts and have someone whose advice you respect—a parent, teacher, or guidance counselor—review the essay for grammar and content.

Finally, if you know in advance which scholarships you want to apply for, there might still be time to stack the deck in your favor by getting an internship, volunteering, or working part time. Bottom line: The more you know about a scholarship and the sooner you learn it, the better.

Follow Directions

Think of it this way: Many of the organizations that offer scholarships devote 99.9 percent of their time to something other than the scholarship for which you are applying. Don't make a nuisance of yourself by pestering them for information. Simply follow the directions as they are presented to you. If the scholarship application specifies that you should write for further information, then write for it—don't call.

Pay close attention to whether you're applying for an award, a scholarship, a prize, or financial aid. Often these words are used interchangeably, but just as often they have different meanings. An award is usually given for something you have done: built a park or helped distribute meals to the elderly; or something you have created: a musical composition, a design, an essay, a short film, a screenplay, or an invention. On the other hand, a scholarship is frequently a renewable sum of money that is given to a person to help defray the costs of college. Scholarships are given to candidates who meet the necessary criteria based on essays, eligibility, grades, or sometimes all three.

Supply all the necessary documents, information, and fees, and make the deadlines. You won't win any scholarships by forgetting to include a recommendation from a teacher or failing to postmark the application by the deadline. Bottom line: Get it right the first time, on time.

Apply Early

Once you have the application in hand, don't dawdle. If you've requested it far enough in advance, there shouldn't be any reason for you not to turn it in well in advance of the deadline. You never know, if it comes down to two candidates, your timeliness just might be the deciding factor. Bottom line: Don't wait.

Be Yourself

Don't make promises you can't keep. There are plenty of hefty scholarships available, but if they all require you to study something that you don't enjoy, you'll be miserable in college. And the side effects from switching majors after you've accepted a scholarship could be even worse. Bottom line: Be yourself.

Don't Limit Yourself

There are many sources for scholarships, beginning with your guidance counselor and ending with the Internet. All of the search engines have education categories. Start there and search by keywords, such as "financial aid," "scholarship," and "award." Don't be limited to the scholarships listed in these pages.

If you know of an organization related to or involved with the field of your choice, write a letter asking if they offer scholarships. If they don't offer scholarships, don't stop there. Write them another letter, or better yet, schedule a meeting with the president or someone in the public relations office and ask them if they would be willing to sponsor a scholarship for you. Of course, you'll need to prepare yourself well for such a meeting because you're selling a priceless commodity—yourself. Don't be shy, and be confident. Tell them all about yourself, what you want to study and why, and let them know what you would be willing to do in exchange—volunteer at their favorite charity, write up reports on your progress in school, or work part time on school breaks and full time during the summer. Explain why you're a wise investment. Bottom line: The sky's the limit.

One More Thing

We have not listed financial aid that is awarded to law students in this section. Why? Because this is a book about what you can do now to prepare for a career, and to earn a law degree, you first need to earn a bachelor's degree. Law schools say that they have no particular preference regarding applicants' choice of undergraduate major. Many aspiring law students pursue undergraduate majors in prelaw, government, history, public policy, business, political science, philosophy, English, or other fields. Many colleges and universities offer financial aid for prelaw students and those pursuing other majors; check with your college for details on available programs. Additionally, you will find many general scholarship Web sites below that will provide you with information on financial aid in a variety of fields, including the aforementioned majors. Use these to help you locate funding sources for your undergraduate education. And when you're ready to attend law school, contact the American Bar Association and other legal associations for information on financial aid for law students.

❑ THE LIST

American Association of Colleges of Nursing (AACN)

After College/AACN Scholarship Fund
One Dupont Circle, NW, Suite 530
Washington, DC 20036-1135
202-463-6930
http://www.aacn.nche.edu/ Education/financialaid.htm

The association awards $2,500 scholarships to students who are seeking baccalaureate, master's, or doctoral degrees in nursing. Preference will be given to students who are enrolled in a master's or doctoral program and plan to pursue a nursing faculty career; completing an RN-to-baccalaureate program; or enrolled in an accelerated baccalaureate or master's degree nursing program. Contact the AACN for more information.

Association on American Indian Affairs

Attn: Scholarship Coordinator
966 Hungerford Drive, Suite 12-B
Rockville, MD 20850-1714
240-314-7155
lw.aaia@verizon.net
http://www.indian-affairs.org

Undergraduate and graduate Native American students who are pursuing a wide variety of college majors can apply for several different scholarships of $1,500. All applicants must provide proof of Native American heritage. There is also a specific scholarship, the Florence Young Memorial Scholarship, available for students who are pursuing a master's degree in law, art, or public health. Visit the association's Web site for more information.

Collegeboard.com

http://apps.collegeboard.com/
cbsearch_ss/welcome.jsp

This testing service (PSAT, SAT, etc.) also offers a scholarship search engine at its Web site. It features scholarships worth a total of nearly $3 billion. You can search by specific major (such as law) and a variety of other criteria.

CollegeNET: MACH 25 Breaking the Tuition Barrier

http://www.collegenet.com/mach25/
app

CollegeNET features 600,000 scholarships worth more than $1.6 billion. You can search by keyword (such as "law" or "government") or by creating a personality profile of your interests.

Daughters of the American Revolution (DAR)

Scholarship Committee
1776 D Street, NW
Washington, DC 20006-5303
202-628-1776
http://www.dar.org

Caroline Holt Nursing Scholarships are available to students who have been accepted or who are currently enrolled in a nursing program in the United States. Selection criteria include academic standing, financial need, and letters of recommendation; applicants need not be affiliated with DAR. The Mildred Nutting Nursing Scholarship is also available; preference for this scholarship will be given to candidates from the greater-Lowell, Massachusetts, area. The Arthur Lockwood Beneventi Law Scholarship is available to students with a GPA of at least 3.25 who are enrolled or currently attending law school. Contact DAR for more information.

Discover Nursing

http://www.discovernursing.com/
scholarship_search.aspx

This Web site, sponsored by Johnson & Johnson, offers a nursing scholarship search engine (as well as extensive career information). You can search for scholarships by keyword, U.S. state or territory, GPA, ethnicity, and grade level.

FastWeb

http://fastweb.monster.com

FastWeb is one of the best-known scholarship search engines around. It features 1.3 million scholarships worth more than $3 billion. To use this resource, you will need to register (free).

Foundation for the Carolinas

Attn: Scholarships
217 South Tryon Street
Charlotte, NC 28202-3201
704-973-4537
tcapers@fftc.org
http://www.fftc.org

The foundation administers more than 105 scholarship programs that offer awards to high school seniors and undergraduate and graduate students who plan to or who are currently pursuing study in nursing and other disciplines. Visit its Web site for a list of awards.

GuaranteedScholarships.com

http://www.guaranteed-scholarships.
com

This Web site offers lists (by college) of scholarships, grants, and financial aid that "require no interview, essay, portfolio, audition, competition, or other secondary requirement."

Hawaii Community Foundation

1164 Bishop Street, Suite 800
Honolulu, HI 96813-2817
888-731-3863
info@hcf-hawaii.org
http://www.hawaiicommunity
foundation.org/scholar/scholar.php

The foundation offers a variety of scholarships for high school seniors and college students planning to or currently studying law, nursing, and other majors in college. Applicants must be residents of Hawaii, demonstrate financial need, and attend a two- or four-year college. Visit the foundation's Web site for more information and to apply online.

Hispanic College Fund (HCF)

1301 K Street, NW, Suite 450-A West
Washington, DC 20005-3317
800-644-4223
hcf-info@hispanicfund.org
http://www.hispanicfund.org

The Hispanic College Fund, in collaboration with several major corporations, offers many scholarships for high school seniors and college students planning to or currently attending college. Applicants must be Hispanic, live in the United States or Puerto Rico, and have a GPA of at least 3.0 on a 4.0 scale. Contact the HCF for more information.

Illinois Career Resource Network

http://www.ilworkinfo.com/icrn.htm

Created by the Illinois Department of Employment Security, this useful site offers a scholarship search engine, as well as detailed information on careers (including law jobs). You can search for law, nursing, or other scholarships based on major (such as law, prelaw, court reporting, legal secretarial studies, paralegal studies, registered nursing, government, business, etc.), and other criterion. This site is available to everyone, not just Illinois residents; you can get a password by simply visiting the site. The Illinois Career Information System is just one example of sites created by state departments of employment security (or departments of labor) to assist students with financial- and career-related issues. After checking out this site, visit your state's department of labor Web site to see what it offers.

National Verbatim Reporters Association (NVRA)

207 Third Avenue
Hattiesburg, MS 39401-3868
601-582-4345
nvra@nvra.com
http://www.nvra.org

The association awards Horace L. Webb Scholarships to students who are currently attending or who have been accepted by a NVRA-endorsed school. The scholarship amount is $250. Applicants must submit a completed application and an essay that details their career interests and background. Contact the association for more information.

Sallie Mae

http://www.collegeanswer.com/
paying/scholarship_search/pay_
scholarship_search.jsp

This Web site offers a scholarship database of more than 2.9 million awards worth more than $16 billion. You must register (free) to use the database.

Scholarship America

One Scholarship Way
PO Box 297
Saint Peter, MN 56082-0297
800-537-4180
http://www.scholarshipamerica.org

This organization works through its local Dollars for Scholars chapters throughout the United States. In 2008, it awarded more than $219 million in scholarships to students. Visit Scholarship America's Web site for more information.

Scholarships.com

http://www.scholarships.com

Scholarships.com offers a free college scholarship and grant search engine (although you must register to use it) and financial aid information. Its database of awards features 2.7 million listings worth up to $19 billion in aid.

United Negro College Fund (UNCF)

8260 Willow Oaks Corporate Drive
PO Box 10444
Fairfax, VA 22031-8044

800-331-2244
http://www.uncf.org/forstudents/
scholarship.asp

Visitors to the UNCF Web site can search for information on thousands of scholarships and grants, many of which are administered by the UNCF. Its search engine allows you to search by major (such as law), state, scholarship title, grade level, and achievement score. High school seniors and undergraduate and graduate students are eligible.

U.S. Department of Education
Federal Student Aid
800-433-3243
http://www.federalstudentaid.ed.gov
http://studentaid.ed.gov/students/pub
lications/student_guide/index.html

The U.S. government provides a wealth of financial aid in the form of grants, loans, and work-study programs. Each year, it publishes *Funding Education Beyond High School*, a guide to available funds. Visit the Web sites above for detailed information on federal financial aid.

Look to the Pros

The following professional organizations offer a variety of materials, from career brochures to lists of accredited schools to salary surveys. Many publish journals and newsletters that you should become familiar with. Some also have annual conferences that you might be able to attend. (While you may not be able to attend a conference as a participant, it may be possible to "cover" one for your school or even your local paper, especially if your school has a related club.)

When contacting professional organizations, keep in mind that they all exist primarily to serve their members, be it through continuing education, professional licensure, political lobbying, or just "keeping up with the profession." While many are strongly interested in promoting their profession and sharing information with the general public, these busy professional organizations do not exist solely to provide you with information. Whether you call ur write, be courteous, brief, and to the point. Know what you need and ask for it. If the organization has a Web site, check it out first; what you're looking for may be available there for downloading, or you may find a list of prices or instructions, such as sending a self-addressed stamped envelope with your request. Finally, be aware that organizations, like people, move. To save time when writing, first confirm the address, preferably with a quick phone call to the organization itself, "Hello, I'm calling to confirm your address. . . ."

❏ THE SOURCES

American Alliance of Paralegals
4001 Kennett Pike, Suite 134-146
Wilmington, DE 19807-2315
info@aapipara.org
http://www.aapipara.org

The alliance offers certification to paralegals.

American Association for Paralegal Education
19 Mantua Road
Mt. Royal, NJ 08061-1006
856-423-2829
info@aafpe.org
http://www.aafpe.org

Visit the association's Web site for information about paralegal education programs and advice on evaluating the quality of educational programs.

American Association of Colleges of Nursing (AACN)
One Dupont Circle, NW, Suite 530
Washington, DC 20036-1135
202-463-6930
http://www.aacn.nche.edu

The association provides resources for nursing students, including information on scholarships for currently enrolled nursing students and online publications for nurses, such as *Listing of AACN-Member Schools*, *Your Nursing Career: A Look at the Facts*, and *What Nursing Grads Should Consider When Seeking Employment.*

American Association of Electronic Reporters and Transcribers

2900 Fairhope Road
Wilmington, DE 19810-1624
800-233-5306
aaert@comcast.net
http://www.aaert.org

Visit the association's Web site for information about digital/electronic court reporting and certification.

American Association of Law Libraries

105 West Adams Street, Suite 3300
Chicago, IL 60603-6225
312-939-4764
http://www.aallnet.org

The association represents law librarians who are employed at law firms; law schools; courts; corporate legal departments; and local, state, and federal government agencies. Visit its Web site for information on education and careers in law librarianship.

American Association of Legal Nurse Consultants

401 North Michigan Avenue
Chicago, IL 60611-4255
877-402-2562
info@aalnc.org
http://www.aalnc.org

The association provides information on careers (via online publications such as *What is a LNC?* and *Getting Started in Legal Nurse Consulting*) and certification. It also offers publications, books, an annual conference, and sustaining membership to anyone with an interest in the goals and activities of the association.

American Bar Association (ABA)

321 North Clark Street
Chicago, IL 60654-7598
800-285-2221
http://www.abanet.org

The ABA is the leading professional association for lawyers in the United States, and represents the interests of other law professionals through standing committees and advocacy branches. Visit its Web site for information about educational programs, career options, the bar examination, publications, conferences, and a variety of other resources for those interested in the legal industry. The ABA also offers membership to law students.

American College of Legal Medicine

Two Woodfield Lake
1100 East Woodfield Road, Suite 520
Schaumburg, IL 60173-5125
847-969-0283
info@aclm.org
http://www.aclm.org

This is a professional organization for attorneys, physicians, dentists, health care professionals, administrators, and scientists "who focus on the important issues where law and medicine converge." It offers membership to law, medical, and dental students.

American Intellectual Property Law Association (AIPLA)

241 18th Street South, Suite 700
Arlington, VA 22202-3419
703-415-0780
aipla@aipla.org
http://www.aipla.org

Visit the association's Web site to read *What Is a Patent, a Trademark and a Copyright?* and *Careers in IP Law.* The AIPLA also offers publications, job listings, and membership for law students.

American Judges Association

300 Newport Avenue
Williamsburg, VA 23185-4147
757-259-1841
aja@ncsc.dni.us
http://aja.ncsc.dni.us

This is a professional membership organization for judges in the United States and its territories (Puerto Rico, Guam, American Samoa and the Virgin Islands), Canada, and Mexico. It offers an essay contest for law students.

Association for Gerontology in Higher Education (AGHE)

1220 L Street, NW, Suite 901
Washington, DC 20005-4018
202-289-9806
http://www.aghe.org

Visit the AGHE's Web site to read *Careers in Aging: Consider the Possibilities,* which discusses the field of gerontology, available careers, how to select a program, and how to find jobs in aging. Other resources include scholarship information, special resources for students, and a directory of more than 750 gerontology programs (which can be purchased online).

Association of American Law Schools

1201 Connecticut Avenue, NW,
  Suite 800
Washington, DC 20036-2717
202-296-8851
aals@aals.org
http://www.aals.org

Visit the association's Web site for information on member schools, the *Journal of Legal Education,* and links to other legal organizations.

Association of Legal Administrators

75 Tri-State International, Suite 222
Lincolnshire, IL 60069-4435
847-267-1252
http://www.alanet.org

This organization represents professionals who manage law firms, government legal agencies, and corporate legal departments. Visit its Web site for job listings and information on careers and certification.

Council on Legal Education Opportunity

740 15th Street, NW, 9th Floor
Washington, DC 20005-1019

866-886-4343
cleo@abanet.org
http://www.cleoscholars.org

The council is "committed to diversifying the legal profession by expanding legal education opportunities to minority, low-income, and disadvantaged groups." It is funded by the U.S. Department of Education. The council offers a variety of publications, programs, and other resources for college students who are interested in exploring law careers. Visit its Web site for more information on available programs and applying to law school.

Federal Bar Association (FBA)

Student Services
1220 North Fillmore Street,
   Suite 444
Arlington, VA 22201-6501
571-481-9100
fba@fedbar.org
http://www.fedbar.org

The FBA provides support for lawyers and judges involved in federal practice. Visit its Web site to read selected articles from *The Federal Lawyer Magazine*.

Federal Judicial Center

Thurgood Marshall Federal
   Judiciary Building
One Columbus Circle, NE
Washington, DC 20002-8003
202-502-4000
http://www.fjc.gov

Contact the Federal Judicial Center for information about educational programs for federal judges. Visit its Web site to read biographies of federal judges since 1789, landmark judicial legislation, and histories of individual U.S. courts.

Hispanic National Bar Association

Ben Franklin Station
PO Box 14347
Washington, DC 20044-4347
202-223-4777
http://www.hnba.com

This is a professional organization for Hispanic lawyers, law students, judges, law professors, and legal assistants. Its foundation offers a scholarship for college students who are interested in studying law.

International Law Students Association

c/o DePaul University School of Law
25 East Jackson Boulevard
Chicago, IL 60604-2201
312-362-5025
http://www.ilsa.org

This organization of students and lawyers promotes the study and practice of international law. It offers several interesting publications, information on study abroad programs, and other resources.

Legal Aid Society

199 Water Street
New York, NY 10038-3526
212-577-3300
http://www.legal-aid.org

Founded in 1876, the Legal Aid Society is the nation's "oldest and largest provider of legal services to the indigent." Visit its Web site for more information on legal advocacy careers.

Legal Secretaries International
2302 Fannin Street, Suite 500
Houston, TX 77002-9136
http://www.legalsecretaries.org

For job listings and information about certification and careers, visit this organization's Web site.

NALS...the association for legal professionals
8159 East 41st Street
Tulsa, OK 74145-3313
918-582-5188
info@nals.org
http://www.nals.org

NALS represents paralegals, legal assistants, legal administrators, office managers, and other legal professionals. Visit its Web site for information about certification, careers, and membership for students at the postsecondary level.

National Academy of Elder Law Attorneys
1577 Spring Hill Road, Suite 220
Vienna, VA 22182-2223
703-942-5711
naela@naela.org
http://www.naela.org

Visit the academy's Web site for information about elder law and a list of law schools that offer programs or classes for students who are interested in studying elder care law. The academy offers membership for law students.

National Asian Pacific American Bar Association
1612 K Street, NW, Suite 1400
Washington, DC 20006-2807

202-775-9555
http://www.napaba.org

This is a professional organization for Asian Pacific American lawyers, law students, judges, and law professors. Visit its Web site for information about moot court competitions and scholarships for law students.

National Association for Law Placement
1025 Connecticut Avenue, Suite 1110
Washington, DC 20036-5413
202-835-1001
info@nalp.org
http://www.nalp.org

Visit the association's Web site for information on choosing a law school, law careers, salaries, and alternative law careers, as well as to access the *Directory of Legal Employers* and the *Directory of Law Schools*.

National Association of College & University Attorneys
One Dupont Circle, Suite 620
Washington, DC 20036-1134
202-833-8390
nacua@nacua.org
http://www.nacua.org

This is a professional organization for attorneys and accredited, nonprofit, degree-granting institutions of higher education. Visit its Web site for information on practice areas, important professional skills, and employment settings.

National Association of Criminal Defense Lawyers
1660 L Street, NW, 12th Floor

Washington, DC 20036-5603
202-872-8600
assist@nacdl.org
http://www.nacdl.org

This is a professional organization for defense lawyers, including those who practice indigent law. It offers membership for law students and "allied non-lawyers," and *The Champion* magazine.

National Association of Legal Assistants

1516 South Boston, Suite 200
Tulsa, OK 74119-4013
918-587-6828
nalanet@nala.org
http://www.nala.org

Visit the association's Web site for information about educational and licensing programs, certification, paralegal careers, and membership for college students and those "who endorse the legal assistant concept."

National Association of Patent Practitioners

3356 Station Court
Lawrenceville, GA 30044-5674
800-216-9588
napp@napp.org
http://www.napp.org

Visit the association's Web site for information on patent law, job listings, and membership for students preparing to become patent lawyers or patent agents.

National Association of Women Judges

1341 Connecticut Avenue, NW, Suite 4.2
Washington, DC 20036-1834

202-393-0222
nawj@nawj.org
http://www.nawj.org

This is a professional organization for female judges, judicial clerks, attorneys, and law students. Male law professionals are also invited to become members. The association offers scholarships and internships to law students.

National Association of Women Lawyers

American Bar Center
321 North Clark Street
Chicago, IL 60654-4714
312-988-6186
nawl@nawl.org
http://www.nawl.org

This professional organization for both female and male lawyers offers career development programs for new lawyers, publications, a mentorship program, and membership for law students.

National Center for State Courts

2425 Wilson Boulevard, Suite 350
Arlington, VA 22201-3320
http://www.ncsconline.org

Information on state courts and the online publications *Survey of Judicial Salaries* and *Future Trends in State Courts* are available at the center's Web site.

National Court Reporters Association

8224 Old Courthouse Road
Vienna, VA 22182-3808
800-272-6272
msic@ncrahq.org
http://www.ncraonline.org

Visit the association's Web site for information about certification, career publications and resources (including *A Career in Court Reporting and Broadcast Captioning*), training programs, a mentor program for college students, membership for college students, and job listings.

National Court Reporters Foundation

8224 Old Courthouse Road
Vienna, VA 22182-3808
800-272-6272
msic@ncrahq.org
http://ncraonline.org/ncrf

The foundation provides scholarships for students who are currently enrolled in court reporting training programs.

National District Attorneys Association

44 Canal Center Plaza, Suite 110
Alexandria, VA 22314-1548
703-549-9222
http://www.ndaa.org

This is the oldest and largest professional association for prosecutors in the world.

National Elder Law Foundation

6336 North Oracle Road, Suite 326,
  #136
Tucson, AZ 85704-5480
520-881-1076
http://www.nelf.org

The foundation offers certification to elder law attorneys.

National Federation of Paralegal Associations

PO Box 2016
Edmonds, WA 98020-9516
425-967-0045
info@paralegals.org
http://www.paralegals.org

For information on education, careers, and membership for college students, visit the federation's Web site.

National Judicial College

University of Nevada-Reno
1664 North Virginia Street
Judicial College Building, MS 358
Reno, NV 89557-0002
800-255-8343
http://www.judges.org

The college provides educational programs for judges.

National Lawyers Guild

132 Nassau Street, Suite 922
New York, NY 10038-2439
212-679-5100
http://nlg.org

The guild "is dedicated to the need for basic and progressive change in the structure of our political and economic system." Its members include law students, lawyers, and other legal professionals. It offers membership to law students.

National Legal Aid and Defender Association

1140 Connecticut Avenue, NW,
  Suite 900
Washington, DC 20036-4019
202-452-0620

info@nlada.org
http://www.nlada.org

This organization is the largest non-profit membership association for public defenders and other equal-justice professionals. It offers membership for law students and private citizens who share its goals. Visit its Web site for information on membership, careers, *Cornerstone* magazine, and the *Directory of Legal Aid & Defender Offices and Resources.*

National Native American Bar Association

1301 Connecticut Avenue, NW,
   Suite 200
Washington, DC 20036-1865
nativeamericanbar@gmail.com
http://www.nationalnativeamerican
   barassociation.org

This is a professional organization for Native American lawyers, law students, judges, law professors, and attorneys who practice American Indian law.

National Paralegal Association

PO Box 406
Solebury, PA 18963-0406
215-297-8333
admin@nationalparalegal.org
http://www.nationalparalegal.org

The association provides information about employment networks and paralegal training opportunities, as well as a pre-student membership category for young people who are considering a career as a paralegal.

National Verbatim Reporters Association (NVRA)

207 Third Avenue
Hattiesburg, MS 39401-3868
601-582-4345
nvra@nvra.com
http://www.nvra.org

The association provides tips on preparing for certification exams, career and educational program information, publications, and a scholarship for students who are currently attending or who have been accepted to a NVRA-endorsed school. Additionally, it offers a membership option for individuals with an interest in the voice writing profession who are not verbatim reporters. Visit the association's Web site for details.

Phi Delta Phi International Legal Fraternity

1426 21st Street, NW
Washington, DC 20036-5947
800-368-5606
http://www.phideltaphi.org

This professional fraternity for law school students is the oldest legal organization in the United States. It "promotes legal ethics and academic distinction in the law schools and the profession at large."

Society of American Law Teachers

Touro Law Center
Public Advocacy Center, Room 223
225 Eastview Drive
Central Islip, NY 11722-4539
http://www.saltlaw.org

This professional organization for law faculty and law school administrators seeks "to make the legal profession more inclusive, to enhance the quality of legal education, and to extend the power of legal representation to under-served individuals and communities." Visit its Web site for more information on earnings for law professors.

United States Court Reporters Association

4725 North Western Avenue,
   Suite 240
Chicago, IL 60625-2096
800-628-2730
info.uscra@gmail.com
http://www.uscra.org

This organization represents court reporters employed at the federal level. It offers membership to court reporting students.

United States Patent and Trademark Office

Office of Public Affairs
PO Box 1450
Alexandria, VA 22313-1450
800-786-9199
usptoinfo@uspto.gov
http://www.uspto.gov

Contact this government agency for information about intellectual property (including patents, trademarks, and copyrights), job opportunities, and recent press releases.

Index

Entries and page numbers in **bold** indicate major treatment of a topic.

A

M

Madonna University 74, 77
magazines. *See* periodicals, law-related
magistrates. *See* judges
Maisami, Ceyda Azakli 46, 47
maritime lawyers 8, 60
Marshall, Thurgood 53
Martin, Joyce 22, 23, 24–25
Mason, Donna 43, 44, 65
McDermott Will & Emery 62
McEldowney, Patricia 81–82, 84
McKenna, Patrick 61–62, 63, 64, 65
Medicaid legal issues 29, 38
Medicare legal issues 29, 38
Medtronic (technology patents) 42
Melendy, Mark E., Law Offices of 30
membership, in general 25, 48, 75, 90,
    118, 128, 131–160. *See also specific
    organizations*
Memphis Bar Association 136
Michigan Supreme Court Historical
    Society Learning Center 143–144
Milwaukee Area Technical College
    90
Minnesota Intellectual Property Law
    Association 48
Minnesota Paralegal Association 90
Missouri Public Defender System 108,
    112, 114
mock trials 44, 121
Mollen, Gerald 100–101, 102, 103
Moritz, Daphne 28, 30–31, 32, 33, 35
Moses 6
Mount Vernon 121
movies, law-related 118–119
museum, visit a 120
Museum of Law 120, 132

N

NAELA. *See* National Academy of Elder
    Law Attorneys
NALA. *See* National Association of Legal
    Assistants
NALS. *See* National Association of Legal
    Secretaries
Napoleon 6
Napoleonic Code 6
National Academy of Elder Law Attorneys
    (NAELA) 30, 35, 36, 188
National Asian Pacific American Bar
    Association 188
National Association for Law Placement
    12, 37, 67, 105, 114, 175, 188
National Association of College and
    University Attorneys 188
National Association of Criminal Defense
    Lawyers 114, 144, 188–189
National Association of Legal Assistants
    (NALA) 81, 83, 118, 144–145, 189
National Association of Legal Secretaries
    (NALS) 81, 83, 188
National Association of Patent
    Practitioners 189
National Association of Women Judges
    189
National Association of Women Lawyers
    189
National Bar Association 145
National Center for State Courts 56–57,
    189
National Court Reporters Association
    (NCRA) 23, 25, 172–173, 189–190
National Court Reporters Foundation 25,
    190
National District Attorneys Association
    190
National Elder Law Foundation (NELF)
    34, 190
National Federation of Paralegal
    Associations 93, 94, 190
National High School Mock Trial
    Championship 145